The Official Website of The New Life Mission
www.nlmission.com or
www.bjnewlife.org

*W*orldwide websites of

 The New Life Mission

Please find your vernacular websites below.
You can download Christian e-books and request Christian books for free.
Feel free to visit our websites below right now!

A
www.nlmafghanistan.com
www.nlmafrikaans.com
www.nlmalbania.com
www.nlmamharic.com
www.nlmangola.com
www.nlmarabemirates.com
www.nlmarabic.com
www.nlmargentina.com
www.nlmarmenia.com
www.nlmaruba.com
www.nlmaustralia.com
www.nlmaustria.com

B
www.nlmbahamas.com
www.nlmbahrain.com
www.nlmbangladesh.com
www.nlmbelarus.com
www.nlmbelgium.com
www.nlmbengali.com
www.nlmbenin.com
www.nlmbhutan.com
www.nlmbolivia.com
www.nlmbotswana.com
www.nlmbrasil.com
www.nlmbriton.com
www.nlmbrunei.com
www.nlmbulgalia.com
www.nlmburkinafaso.com
www.nlmburundi.com

C
www.nlmcameroon.com
www.nlmcanada.com
www.nlmcebuano.com
www.nlmchichewa.com
www.nlmchile.com
www.nlmchin.com

www.nlmchina.com
www.nlmcolombia.com
www.nlmcongo.com
www.nlmcostarica.com
www.nlmcotedivoire.com
www.nlmcroatia.com
www.nlmczech.com

www.nlmelsalvador.com
www.nlmequatorialguinea.com
www.nlmethiopia.com
F
www.nlmfinland.com
www.nlmfrance.com
www.nlmfrench.com
G
www.nlmgabon.com
www.nlmgeorgian.com
www.nlmgerman.com
www.nlmgermany.com
www.nlmghana.com
www.nlmgreek.com
www.nlmgrenada.com
www.nlmguatemala.com
www.nlmgujarati.com
H
www.nlmhaiti.com
www.nlmhindi.com
www.nlmholland.com
www.nlmhonduras.com
www.nlmhungary.com

Turn over

Worldwide websites of
 The New Life Mission

I www.nlm-india.com
www.nlmindonesia.com
www.nlmiran.com
www.nlmiraq.com
www.nlmisrael.com
www.nlmitaly.com
J www.nlmjamaica.com
www.nlmjapan.com
www.nlmjavanese.com
K www.nlmkannada.com
www.nlmkazakhstan.com
www.nlmkenya.com
www.nlmkhmer.com
www.nlmkirghiz.com
www.nlmkirundi.com
www.nlmkorea.com
L www.nlmlatvia.com
www.nlmluganda.com
www.nlmluo.com
M www.nlmmadi.com
www.nlmmalagasy.com
www.nlmmalayalam.com
www.nlmmalaysia.com
www.nlmmarathi.com
www.nlmmauritius.com
www.nlmmexico.com
www.nlmmindat.com
www.nlmmizo.com
www.nlmmoldova.com
www.nlmmongolia.com
www.nlmmyanmar.com
N www.nlmnepal.com
www.nlmnewzealand.com
www.nlmnigeria.com
www.nlmnorthkorea.com
www.nlmnorway.com
P www.nlmpakistan.com
www.nlmpanama.com
www.nlmperu.com
www.nlmphilippines.com

www.nlmpoland.com
www.nlmportugal.com
www.nlmportuguese.com
www.nlmprcongo.com
Q www.nlmqatar.com
R www.nlmromania.com
www.nlmrussia.com
S www.nlmsaudiarabia.com
www.nlmserbian.com
www.nlmshona.com
www.nlmsingapore.com
www.nlmslovakia.com
www.nlmslovene.com
www.nlmsolomon.com
www.nlmsouthafrica.com
www.nlmspain.com
www.nlmspanish.com
www.nlmsrilanka.com
www.nlmsuriname.com
www.nlmswahili.com
www.nlmswaziland.com
www.nlmsweden.com
www.nlmswiss.com
T www.nlmtagalog.com
www.nlmtaiwan.com
www.nlmtamil.com
www.nlmtelugu.com
www.nlmthailand.com
www.nlmtogo.com
www.nlmtonga.com
www.nlmturkey.com
U www.nlmuganda.com
www.nlmukraine.com
www.nlmurdu.com
www.nlmusa.com
V www.nlmvenezuela.com
www.nlmvietnam.com
Z www.nlmzambia.com
www.nlmzimbabwe.com
www.nlmzou.com

FROM THIS CORRUPTED WORLD TO HEAVEN ABOVE

FROM THIS CORRUPTED WORLD TO HEAVEN ABOVE

PAUL C. JONG

Hephzibah Publishing House
A Ministry of THE NEW LIFE MISSION
SEOUL, KOREA

From This Corrupted World to Heaven Above
Copyright © 2008 by Hephzibah Publishing House
Scripture quotations are from *the New King James Version.*

ISBN 89-8314-439-4
Cover Art by Min-soo Kim
Illustration by Young-ae Kim
Printed in Korea

Hephzibah Publishing House
A Ministry of THE NEW LIFE MISSION
P.O. Box 18 Yang-Cheon Post Office
Yang-Cheon Gu, Seoul, Korea

♠ Website: http://www.nlmission.com
　　　　 http://www.bjnewlife.org
　　　　 http://www.nlmbookcafe.com
♠ E-mail: newlife@bjnewlife.org
♠ Phone: 82(Korea)-11-1788-2954

Table of Contents

Preface

"A long, long time ago..." There is no story that is not boring when it begins in this way. Yet I am opening my preface with such a trite expression in order to ascend from the face of this earth, where I am now, to the glorious Kingdom of Heaven, where Jesus Christ, God Himself is.

A long, long time ago, God created this universe. In the universe filled with countless stars, there is a planet called earth, a planet that is no more than a tiny dot. In this planet earth there are five oceans and six continents which the human race calls its home, and I am just one of the billions of human beings. My existence is rendered infinitely humble before the universe. Yet for such an insignificant being like me, God made this universe.

From this creation of the heavens and the earth, it is me whom God loved the most. Because God loved me, He gave human beings an innocent heart, but tempted by Satan, they lost this heart and became one with sin. As hundreds and thousands of years went by, the wall of sin built between God and the human race became even stronger, and everyone ended up being hardened into a pile of sins. As a result, I turned my back against God who had made me, loved me, protected me, and abided with me; I built a wall and imprisoned myself in a chamber of suffering; and I came to believe that the face of this earth was the only world where I had to live the rest of my life. Because of sin, I went astray and came to forget all about God, who was my beginning and the reason for my existence. It was because of my heart's sins that I drifted away from God, who had breathed life into me.

I had to be freed from all sins and meet God my Creator. But finding this way was extremely difficult and hard. Since I had no sight even though I had my eyes, I could not find the way to become one with God; and since there was no one to teach me, my heart was filled with an unquenched yearning to discover the Truth.

However, when I realized from the Word of God that I was fundamentally a depraved sinner by nature, and came across the gospel of the water and the Spirit, I finally understood what was causing this deep unexplainable sorrow that had made me wander in darkness, not knowing where to turn and moaning in pain. And I came to break down this thick wall of sin which was separating me from God, and I opened my spiritual eyes to finally see the everlasting God who had been with me from the beginning, and whom I had yearned and longed for from the depth of my heart. God had known me before I knew myself, and He had been waiting for me silently even when I had turned my back against Him. And through the God-given Law, I was awakened to the fact that I was a grave sinner destined to suffer helplessly for my sins.

I also realized that God had sent His only begotten Son Jesus Christ to this earth for my sake, and that this Son had saved me from the sins of the world through the gospel of the water and the Spirit. When I realized and admitted just how sinful I was, God showed me the gospel Truth of the water and the Spirit, and by believing in this gospel with my heart, I received the remission of all my sins which freed me from my every sin. As a result, I attained true peace and tranquility in my spirit.

Did God create only the visible world? Are the things that our eyes see all that exist? No, this visible world is no more than a shadow of the good things to come, the real Kingdom of

God that is not visible to our naked eyes. I'd like to then ask you this question: Have you moved yourself from the earth to the dominion of the gospel of the water and the Spirit?

I'd like to now invite you to the Kingdom of Heaven prepared by God. Yet just as God said that many are invited to the celestial wedding but only a few put on the wedding garments, there are extremely few people who will actually be moved from this earth to Heaven. The incontrovertible evidence proving that one will live in Heaven is the perfect salvation of the remission of sins that's received through the gospel of the water and the Spirit. Those who have been moved to Heaven are none other than those who have been saved perfectly by believing in the gospel of the water and the Spirit and put on the garments of the remission of sins.

Thanks to the gospel of the water and the Spirit, I have recovered my soul's health that had been lost. Now it's your turn. ✉

SERMON

1

Look at Your True Self And Believe in The Gospel of the Water And the Spirit

< Mark 7:1-23 >

"Then the Pharisees and some of the scribes came together to Him, having come from Jerusalem. Now when they saw some of His disciples eat bread with defiled, that is, with unwashed hands, they found fault. For the Pharisees and all the Jews do not eat unless they wash their hands in a special way, holding the tradition of the elders. When they come from the marketplace, they do not eat unless they wash. And there are many other things which they have received and hold, like the washing of cups, pitchers, copper vessels, and couches. Then the Pharisees and scribes asked Him, 'Why do Your disciples not walk according to the tradition of the elders, but eat bread with unwashed hands?' He answered and said to them, 'Well did Isaiah prophesy of you hypocrites, as it is written:

'This people honors Me with their lips,
But their heart is far from Me.
And in vain they worship Me,
Teaching as doctrines the commandments of men.'

For laying aside the commandment of God, you hold the tradition of men the washing of pitchers and cups, and

many other such things you do.' He said to them, 'All too
well you reject the commandment of God, that you may
keep your tradition. For Moses said, 'Honor your father
and your mother'; and, 'He who curses father or mother,
let him be put to death.' But you say, 'If a man says to his
father or mother, 'Whatever profit you might have
received from me is Corban' (that is, a gift to God), then
you no longer let him do anything for his father or his
mother, making the word of God of no effect through your
tradition which you have handed down. And many such
things you do.' When He had called all the multitude to
Himself, He said to them, 'Hear Me, everyone, and
understand: There is nothing that enters a man from
outside which can defile him; but the things which come out
of him, those are the things that defile a man. If anyone has
ears to hear, let him hear!' When He had entered a house
away from the crowd, His disciples asked Him concerning
the parable. So He said to them, 'Are you thus without
understanding also? Do you not perceive that whatever
enters a man from outside cannot defile him, because it
does not enter his heart but his stomach, and is eliminated,
thus purifying all foods?' And He said, 'What comes out of
a man, that defiles a man. For from within, out of the heart
of men, proceed evil thoughts, adulteries, fornications,
murders, thefts, covetousness, wickedness, deceit, lewdness,
an evil eye, blasphemy, pride, foolishness. All these evil
things come from within and defile a man.'"

Dear fellow believers, we must read the Word of God
every day and think what kind of person we are. What kind of
person are we really? We were originally born as the

descendants of Adam who commit sins because we have inherited all the sins from our parents. In other words, we are originally *"a brood of evildoers" (Isaiah 1:4)* that cannot but commit sins; we all are people who cannot do any righteous deeds even if we really want to do such deeds. However, in order to save all of us we who cannot but commit sins like this, our God came and saved us from all the sins of the world once and for all by the gospel of the water and the Spirit. We must know this gospel of the water and the Spirit. We really come to give thanks and praise to our Lord when we think of this gospel of truth of salvation which God has given to us.

Do Not Become Hypocrites

In today's Scripture passage, we can see that the Pharisees and the scribes were full of hypocrisy. That they were hypocrites before the presence of God means that their heart and their behavior were very different. These spiritual hypocrites decorate their outward appearances cleanly although their inside is filthy. This is the life of the spiritual hypocrites. And when we look into all these religious people of this world who live like Pharisees, we can see that they all are giving up themselves just to become successful in a fleshly sense. They just wash their hands and feet cleanly and polish their outward appearances when they go before the presence of God. They clean up their outward appearance and think that everything concerning themselves has become clean. Some people look at themselves and think that they are clean enough. However, one has not become a clean person before the presence of God just because his outward appearance is clean. One is not truly clean just because his outward appearance is clean.

The Pharisees who appears in the Scriptures here claimed to believe in Jehovah God, but they were actually people who believed in the elders of their denomination and not God. Thus, they believed that the teachings of humans had more authority than God and His Word. So, they followed these inherited traditions of the elders instead of the Word of God.

In the Gospel of Mark chapter 7 verses 1 to 2 it is written, *"Then the Pharisees and some of the scribes came together to Him, having come from Jerusalem. Now when they saw some of His disciples eat bread with defiled, that is, with unwashed hands, they found fault."* The Pharisees at that time followed the custom of washing their hands and feet cleanly when they entered into their homes. The practice of splashing water on the yard and washing the cups, pitchers, and copper vessels cleanly before eating when they returned from the marketplace still remained a strong tradition.

Now, what is the problem with this custom of the Pharisees? Is there anything that could be a problem in a fleshly sense? There is nothing wrong from a fleshly viewpoint. They were the people who lived a very ordinary life, washing their hands and feet before eating when entering a home. Also, even splashing water on the yard and washing the dirty things in the house and then eating do not seem to be special behaviors either.

Then, let's look at what the problem was with such traditions of the Pharisees that prompted Jesus to rebuke their faith like this. The Pharisees had thought that such things ordinary people did normally as an important duty in believing and serving God. This was the problem spiritually. Put differently, those Pharisees had thought that they had to take a bath, wash the bowls cleanly, and splash water over the yard before eating when they returned from the marketplace to be considered as a faithful person to God. This was the problem. The problem was that they approved only someone with such faith as a proper and pure person before the presence of God. Because of this reason, the religious life of all the Pharisees became more and more hypocritical and was becoming increasingly more distant in the matter of believing and following God with a sincere heart of faith. They were respected when they went around looking upright with clean clothes, clean hands and feet, and washed their bodies cleanly.

Let's read what the Lord said to these Pharisees. Then Jesus said to the Pharisees, *"All too well you reject the commandment of God, that you may keep your tradition. For Moses said, 'Honor your father and your mother'; and, 'He who curses father or mother, let him be put to death.' But you say, 'If a man says to his father or mother, "Whatever profit you might have received from me is Corban"-' (that is, a gift to God), then you no longer let him do anything for his father or his mother, making the word of God of no effect through your tradition which you have handed down. And many such things you do"* (Mark 7:9-13).

What did Jesus say to the Pharisees? He said, "For Moses said, 'Honor your father and your mother'; and, 'He who curses father or mother, let him be put to death.'" Jesus was rebuking the Pharisees like this. When they had something worthy to give to their parents, they should have gladly given it to their parents. However, the Pharisees said that they could not give it to their parents or any other person because they had already given it to God. Thus, no matter what wonderful thing they had, they did not have to use it to honor their parents since they could say that they had already offered it up to God.

Let's compare this with a business of a certain believer. A certain Christian was working as a realtor. And there was a

Bible and a hymnal on his desk in his office. It seemed like a custom especially for Korean Christians to do this when they were in the workplace. What do you think is the reason for them doing this? When there is a Bible and a hymn on the desk in the office, it makes people think, "Ah! This person believes in God. He must be upright and honest."

However, people generally thought like this before, but it is not like this in these days. These days, when a person has a Bible and a hymnbook on his desk, people look at that and think, he must be a "thief." People's presumptions have changed like this today. A few decades ago, people of this world at least thought of Christians as upright and honest. But the faith of believing in God does not work in business transactions any more. Before even in a place like a supermarket, business usually was better when they had a Bible and a hymnal on their cash desks.

People of this age have been hurt so much by these hypocrites that they no longer are deceived by such false Christians anymore. There are many among today's Christian believers who go to a church to do business. There actually are many people who believe in God but have nothing to do with God. They don't believe in the Word of God. They just believe in the false doctrines their respective church teaches and they give up themselves to seek only material things of this world. Thus, they should learn even now about the gospel of the water and the Spirit and believe in God through His Word.

However, they are trying to live out their faith without knowing the will of God. Therefore, they actually do not know the righteousness of God or believe in God although they claim to believe in God. They believe the teachings of their leaders of their respectful denominations as if they are of the Word of God, instead of believing in God or His Word. The humanistic teachings of these so-called great pastors of today have become the bases of their faith. So they claim to believe in the Word of God, but they really believe in their own fleshly thoughts and false doctrines rather than the righteousness of God.

The faith of most Christians these days is like this. The Presbyterian denominations are following Christian doctrines, which was made up by John Calvin a long ago. In other words, Christian doctrines proclaimed by Calvin became the central doctrines of the Presbyterian denominations. And so those from the generations thereafter thought that the theology of Calvin had discovered many things from the Bible and have thus come to consider Calvin's teachings more important than the recorded Word of God. All these people who advocate the Christian doctrine of Calvin these days consider what Calvin said about certain things as more important than the recorded Word of God.

Therefore, they are making a terrible mistake because they do not even try to know about the gospel of the water and the Spirit. They come to consider the teachings of sinful theologians more important than the gospel of the water and the Spirit which is the gospel of the righteousness of God. It is a problem to think that the words spoken by these theologians have greater authority than the Word of God. Therefore, they come to stand against the righteousness of God with this wrong faith. This was the mistake and misunderstanding of today's Pharisees.

Long Ago the Pharisees Misunderstood as If Only They Believed in God Correctly

They could not preach the gospel of the righteousness of

God as recorded in the Scriptures because they did not know this Truth. Not only that, but they also taught theological doctrines that they have learned from their theologians to many other people. Thus the situation had become so bad that increasingly more and more people were learning these theological doctrines instead of facing the gospel of the righteousness of God. Therefore, this evil yeast of the Pharisees had been handed down to even lay Christians from generation to generation. The Scriptures referred to these teachings which were handed down through the generations as the "tradition" of the elders. Therefore, the core of the gospel of the remission of sins that is in the Word of God namely, the gospel of the water and the Spirit had consequently disappeared and only these academic assertions of theologians became abundant. Because of this Jesus rebuked them citing the Word from Isaiah,

"These people draw near to Me with their mouth,
And honor Me with their lips,
But their heart is far from Me.
And in vain they worship Me,
Teaching as doctrines the commandments of men'"
(Matthew 15:8-9).

Likewise, Christians of today have come to consider these theological doctrines mentioned here more important than the gospel of the water and the Spirit which is the Word of God.

The faith of most Christians throughout the entire world is becoming like this. Christians today are becoming hypocrites just like these theologians. The Methodist denomination in Korea absolutely believes and follows the teachings of John Wesley. And the doctrines of Calvin are critically important to the Presbyterian Christians. They say that they believe and follow the teachings of Calvin not because his teachings are important but because he had interpreted the Word of God correctly. They open up the Bible and read the Word of God and teach that John Calvin said it like this, John Wesley said it like this, and a certain theologian said this. They open the Scriptures and teach what certain theologians said about this and that, instead of teaching the pure Word of God just as it is.

Most Christians today attend church to believe in God at first. While attending church, they learn how to offer these prayers of repentance, how to fast and prayer, the doctrine of sanctification, the doctrine of salvation by believing in Jesus, and various hymns, and they even attend all night prayer meetings. They learn all the doctrines taught in the church. They respond with "halleluiah's" when a preacher occupies the pulpit and says "halleluiah" and they respond with "amen" when the preacher says, "Do you believe?" In other words, these believers learn these Christian doctrines that these theologians have fabricated rather than learning the pure Word of God from the time when they started attending a church. The longer someone has been going to a church the more that person becomes someone who knows only Christian doctrines and advocates them. Now what does this all mean? It means that the longer a Christian has been attending church the more he knows only these Christian doctrines and does not know the gospel of the water and the Spirit that he really should know. And in order to seem like a person with strong faith befitting many years of attending church, such a person fasts and prays even more, carries the Bible around in humble manner, tries to sing hymns gracefully, and prays hypocritically just so that other people can see.

In Korea, a Christian is usually given the privilege of voting in church when he has attended church for a year and becomes a baptized member of that congregation. Then this layperson gains the right to vote in some matters of decision-making in church from that time on. But to be a member of a presbytery, which is the actual decision-making office in a Presbyterian Church, that layperson should become an elder. What is the highest position a layperson can attain in a church? It is eldership. However, a layperson should have offered up much money in order to become an elder in a church. Only then can that person become an elder in a church and be respected. Therefore, elders must be faithful to do such things like attending early Morning Prayer meetings; all night prayer meetings, mountain prayers retreats, and offering up money at all worship services. And they must also adhere honorably to the rules of the elders. But they have become people in high positions in the church with all kinds of sins in their hearts. They have become imprisoned in sins because they have not believed in the gospel of the water and the Spirit which can make them righteous. They have as a consequence of this become great religious people. They have come to be rebuked by Jesus who said to the Pharisees, "Woe to you, hypocrites, the scribes and the Pharisees." Such people are the hypocritical believers.

Jesus rebuked the hypocrisy of the Pharisees, saying, *"Not what goes into the mouth defiles a man; but what comes out of the mouth, this defiles a man" (Matthew 15:11)*. Jesus thus rebuked the hypocritical faith of these Pharisees by saying, *"Did not He who made the outside make the inside also? (Luke 11:40)* You must clean the inside first." The Lord is saying this also to us in this era. The Lord told all the Christians these days not to be hypocrites.

What Kind of Sins Are in the Hearts of Christians These Days?

Let's read Mark chapter 7 verses 20-23 again, *"What comes out of a man, that defiles a man. For from within, out of the heart of men, proceed evil thoughts, adulteries, fornications, murders, thefts, covetousness, wickedness, deceit, lewdness, an evil eye, blasphemy, pride, foolishness. All these evil things come from within and defile a man."*
Jesus told us here that this sinful nature inside someone's heart makes that person commit sins. We should therefore know that evil thoughts exist in everyone's heart. It is not as though these evil thoughts are in some people's hearts and not in the other people. It is because everyone was born with these twelve kinds of sin in his heart. Everyone is born with these twelve kinds of sins from their very birth. Thus, everyone has evil thoughts in his heart. We are therefore "a brood of evildoers." Because such sinful nature is in us, God said, "You are originally a brood of evildoers." As a brood of evildoers, we were born with sin from our fleshly parents from our births. Therefore, we commit these twelve kinds of sins while living in this world.
Because humans are scrupulous, they can commit all twelve kinds of sins in turn. Someone can commit three kinds of sins even in one night. An impatient person schemes many sins at once to tear down another. The Scriptures speak about the sin of adultery. You know what "lewdness" is, don't you? Lewdness is in the heart of every one of you. There is no one in this world who does not have lewdness in his heart.
Jesus said, *"What comes out of a man, that defiles a man"* *(Mark 7:20)*. And He also said, "Humans are this kind of offspring of sin who were originally born with twelve kinds of

sins. Humans are offspring of sin." Therefore, everyone has a lewd heart. Because humans have such a lewd heart, humans find lewd things and continue to commit such lewd deeds even if no one teaches them. They also invent new items that make them enjoy lewdness even more. Do you know the most successful business on the internet is? There are millions of porno websites with a collection of all kinds of lewd photos and movies. One can turn on a personal computer, connect to the internet, and log on to such a website and pay some fee and see all these lewd things. There are all kinds of lewd photos and movies in such websites. Humans make these things and also look such things because they are a brood of evildoers.

All vegetables show themselves purely according to what God has told them. You don't get two kinds of flowers on a tree. Each one shows itself only in one form that God has allowed. The flowers of azaleas show themselves exactly as an azalea. It cannot show itself in any other form. This azalea propagates azaleas until the end of the world. It will bloom and wither away as an azalea. This is true. It is unable to blossom other kinds of flowers. Of course, it will show itself in various kinds of flowers when humans cross-breed them artificially. But the fact is that it shows itself exactly in one form naturally. This means that it has the original form purely forever. How is grass then? Grass is grass until the end of the world. What about a pine tree? A pine tree continues to show itself as a pine tree.

But how are humans? Because humans always have twelve kinds of sins in their hearts, these lewd hearts will arise; evil thoughts will come up, and it will also manifest behaviors of thievery. Therefore, everyone is a sinner in the presence of God. And so we always have sins in our hearts if we do not receive the cleansing of all these sins. Therefore the Lord said that we must receive the cleansing of our sins.

Before the presence of God, there are some sins which are harbored in the heart and some sins that are physically carried out. The sins humans put into action are called trespasses or personal sins since they actually violate the statutes of the Law. And the sins mankind holds onto quietly in the heart are called original sins. Humans have such sins in their hearts.

Humans are originally lewd offspring. Humans are a brood of evildoers who always harbor evil thoughts. Humans are the offspring that steals. Humans are the species that commits murder. They are the species that commits adultery. They are the species that covets. They are an evil species. They are a deceitful species. They are a lewd species. They have evil eyes. They are the offspring that blasphemes. They are arrogant. Humans are crazy a species.

If a human does not know his fundamental nature, he will not seek salvation from God and also cannot receive the remission of his sins because he does not need to believe in the righteousness of God which is manifested in the gospel of the water and the Spirit. Thus, we must know that a human is originally an offspring of evil. God says to us, "You are sinners. The wages of sin is death. You shall die if you have sin. You will go to hell if you have sin." If one has sin in the light of the Word of God, the consequence of this is death. Death here refers to spiritual and eternal death that is, being cast into hell.

Then How Must We Believe to Receive Salvation from All Our Sins?

Let's think about the gospel of the water and the Spirit that makes us receive salvation from our sins. Let's think about how the Lord saved us and from what sins He saved us. The Lord spoke the Truth, that is, the Word of the water and the Spirit to us. And the Lord taught us that we are really people who are full of sins. We are the people who commit sins with our hearts and with our actions before the presence of the Lord. We are the people who commit sins throughout our lifetime until the moment of death. Jesus came to save us who cannot but fall into sins and be cast into hell from all sins. Hence, Jesus is our Savior. The Lord has become our Savior and blotted out all our sins by His righteousness and, therefore, we must receive our salvation by faith.

Jesus said that we must cleanse away the sins from our hearts completely. But cleansing all our sins cannot be achieved by our fleshly works. It means that we cannot do this even by weeping or trying hard. We must receive the remission of sins only by believing in the righteousness of the Lord. What does the righteousness of the Lord mean here? It means that the Lord has blotted out all our sins by the gospel of the water and the Spirit.

Jesus rebuked the hypocrisy of the Pharisees. He said, "Such and such sins spill out from the heart of humans and these things defile them. You cannot become clean by your hypocritical works. Your sins are not blotted out no matter how much you wash your hands and take a bath. And your hearts do not become clean no matter how you eat clean food with your washed hands. Therefore, you must receive the remission of your sins by believing in Jesus Christ."

Those who just believe in Christian doctrines, that is, those who do not know that they have twelve kinds of sins in their hearts while believing in Jesus as their Savior, do not know that Jesus came to this world and blotted out all our sins by receiving baptism from John the Baptist and shedding blood on the Cross. Yet many Christians still just piously carry their Bible's, and their positions in the church continue to move up. They then offer up money and polish their outward appearances while learning worship rituals and formalities. Such people must return back to the gospel of the water and the Spirit. They must turn to Jesus Christ with a sincere heart and listen to the Word of the gospel of the water and the Spirit which Jesus spoke about.

Do you really have filthy sins in your heart? Have you committed sins until now? And will you commit sins again in the future? You must ask these hard questions and look into yourself honestly. If you still are a sinner before the presence of God, you must acknowledge before Him that you are a sinner. And you must really learn what God says about this genuine salvation. You must receive the remission of your sins by understanding the gospel of the water and the Spirit and you must believe in it. You must really become a beautiful believer. People must now stop leading a wrong spiritual life of just decorating their outsides while believing in Christianity. Such people are today's Pharisees spiritually.

If some among you happen to think that Christianity is one of the religions of the world, then you must immediately turn to the gospel of the water and the Spirit as early as you can. Christianity that only clings to various kinds of formalities must turn from such wrong faith because no one can receive the remission of their sins by offering prayers of repentance. We must depart from Christianity that emphasizes only the outward appearance and return to the gospel of the water and the Spirit. Some Christians say, "I have always had sins in my heart although I had believed for three years. And I believed in Jesus for three more years after that, but I became an even more treacherous sinner." They say that their sins have become

heavier because they have increased so much more while they
had believed in Jesus for 10 years. We must now turn from
such formalistic faith immediately and believe in the gospel of
the water and the Spirit if we do not want to lament in this way.
"Jesus said, 'Come to Me, all you who labor and are heavy
laden, and I will give you rest,' but my sins have instead
increased, and my heart has become heavy laden. I have
believed in Jesus as my Savior for ten years, but my sins have
been added onto my back. They are too heavy. I had hope
when I first believed in Jesus and my heart also was not so
heavy then. But my sins oppress me even more now that I have
believed in Jesus for these ten years. How heavier would my
heart become if I believe in Jesus for 20 years?"

I asked this question to a Christian who had believed in
Jesus as his Savior for 50 years: "Do you have sins? The Word
in the Old Testament Book of Isaiah chapter 1 verse 18 states,

'Come now, and let us reason together,'
Says the LORD,
'Though your sins are like scarlet,
They shall be as white as snow;
Though they are red like crimson,
They shall be as wool.'

If this is so, then has your sins been blotted out as white as
snow?"

That person then replied, "How can my sins be blotted
out? The sins in my heart have increased since I have believed
for 50 years. I am trying to receive the cleansing of sins by
offering these prayers of repentance every day! I am thus
praying hard to attain sanctification."

Why does this Christian say this? It's because this person
has believed in Jesus as his Savior by legalistic faith! It's
because he has believed without knowing the righteousness of

God so far! A person who has believed for 50 years and a person who has believed for 10 years are the same in that they both have sins since they do not know the gospel of the water and the Spirit. Of course, the weight of their sins would be different. However, we cannot say that a person who has believed for 50 years has more sins, and a person who has believed for 10 years has less sins. They just feel that they have more or less sins. It just means that their understanding of the amount of sins they have is more or less, but they are all the same in that they both have sins.

Why are you still a sinner although you have believed in Jesus as the Savior? It's because you do not believe in the Word of God and have not accepted the gospel of the water and the Spirit. Jesus has come to us who are such sinners by the gospel of the water and the Spirit in order to blot out all our sins once and for all. Although the Lord has saved you from the sins of the world once and for all by this gospel, you have not been able to receive salvation because you could not recognize that you are a brood of evildoers, and therefore could not receive the remission of sins by believing in the gospel of the truth which the Lord has given to you. You have become a sinner because you have not believed in the Lord's love that gave the remission of sins through the gospel of the water and the Spirit, not because God has not bestowed salvation on sinners like you.

Therefore, you must return back to the gospel of the water and the Spirit immediately. And you must learn what the Scriptures say about the righteousness of God. When you study about the righteousness of God in the Word of God, you come to know the truth of salvation that has come by the gospel of the water and the Spirit and come to receive this genuine freedom by believing in this gospel Truth. And you come to know your true self also.

Every sinner should know first that everyone commits these twelve kinds of sins until the moment of their deaths. This is correct. Sins are not cleansed no matter how much people offer prayers of repentance because they continue to commit such sins. Your sins cannot be cleansed away even if you lament over your sins. Your sins cannot be cleansed even if you offer up money to God for the remission of your sins. Your sins cannot be cleansed even if you die a martyr for the Lord. Your sins can only be cleansed away by believing in the gospel of the water and the Spirit with which the Lord saved us from all our sins. Only then can your sins be washed away perfectly.

In the region of the Himalayan Mountains, many believe in Buddhism. They believe that they must practice asceticism to blot out their sins and to be born in a better circumstance when they are reincarnated in the next world. There is a place called "the holy land" for them. It is very far from their homes. However, they go to that holy place by walking a few steps and then bowing known as the five point prostrations, and they do this repeatedly. They bow towards this holy place touching ground with the five parts of their bodies and get up. And they fall on their stomach again. They repeat such behavior until they reach that far away so-called holy place. After worshipping Buddha at this holy place, they return all the way back to home in the same way they came. They practice asceticism like this.

All the religions of this world are like this. They think that they receive the remission of their sins by practicing asceticism, by sacrificing, and by knowing the Christian doctrines very well. But I am telling you clearly that you can only receive the remission of your sins only by believing in the gospel of the water and the Spirit, and not by doing such absurd things. Do not believe in Christianity like one of the religions of this world. The religions of this world are like an addictive drug. People say that such drugs make them feel great when they use it for the first time. They say that they feel like they own the entire world when they use drugs for the first time. However, the strength of the drug soon wears out. Then their hands and feet begin to tremble. And then begin suffering from so-called "withdrawal symptoms." And so they have to take it again. And when they have used drugs for a long time, they have to inject this drug into themselves with a syringe within 5 minutes repeatedly. They go crazy when they stop doing this. The religions of the world are so different to this. We must throw away such religious faith that comes from any worldly religion. And we must really know how the Lord has saved us from the sins of the world through the gospel Truth of the water and the Spirit.

We must know our original sin through the recorded Word of God. And we must know such things, like why we humans were born; what we were born with; and how we live and where we are destined to go after we die. We can learn all these things through the Word of God. We must know that we receive the remission of sins only by believing in the gospel of the water and the Spirit. Therefore, we must without delay learn the gospel Truth of the water and the Spirit. We must cut the bondage of any formalistic faith of Christianity that has bound us so tightly. Among those sitting here today, there probably are many who have received the remission of sins by believing in the gospel of the water and the Spirit, but I think some of you have not received the remission of sins perfectly yet. Even if there are some people who have not received the remission of sins yet, you can be freed from all sins if you learn the righteousness of God step by step and then to believe in it.

You and I commit sins until the moment of our deaths. Can these sins then be blotted out by offering prayers of repentance? Christianity of this world understands prayers of repentance as a means to reach sanctification. However, did Jesus say that He blotted out our original sin but He did not blot out our personal sins and, therefore, we had to cleanse our personal sins by offering prayers of repentance every day? Where in the Scriptures does it say this?

Let's think about this seriously for a moment. Does it make any sense? We would have to cleanse the sins we commit until the moment of our death by offering these prayers of repentance, but would this be at all possible? Let's think about this today. We would have to think of all the sins we have committed from when we woke up until we go to bed. If this is possible can we offer prayers of repentance for all those sins? However, there are so many sins that we have forgotten about and only one or two sins that we have really done wrong remains in our memory, but can even those few sins be blotted out by offering prayers of repentance? No, they cannot be blotted out by this means. Sin cannot be blotted out like this. Every sin is blotted out absolutely by believing in the baptism Jesus received from John the Baptist and the blood He shed on the Cross.

Because Adam and Eve committed sin, we their descendants inherited this sin and could not but commit sins and be destroyed since we were born with sin. Moreover, humans commit sins until the moment of their deaths. Therefore, the people of this world make up a religion like this and try to cleanse their sins away only by offering prayers of repentance. But would your sins be blotted out just because you offered up prayers of repentance? Where in the Scriptures does it say that only our original sin was blotted out? Did the Lord not say that He would blot out all the sins of the world?

Jesus said, *"It is finished!" (John 19:30)* while dying on the Cross after receiving His baptism. Jesus came to this world once in the flesh of man, received baptism to take all the sins of the world once and for all, and bore the condemnation for all those sins by dying on the Cross once and for all. And the Lord was resurrected once and for all and ascended to the Kingdom of Heaven. The Lord has thus become the Savior of humanity and now rests on the seat at the right hand of the throne of God the Father. Now you can receive salvation from all your sins just by believing in Jesus Christ who came by the gospel of the water and the Spirit. It is because Jesus is your Savior.

Dear fellow believers, it is useless even if you go before the presence of God and offer these prayers of repentance every day by saying, "God, I have committed such and such sins. Please forgive me." Jesus does not go to the Cross and blot out your sins every day for you. Jesus fulfilled the work of blotting out all your sins once and for all by receiving the baptism from John the Baptist and shedding His blood on the Cross about 2000 years ago. We must know this gospel Truth of the water and the Spirit well.

We must not believe in Jesus like the people of this world who believe in their worldly religions. Religion is like a powerful drug. You must boldly throw it away. What have you received by knowing and believing in Christianity so far as a system of religious rituals? You only have gotten more sins, and you have wasted your time and money.

Are we not all the offspring born with sins, the people who really cannot but commit sins until the moment of their deaths? But the Lord came to this world to save us from the sins of the world. And the Lord has saved us from all these sins by the baptism He received from John the Baptist and the precious blood He shed on the Cross. We praise the love of God and His righteousness.

I really give praise and thanks to the Lord who saved us from all sins by the gospel of the water and the Spirit. ✉

SERMON

2

Acknowledge the Word And Seek God's Mercy

< Mark 7:1-23 >

"Then the Pharisees and some of the scribes came together to Him, having come from Jerusalem. Now when they saw some of His disciples eat bread with defiled, that is, with unwashed hands, they found fault. For the Pharisees and all the Jews do not eat unless they wash their hands in a special way, holding the tradition of the elders. When they come from the marketplace, they do not eat unless they wash. And there are many other things which they have received and hold, like the washing of cups, pitchers, copper vessels, and couches. Then the Pharisees and scribes asked Him, 'Why do Your disciples not walk according to the tradition of the elders, but eat bread with unwashed hands?' He answered and said to them, 'Well did Isaiah prophesy of you hypocrites, as it is written:

'This people honors Me with their lips,
But their heart is far from Me.
And in vain they worship Me,
Teaching as doctrines the commandments of men.'

For laying aside the commandment of God, you hold the tradition of men the washing of pitchers and cups, and many other such things you do.' He said to them, 'All too well you reject the commandment of God, that you may keep your tradition. For Moses said, 'Honor your father and your mother'; and, 'He who curses father or mother, let him be put to death.' But you say, 'If a man says to his father or mother, 'Whatever profit you might have received from me is Corban' (that is, a gift to God), then you no longer let him do anything for his father or his mother, making the word of God of no effect through your tradition which you have handed down. And many such things you do.' When He had called all the multitude to Himself, He said to them, 'Hear Me, everyone, and understand: There is nothing that enters a man from outside which can defile him; but the things which come out of him, those are the things that defile a man. If anyone has ears to hear, let him hear!' When He had entered a house away from the crowd, His disciples asked Him concerning the parable. So He said to them, 'Are you thus without understanding also? Do you not perceive that whatever enters a man from outside cannot defile him, because it does not enter his heart but his stomach, and is eliminated, thus purifying all foods?' And He said, 'What comes out of a man, that defiles a man. For from within, out of the heart of men, proceed evil thoughts, adulteries, fornications, murders, thefts, covetousness, wickedness, deceit, lewdness, an evil eye, blasphemy, pride, foolishness. All these evil things come from within and defile a man.'"

What Is the Sin of a Human Being?

I want to speak about the 'human sin' that the Lord spoke of here in today's Scripture reading. What is the sin of human beings? The Gospel of Mark chapter 7 records our sins in detail.

People have their own standards about sin. Some people define a sin as a flaw. And some people think sin is a wrong behavior of a person. In Korea, when parents pass away, their sons and daughters dig a large grave and lower them into the grave carefully and then build a mound over the grave with earth, and cover it with grass. Then the surviving children regularly go to this gravesite and take care of the grass that covers the grave. And they say this is the faithful duty of children. So, if someone does not do this, he would be reproached as a grave sinner

How about other countries? There are some remote regions in Papua New Guinea or the Amazon forest where civilization has not reached yet. Native tribes live there. But we are told that if one dies, his or her descendants gather around their dead parent and eat the corpse so that the animals would not eat it. I don't know whether they boil the dead bodies or they just eat the flesh raw, but they think it is the filial piety of the children to gather together to eat the flesh of their parents so that the worms would not eat them. Therefore, even the concept of filial piety to parents is different from each culture with its own distinction in different societies.

There are many different concept of sin according to human thinking as there are many concept of filial piety to parents. Some people say that a wrongdoing is a sin. Like this, people define the concept of sin according to their value system or their standards. Some people judge the sin according to their ethics and moral standards. They look at a behavior in the light of the social norms that must be kept and they consider it sin when it deviates from those standards.

In Korea, some people stipulate sin in the light of the teachings of Confucianism that has been handed down. So they think it's a grave sin for a person not to follow the virtues such as not honoring their parents faithfully. They think it is very important to abide by Confucian norms. They believe that they don't have sin if they worship their dead ancestors and take care of their parents faithfully with all their devotion. Like this, there are many different concepts of sin in this world.

Therefore, we must know what sin is in the light of God's Word. Then what is the sin of a human being which God is talking about? What part of us constitutes sin? People generally do not know this correctly even though God told us clearly what sin is. That's why we must pay close attention to the Word. That's the only way we can understand correctly about the sin of humans. What is the human sin? It is a sin to try to just keep God's Word without believing in His Word of mercy.

Let's look at the Scripture passage here. When Jesus was in this world, a few Pharisees and the scribes came together around Jesus in Jerusalem and saw that the disciples of Jesus were eating bread without washing their hands. Therefore, the Pharisees and the Scribes pointed to Jesus and His disciples and thought, "Why do they sin?" They stipulated that it was sin according to the tradition of the elders which was made up by their ancestors. The Scriptures records that the Jews thought only the man-made traditions were important and because of this they threw away God's Word.

What would happen when people of Palestine went around together with dust all over their bodies and then returned back home? Their hands and feet as well as their clothes would have been covered in dust. In a word, they would be covered in dust. Therefore, when they got home, those people poured water into a washing basin first and washed their hands and feet clean and dusted off their clothes before entering the house. And before they eat anything and even before they made food, they took out the necessary kitchenware that was previously washed clean and washed it again. And so it is written that they washed "the cups, pitchers and copper vessels."

What would be different with the things at home when even people become completely covered with dust? How much more would they be covered with dust? That's why people washed their hands and feet as well as the kitchenware. And this became the inherited tradition of the people. In other words, this custom was made and inherited because of the natural environment of that dusty region.

Therefore, they needed to wash their hands and feet cleanly if they wanted to eat after going around here and there. Of course we Koreans also wash our hands before eating, but we don't have to absolutely wash our hands and feet before we eat. That's why people in Korea cannot understand such behavior of the Jews. But you will understand a little better if you understand the background of their tradition. The Jews taught their children after playing outside to "wash hands and feet in this manner." And they also taught their children, "Eat food only after washing all the dishes in the house." The teaching that was made necessary because there was so much dust in that region was passed down through many thousands of years. Through about four thousand years of the history of Israel, adults have been teaching their kids like this continuously and their children grew up and passed down this same custom in the same manner to their descendants. And they told them, "You must definitely wash your hands and feet before coming inside and then you can eat food." Therefore, it became the tradition of the elders.

Then one day, Jesus was born to the little village called Bethlehem near Jerusalem in the region of Judea. And when Jesus was grown up He went to Jerusalem with His disciples. And the scribes and Pharisees were also gathered together there. There was a group of the disciples of Jesus and there were some who were not His disciples. And it was the custom that the owner of that house usually served food to the guests when people gathered together there. This is similar to Korean custom. This is the proper custom. There are many similarities between the Israeli custom and Korean custom.

Now, what happened? The disciples of Jesus took the food and ate it without washing their hands and feet. They did this before the people who thought that everyone had to wash their hands and feet before eating. The Pharisees and the scribes who were there with Jesus thought like this, "What ignorant bastards! They are so ignorant." Who did they point the fingers at because the disciples of Jesus behaved like this? It was Jesus who was insulted here. It is recorded in the Scriptures, *"Then the Pharisees and scribes asked Him, 'Why do Your disciples not walk according to the tradition of the elders, but eat bread with unwashed hands.'"* They challenged Jesus in this manner. How did Jesus respond? He said, *"Well did Isaiah prophesy of you hypocrites, as it is written: 'This people honors Me with their lips, But their heart is far from Me. Teaching as doctrines the commandments of men.'"* And He also said, *"All too well you reject the commandment of God, that you may keep your tradition."*

God looks at the center of people's hearts and not the outward appearance. Jesus saw their hearts' when the Pharisees and the scribes told Jesus, "Why don't your disciples keep the tradition passed down by the elders? Why don't they keep the teaching passed down by the elders to wash hands and feet before eating?" Then Jesus answered and said to them, *"Well did Isaiah prophesy of you hypocrites, as it is written: 'This people honors Me with their lips, But their heart is far from Me.'"*

Generally, people thought that it was a sin to discard the tradition and the teachings of people that were passed down from their ancestors. So what did the people of Israel do? They threw away God's commandments and followed after human tradition that were passed down as their ancestors' teachings.

But our Lord said, "Throwing away God's Word is a sin." Then, what is sin? Sin is to throw away God's Word. Of course, trespasses committed by humans, wrongdoings, shortcomings, and not doing what we must do are all sins. But throwing away God's Word is the real and fundamental sin.

What Does Our Lord Dislike the Most?

It is throwing away God's Word instead of believing it as the Truth. He dislikes this the most. And He dislikes not believing in His Word the most. What is the difference in the concept of sin between the Lord and the Pharisees? What is the difference between our thinking and God's thinking? God says it is upright when we believe and accept God's Word of Truth and tells us that we have done well. But God says that it is a sin if we do not believe in His Word and ignore it.

What is the sin of a human being? The original definition of sin (*Hamartia* in Greek) is "to miss the mark." Not believing in the Word according to God's will is sin. Believing in God's Word is hitting the mark perfectly. Put differently, not acknowledging God's Word is committing sin. Not believing in God's Word and throwing it away is sin. God existed even before the creation and then God created this world. Therefore, God Himself is the Master of this world.

What did God say about the sin of the Pharisees? We can see in the Scriptures that Jesus said that people throwing away God's Word and considering human traditions more important is sin. Do you understand what I am saying? The Pharisees are absolute hypocrites in Jesus' eyes; they were people who only decorated themselves splendidly on the outside.

Jesus looked at the Pharisees and judged them, "How could you believe in God and how could you admire and revere Me, and with what could you say that you honor Jehovah God?" They are sinners in God's eyes. They judged others only based on their outward appearance and totally ignored God's Word. Furthermore, they considered the human word very important. That is sin. This is the greatest sin of them all. Not acknowledging God's Word and throwing it away, that is the greatest sin.

Ephesians 2:1 says, *"And you He made alive, who were dead in trespasses and sins."* Here the Bible classifies two kinds of sins namely, trespasses and sins. We sometimes have shortcomings as we live in this world. We refer to it as a trespass or a transgression. The sin we commit due to our shortcoming is referred to as a trespass. The sin we commit with our action because of our shortcoming is also a trespass. But a mistake, a transgression is referred to as a shortcoming or a defect in the Scriptures. As such, sin is divided into trespasses and sins.

But the great sin committed before the presence of God is not acknowledging God's Word. This is the great sin before the presence of God. Those who have not believed in God's Word essentially become the greatest sinners before the presence of God. That's why Jesus rebuked the Pharisees in today's Scripture passage. He was saying that they had thrown away the commandments of God. He was saying that they had thrown away the Word of God as recorded in the Pentateuch, the first five Books recorded by Moses in the Old Testament from Genesis to Deuteronomy. It means that the Pharisees had thrown away the do's and don'ts of God's Word.

What Is the Commandment of God?

Jesus referred to the commandment of God in today's Scripture passage. There are 613 statutes in God's commandments. "Do this, and don't do this. Sleep this way, and do not do this. But do certain things this way." They all say such things. The Ten Commandments that we know well also speak of the do's and don'ts. The Book of Leviticus in the Old Testament records, "Men must do this and women must do that; lift out an animal when it falls into a ditch; and do this but don't do that." There are 613 such statutes that God has spoken of. The 613 statutes constitute the Law. We must reconfirm these commandments continuously and obey them because the do's and don'ts that God has commanded us are God's Word, not the words of mere human beings. We must keep them with faith. We must acknowledge that it is God's Word even though we do not have the ability to live by them. I am saying that we must acknowledge that the Word is right.

Is there any part of God's Word that is not correct? There isn't a single verse that is not right. But the Israelites had essentially thrown away the Word of God. Whether God's commandments consisted of 613 or 1000 statutes, they just did not acknowledge any of them. What the elders said was more important and more respected than what God said. Therefore even during the period when Jesus was in this world, the Israelites believed and acted according to the tradition of the elders instead of on God's Word. And Jesus abhorred that the most.

And what does God say to us? It is written, *"For God has committed them all to disobedience, that He might have mercy on all" (Romans 11:32).* God knows that we will not be able to keep His Word perfectly. But God wanted to make us His children because He had mercy on us.

There Is a Purpose for Which God Gave Us the Law

Of course God knew that we humans could not keep the Words of the Law perfectly that was given to us. But the thing that we must understand is that we should not forget about or ignore every Word that God has spoken to us. What we must do is acknowledge before the presence of God clearly that His Word is always right and that we are really corrupt. Therefore, to make us acknowledge that we are truly great sinners, our Lord gave His Law to us.

For what purpose did God give us the Law? Our female believers, our dear sisters, for what purpose did God give us the Law? What is that purpose? You really understand this well don't you. For what purpose did God give us the Law? It is to make us realize our sins. That's right. It means that God gave us the Law to make us recognize our sin.

Did God give the Law to us thinking that we could keep the Law to the letter? Or, did He give us the Law to make us understand our shortcomings and sins? For what purpose did God give us the Law? The purpose for which the Lord gave us the Law was to make us understand sin (Romans 3:19-20).

Therefore, it was okay that the Israelites including the Pharisees and the scribes were not able to keep the Law. But they should have acknowledged God's Word as God's Word. It was wrong for them to ignore God's Word or throw it away. But the Israelites disrespected God's Word. They disrespected the authority of God's Word.

Romans chapter 3 says that God gave the Law to make us

have the knowledge of sin. Therefore, we fail to understand that God did not give us the Law to keep it. Then what did we understand through the Law? What should we understand through the 613 statutes that say the dos and don'ts of God's commandments? We must think about these things.

We must realize our shortcomings and sins by the Law. We must realize our sins before the presence of God. What should we do if we have realized our sins before the Law? Of course, we must try to keep it even though we are lacking. But what is more important is that we must know our sinful selves through the Law. God gave the Law to us humans for the purpose of making us realize sin and understand that we are really sinners and seek help from God and believe in Jesus Christ. Like this, God gave the Law to us in order to make us His children and His people through faith in Jesus Christ.

Even now, there are so many people who are trying hard to keep the Law. But Jesus said in this verse, *"For laying aside the commandment of God, you hold the tradition of men."* We are people who cannot keep all the Law perfectly. But we must not reject even all God's Word just because we cannot keep the Law. In other words, it is wrong not to acknowledge God's Law. We can acknowledge our shortcomings the moment we acknowledge God's Law. What does this mean? A person comes to acknowledge that he is a sinner by understanding his helplessness and his sin through God's Law.

Do you acknowledge the Word of God's Law with your heart? Let's acknowledge God's Word of the Law right now. We must acknowledge that we are sinners before the presence of God. We must acknowledge that we have many shortcomings when we stand before God's Law. We then ask God for our salvation after we acknowledge God's Law. We must go before the presence of Jesus the only Savior and God who can save us from all our sins and seek His help. God sees whether we have such an attitude or not.

But for what purpose did God give us the Law? We cannot stand before the presence of God uprightly with our own efforts because God gave us the Law to teach us painstakingly that we have shortcomings and that we are sinners. To save those who have come to acknowledge their sinfulness, God sent His Son Jesus Christ to this world to cleanse all the sins away from all human beings and made Jesus Christ receive the baptism and shed His blood on the Cross. Therefore, our God gave us the Law to make us receive the remission of sins and become His children by believing in the gospel of the water and the Spirit.

God gave the Law to us all who are the descendants of Adam. And thereby made us understand our sins. And then He made us acknowledge that we are really complete sinners. Therefore, God gave us the blessing of becoming His children by believing in the righteousness of Jesus and being freed from all our sins. God gave the Law to the descendants of Adam to make them receive all the blessings that He has fulfilled for all human beings. Those who still do not understand the reason why God gave this Law and try to keep the Law even though they are weak are people who dwell under the curse of God.

We must clearly understand the intention of God by giving us the Law. God in the beginning created this universe and you and me with His Word. Therefore, we must start our faith from God's Word. And our thinking must begin to unfold within God's Word as well. We must think, judge, and believe all things according to God's Word. This is the most correct notion.

We must believe in God based on the criteria in His Word. We will definitely fall into errors if we do not do this and if we think of God with our own criteria and act according to our own thinking. The Pharisees and the scribes in today's Scripture passage could not have rebuked the disciples of Jesus for eating the bread with dirty hands if they had seen themselves in the light of God's Word. That's because the things that go into a person's mouth cannot defile that person because they do not enter his heart but his stomach, and then pass through. It's because what really defiles a person is not the food of this world. People are defiled because of the sins that arise out of their hearts, not because of food that goes into their stomachs. Do you understand this?

We Are the Descendants of Adam Who Have Inherited All Sins

The things that come out of human beings are evil thoughts, adulteries, fornications, murders, thefts, covetousness, wickedness, deceit, lewdness, and an evil eye. All these dirty sins come out of a person and defile that person. As Jesus said in the Scriptures, it is the sin inside of someone that defiles him not food.

Romans chapter 11 verse 32 says, *"God has committed them all to disobedience, that He might have mercy on all."* What did God say about human beings? God says that He has mercy on them. God made us His children by bestowing His mercy on people through the gospel of the water and the Spirit. God's purpose and His will were aimed to make us His people. Do you understand this? That's why He made us all be born as the descendants of Adam. And He made us a little less than angels because God originally had love for us; He wanted to make us His children because He had pity on us. God planned and brought His plan into being to make us His children out of His love.

We creatures have become God's children not because we are perfect. We have become God's children by His love for He gave us the gospel of the water and the Spirit out of His mercy. God clothed us with the grace of salvation that makes us His children through the gospel of the water and the Spirit. Do you think that we have become God's children and become sinless because we are righteous and blameless, and because we have acted in an upright manner? No, this is not the case. If our salvation was given to us by our merits, then this would not be the mercy of God. We believers have become God's children by His grace of salvation because Jesus Christ took all our sins upon Him at once through the baptism He received from John the Baptist and because He had pity on us.

We became absolute sinners through God's Law, and then we have entered into that grace of God by believing in the gospel of the water and the Spirit. God made us become His children by making us enter into the grace of salvation by faith. It means that He lifted us creatures up as beings like the creator. Do you understand this work God has done?

The Scriptures say, *"Oh, the depth of the riches both of the wisdom and knowledge of God! How unsearchable are His judgments and His ways past finding out!" (Romans 11:33)* How great is God's wisdom? The riches of perfect wisdom and knowledge are in our Lord. His judgment is unfathomable and His ways are unsearchable. Who knows why people were born with such shortcomings? But we get to know the reason why when we meet Jesus Christ. Oh, how unfathomable the depth of the riches is!

Apostle Paul was born again by believing in the gospel of the water and the Spirit just like us. He was able to say, *"Oh,*

the depth of the riches both of the wisdom and knowledge of
God! How unsearchable are His judgments and His ways past
finding out! For who has known the mind of the LORD? Or
who has become His counselor?" (Romans 11:33-34) That is
because he was born again from sin by believing in the gospel
of the water and the Spirit. Who became the counselor of God?
Who dared to share God's plan with Him? It was God Himself
who thought this and did this. We as mere creatures became the
children of God just by His thought and plan, not because
someone taught us how to become His children. Do you
believe so?

Therefore, even all the angels in the Heaven were
astonished. The angels had higher status than us human beings.
The Scriptures tell us clearly that God created us a little lower
than the angels, saying,

"When I consider Your heavens, the work of Your fingers,
The moon and the stars, which You have ordained,
What is man that You are mindful of him,
And the son of man that You visit him?
For You have made him a little lower than the angels,
And You have crowned him with glory and honor" (Psalm
8:3-5). Human beings were made a little lower than the angels
in the beginning, but suddenly they were in a higher position
than the angels. Those who believed in the gospel of the water
and the Spirit had already become the children of God. That's
why the angels were astonished.

Then, what sort of beings are the children of God? They
are beings similar to God. Of course they are not God. But
those who have received the remission of sins are those who
belong to Heaven. That's why the Book of Psalms states,

"When I consider Your heavens, the work of Your fingers,
The moon and the stars, which You have ordained,

What is man that You are mindful of him,
And the son of man that You visit him?"

God did not just leave us in the midst of destruction, but instead loved us unilaterally and had mercy on us who could not help but be destroyed due to our sins and made us His children by blotting out all our sins. God made us His children and His people by making us sinless. So the writer in the Psalms said, *"O LORD, our Lord, How excellent is Your name in all the earth!"*

And the Apostle Paul said the same exclamatory sentences in the New Testament here. He said that this Truth of salvation is so wondrous and deep. That we mere creatures have reached the status of God is done clearly through His mercy. It is done out of His pity on us. It is impossible for us to become the children of God if not for the grace of the salvation of God. All this is the love of God.

Is it right for us to try hard to keep God's Law even though we are essentially lacking, and is it right for us to dwell in the Law of God and try a little harder and put forth a little more effort to go before the presence of the Lord? Or, isn't it right for us to understand the meaning and the purpose of the Law God has given to us to understand our sin properly, and to understand that we are treacherous sinners, and therefore, desire His mercy before Him? This is right, isn't it? It is right for us to truly realize before the presence of God that we are grave sinners and seek God's mercy. But is it right for you to still try to become righteous by yourself without understanding the purpose of the Law God has given to us?

Therefore the important thing is how we understand God's Word? What is sin? Not believing in God's Word is sin, not acknowledging God's Word is sin, and every lacking before the presence of God is sin. Not believing in this Bible as God's

Word is sin. Not believing and ignoring the gospel of the water and the Spirit even though one understands it is sin.

The Word is God. Therefore, not believing in God's Word is a great sin. So we all must know God through His Word and receive the remission of sins through faith. We receive our salvation from sin only by thinking according to God's Word and believing according to the recorded Word. Then we can receive the remission of our heavy sins inside us through faith only.

A person becomes a sinner thoroughly the moment he understands and acknowledges God's Word and God's Law. Someone who acknowledges God's Law becomes a sinner thoroughly and such a person seeks after the righteousness of God and desires mercy from God and becomes freed from all his sins perfectly by believing in the gospel of the water. Such a person can come to know just how imperfect he really is when he acknowledges God's commandment which is God's Word. He comes to understand what an inadequate sinner he is before the presence of God. He does not boast about his own righteousness just because he kept the Law a little bit or not. When we understand the 613 statutes of dos and don'ts recorded in the Scriptures, we get to cry out for help, "God, I have not kept this Law, but did not keep this other Law either. And God, I cannot keep Your commandments perfectly. God, I cannot keep all Your commandments. I cannot keep them all. Save me from sin." That person who understands thoroughly that he is a sinner seeks God in this way. We do not become a sinner because of our wrongdoings, but we acknowledge that we are sinners because we are essentially born to this world as a mass of sin. And we only have inside us these sins that completely stand against God's commandment. Those who acknowledge God's Law come to understand this fully.

What did Jesus say? He said, "The things that come out of a person defile him. All food that God gives can never defile anyone. All the things of the world are clean." And He said further, *"But the things which come out of him, those are the things that defile a man."*

Human Beings Are Originally Sinners

What does it mean to be born as the descendants of Adam? It means that we are born with sin from our birth. And we commit sin throughout our entire life with the sin that comes out from our hearts because we were essentially born with sin. All God's Law and commandments are upright. There isn't anything wrong with the Word God which speaks to us. Therefore, we come to know that we are sinners who are completely opposite of the commandments of God when we come to know His Law. This Truth speaks about the human proneness to sin, original sinfulness, inherited from the first sinner, Adam. Therefore, such people should kneel before the presence of God and seek pity from Him. Only God's love can truly make us sinless. We humans can only seek this before the presence of God. We come to understand that we cannot do any merits with our own work and that we cannot reduce even a little bit of our sins and therefore seek God's mercy and the salvation of His love. Therefore, we come before the presence of the Lord and kneel before Him unconditionally. We then say, "Lord! Have pity on me."

Look at David's account recorded in the Scriptures. David said, "Lord, I am righteous if You say that I am righteous and it is done according to the judgment of the Word of the Lord. I am a mass of sin if You say that I am a sinner and I more than deserve to go to hell. But I am a righteous person if You say I am righteous. I shall receive salvation if God saves me and I shall go to hell if God sends me to hell. It is all up to You, Lord!" David acknowledged God as such.

This is a truly upright faith. This is the faith and the proper attitude that is able to receive the remission of sins. Some of you may say, "Why are you saying this so emphatically and tediously when we hear this all the time?" But we must understand correctly what sin really is and what constitutes our sin.

I have said that we are the descendants of Adam; and we know that we are sinners. Then is there lewdness in your heart, or isn't there? There is. But what does God tell us? God tells us not to commit adultery. Is there a heart of murder in your hearts, or isn't there? There is. But God's Word tells us not to commit murder. But is there a heart to molest other people in your hearts, or isn't there? There is. God's Word tells us to honor our parents, but do we really honor our parents properly? God's Word is so correct. We are truly evil people when we look at our selves in the light of God's Word. Is this correct, or not? It is correct.

Then What Must We Believe to Be Saved from Sin?

We must first become a mass of sin completely before the presence of God. Then we can acknowledge by ourselves that we are sinners before Him. We are sinners even if we have done some good deeds today. In the same way, we are also sinners even when we have not done any good deeds. People are complete sinners with a mass of sin before the presence of

God if we were born with human flesh even if we did not commit even one iota of sin and we have not done any wrong, not only if we have actually committed sin with our work. It means that we are beings that are doomed to go to hell eventually. Do you believe this?

We did not become sinners by committing wrong deeds, in other words, by committing adultery, stealing, beating up other people, and molesting others. We are sinners because we were originally born with sin. We are sinners who cannot help but go to hell because we were born with a nature that is completely opposite to God. Can a person who was born with sin say that he is righteous just because that person who was born with the heart of murdering did not commit murder or just because that person who has a heart of committing theft did not commit theft? What do you think about this? I am saying that we humans are not essentially righteous.

The Scriptures clearly tells us that a work-oriented faith or a Law-oriented faith is 'hypocritical.' Jesus reproached the Pharisees and the Scribes, "Woe to you, scribes and Pharisees, hypocrites!" He was saying their behaviors were hypocritical. People sin throughout their lifetime because they were already born as a mass of sin. This is the perfectly correct perspective of God concerning human beings. But there probably are some people who say, "I have never used my fist in my whole lifetime and I have never stolen anything either. Therefore I have not sinned even once. Therefore I am not a sinner," even though they were born as a mass of sin. But that is lying before the presence of God. God judges us, "You are a mass of sin. You are a sinner." That's why we are sinners born as a mass of sin even if we did not commit any sin even once, and therefore deserve to go to hell. We are still sinners even if we kept the Law a little bit and obeyed the commandments a little. We cannot help but go to hell in the end.

What then should we do? We must receive pity from God. This is the only thing we can do. We can receive the remission of our sins only if God remits our sins; but we cannot help but to carry our sin and go to hell if He does not blot out our sins. We human beings were born with such a fate.

It is written, *"For of Him and through Him and to Him are all things, to whom be glory forever. Amen" (Romans 11:36)*. All things of this universe are of the Lord, through the Lord and to the Lord. All things in this universe have been created through God. And God created all human beings. The reason God created mankind is to make us His children and live forever together with us in the Kingdom of Heaven. God created you and me for that purpose. Genesis chapter 2 tells all about this. Furthermore, it tells us that our becoming the children of God does not depend on our works but on His love and grace that He has granted upon us unilaterally. Isn't that right?

The People Who Acknowledge God's Word Admit That They Are Complete Sinners

They come to acknowledge that they are sinners that cannot help but go to hell no matter what they do. And these kinds of people who acknowledge the Word in this way eventually come to understand that they are perfectly righteous people by the very Word of God. Therefore, throwing away the Word and not acknowledging God's Word is sin. People who commit such sin remain sinners forever. But those who acknowledge God's Word become sinners first and then become perfectly the righteous. This is being born again through God's Word. This is being clothed with God's grace.

What is sin? Not acknowledging God's Word is sin and throwing away the Word is sin. In the Gospel of Mark chapter 7, Jesus tells us clearly about sin. Through this illustration of the misconception of the Pharisees and the scribes, Jesus clearly defined what sin is all about.

God wanted us humans who were created by God to become sinners first by acknowledging God's Word and then become righteous by believing in His Word of salvation by faith. It means that God wanted to fulfill His plan towards us perfectly because He was the Creator. Therefore, if one throws away God's Word and does not acknowledges His Word, that person will become the biggest sinner and deserves to be sent to hell. That's why we must understand God's Word properly and clearly. We must understand clearly what sin is. I will reiterate this again. We used to be doomed complete to death, but we become perfectly righteous people when we truly acknowledged and believed in God's Word.

Let's look at the Book of Galatians chapter 3 verses 10-11: *"For as many as are of the works of the law are under the curse; for it is written, 'Cursed is everyone who does not continue in all things which are written in the book of the law, to do them.'"* What is recorded here? It says that people who are under the works of the Law are under the curse. People who still try hard to keep God's Word, the Law of God, with their works even now are under the curse of God. It's telling us that those who are trying to cleanse their sins away by offering up prayers of repentance and by doing meritorious deeds are still under the curse of God.

It is written, *"Therefore by the deeds of the law no flesh will be justified in His sight, for by the law is the knowledge of sin" (Romans 3:20).* God gave us the Law to make us have the knowledge of sin. God did not give us the Law because He thought we could keep the Law. Then why did God give us the Law if He did not expect us to keep it? He gave us the Law to make us know our sinful nature. This is the purpose why He gave us the Law. Therefore, it is a great sin not to acknowledge God's Word.

You may then ask, "How can trying to live according to the Word be a sin?" Of course, to fear God and try to obey Him in itself is not wrong. However, God said the heart of a human essentially is a heart of murder, adultery, and pride. And it is arrogant to think that we can keep the Law when we have such an evil heart. Then what sort of person receives salvation from all his sins before the presence of God? Someone who believes in God's Word, someone who acknowledges God's Word, someone who seeks for the remission of his sins from God by acknowledging His Word, is saved from all his sins. Only such people can become the people of God and His children and go to the Kingdom of Heaven. We receive salvation from sin only by believing in all of God's Word.

We receive all the blessings of God only through having faith in His Word. We receive salvation by believing in God's Word, not by keeping the Law. Only such people can receive the remission of their sin by believing in the gospel of the water and the Spirit that God gives. But most Christians today try very hard to keep the Law even though God has given it to us to understand our sinful nature. Most Christians are like this. Their notion of trying to keep the Law is laudable, but they must truly believe that God gave the Law to them to make them have the knowledge of sin (Romans 3:20). Put differently, they must throw away their arrogant thinking that they can live according to God's Law if they just try to keep it. Only then can they receive the merciful love of God. Let me say this again: You must first get rid of your arrogance in order to receive the remission of your sins.

God says that those who try to keep the Law and who are of the works of the Law are under the curse. God says that people who think and believe that they can become sanctified and clean and become righteous to enter the Kingdom of Heaven only by living by the recorded Word of God are still under the works of the Law even now and therefore they are under the curse of God. They still take this for granted and think, "I believe in God as my Savior, but I still must live according to the Word."

Then do people become righteous by living according to God's Word? No, never! They must become a complete sinner first by acknowledging God's Word. They must first become sinners who cannot help but go to hell because of their sins. And then they become perfectly righteous people through faith of believing in the Word Jesus Christ. That's why God established the gospel of the water and the Spirit which saves us from sin through the law of faith. God saved us from sin through faith of believing in the God's gospel of the water and the Spirit, not through the works of any human being. God decided on such salvation to save us from the sins of the world.

It is the sin of human beings to not acknowledge God's Word that came by the gospel of the water and the Spirit. Why then could those sinner Christians not receive the remission of their sins? They did not receive the remission of sins because they did not acknowledge the Word of the gospel of the water and the Spirit that God had spoken about. We who have received this grace from God, have received the remission of our sins because we acknowledged His gospel of the water and the Spirit even though we are lacking just as all other human beings are.

The Scriptures tell us, *"Two women will be grinding at the mill: one will be taken and the other left" (Matthew 24:41).* Then would the woman who was left here continue to spin the millstone, or would she not? Of course she would continue to spin it. Why would one person be taken while the other person is left behind? That's because the one taken up is someone who heard God's Word that came by the gospel of the water and the Spirit and believed in it. But the person who was left behind was cast away after only doing the work that belonged to this world and trying earnestly to keep the Law. Therefore, that person went to hell.

Then why was she cast away? It's because she tried to keep God's Law, God's Word, instead of believing it. She became like this because she tried to become perfect before the presence of God with her arrogant heart instead of just believing in God's Word. What this means is that this person fell into hell while trying to challenge God with his arrogant heart.

We smack the bugs away from us when they try to climb up our legs. Likewise, human beings fall into hell when they try to climb up to God with their works instead of believing in His Word of salvation before the presence of God. God smacks them down when they try to live by keeping the Word with an arrogant heart before His presence. He sends people like this to hell. Therefore, you will indeed go to hell when you climb up to God and go against His righteousness. Do you understand this?

The Scriptures say, *"For as many as are of the works of the law are under the curse; for it is written, Cursed is everyone who does not continue in all things which are written in the book of the law, to do them. But that no one is justified by the law in the sight of God is evident, for the just shall live by faith" (Galatians 3:10-12).* What is recorded here? That's right. It says, *"The just shall live by faith."* Then how can anyone become a righteous person? The righteous can become righteous by faith and the righteous can also live by such faith. The righteous live by faith even though their works are lacking. As it is written, *"For there is not a just man on earth who does good and does not sin" (Ecclesiastes 7:20),* we have not become the righteous because we have not sinned.

Trying to keep God's Word instead of believing in it is sin. Not acknowledging God's Word is sin. I will say this again. Not believing in God's Word is a sin that sends that sinner to hell. I want you to know that this constitutes a grave sin.

We cannot keep God's Word properly because we are essentially the descendants of Adam from our birth. Put differently, it is easy for us to believe in God's Word but it is difficult to keep it because we sin throughout our entire lifetime after being born as a mass of sin fundamentally. Therefore, there is not even a little hope to us as humans. There isn't any hope in our own selves for we also cannot but sin throughout our entire lives. The only hope for us who are such sinners is to believe in Jesus Christ who saved us from all sins through the gospel of the water and the Spirit. We have hope in Him only. Therefore we have received salvation from sin by faith of believing in Jesus Christ who came by the gospel of the water and the Spirit. We believe that He has blotted out all our sins through the gospel of the water and the Spirit, and furthermore, He has blotted out the sins of the whole world. We have received salvation from all our sins through faith of believing in Jesus Christ.

Are you insufficient? Yes, you are. But what is your status now? Have you become the righteous through the gospel of the water and the Spirit? Yes, you have become the righteous.

Then have you become righteous through your works? Have you become righteous by keeping the Law? Or have you become righteous because you tried hard to live according to God's will? No, you have not. Rather, you have become the just through faith of believing in God's Word.

Although God's Word of righteousness was announced to everyone in the same manner, some people believed the Word and the others did not. Those who did not believe went to hell and the believers in the gospel of the water and the Spirit became the children of God and went to Heaven. That they refused to believe in the gospel of the water and the Spirit means that they did not acknowledge God's Word. Trying to live according to God's will even though they don't believe in His Word is arrogance. The Scripture talks about this.

We must get rid of our own righteousness. We can return to the bosom of God when we acknowledge that we are sinners before the presence of God and acknowledge the gospel of the water and the Spirit with faith with the understanding that we are people who cannot help but go to hell. We must understand this Truth of how God saved us with His Word and hold onto it with faith. We must receive the grace of the remission of sins through faith in this manner.

We have received the remission of sins by believing in God's Word. Therefore, we give thanks to God. We have become righteous through God's Word, not through our works. We do not become righteous by trying hard to keep the Word of commandments, but we become righteous at once by faith. We become the righteous just by faith in the gospel of the water and the Spirit. ✉

SERMON

3

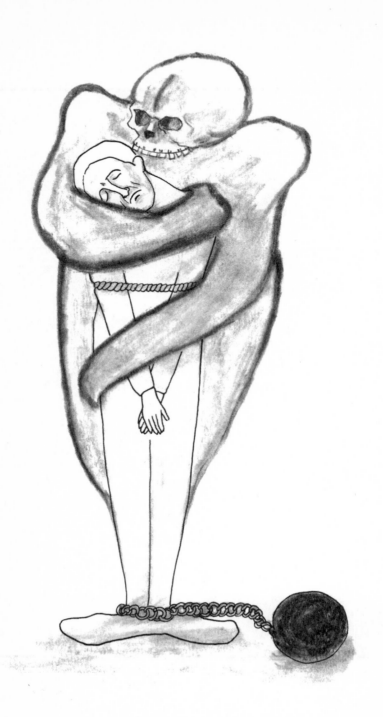

Admit Your
Human Nature

< Mark 7:14-23 >

"When He had called all the multitude to Himself, He said to them, 'Hear Me, everyone, and understand: There is nothing that enters a man from outside which can defile him; but the things which come out of him, those are the things that defile a man. If anyone has ears to hear, let him hear!' When He had entered a house away from the crowd, His disciples asked Him concerning the parable. So He said to them, 'Are you thus without understanding also? Do you not perceive that whatever enters a man from outside cannot defile him, because it does not enter his heart but his stomach, and is eliminated, thus purifying all foods?' And He said, 'What comes out of a man, that defiles a man. For from within, out of the heart of men, proceed evil thoughts, adulteries, fornications, murders, thefts, covetousness, wickedness, deceit, lewdness, an evil eye, blasphemy, pride, foolishness. All these evil things come from within and defile a man.'"

Warm greetings to all of you! I have been mostly ministering in a country church, and so I feel a bit out of place to meet and preach to you in such a huge metropolitan city as Seoul. But I am nevertheless still very glad to meet you all. I actually get quite nervous when I stand before a large crowd, and it takes me a while before I get used to it. So let me ask you for your understanding beforehand.

All our workers ministering across Korea and beyond have been very busy. The past few years have been particularly busy, but even amidst all this work God has bestowed abundant blessings on us. Words cannot express just how grateful we are to the Lord for saving so many souls from their sins, and also for making it possible for us His saints to preach His righteousness. I thank God for enabling us to carry out even more of His work and joyfully serve the Lord every day. While carrying out so much work of God, we have faced many difficulties in our busy schedule, but we've been so happy with our work that we have not felt any burden. And we also appreciate the fact that what we have labored for God's work is only a small part of the work needed to fulfill all the will of the Lord. So let us renew our hearts and faithfully carry out all the remaining work of God in these end times.

We have struggled a lot in recent years, facing numerous challenges while trying to broaden our ministry into new areas unfamiliar to us. Our new series of books for spiritual growth are the products of such an endeavor, and we have made some of our books available to you for free today. Feel free to take them and read them for yourself, as well as share them with everyone around you, including those who still have not heard the gospel of the water and the Spirit and those who already have. I am sure that everyone will find many things in our books that are spiritually beneficial.

It takes little effort for you to receive and read our free gospel books, but it takes a lot of labor for me to actually publish them. In fact, I struggled so much with the first book that I even felt like never publishing another book again. But we have persevered through all our difficulties, and I would like to take this opportunity to thank each and every one of our ministry workers for their diligent labor.

Of course, I am not the only one who has worked so hard. I'm sure that all of you realize just how much work our saints in the Church have done at my request, not to mention our brothers and sisters at the Mission School. Many brothers and sisters there as well as all our saints in the Church, have worked so hard that some of them are totally exhausted. Whenever I see them like this, I am very grateful, but at the same time I feel sorry for giving them so much work.

I've even heard some brothers and sisters talking about how much they are struggling with all this work. Of course, they don't say this to me directly, but I've heard a few grumbling words behind my back. Yet even amidst all this hardship, we recently published a few pamphlets. And this was achieved, thanks to all our saints' hard work, devoting their precious time and effort to our ministry. Each and every one of our achievements is a product of our collective labor. And if there are any shortcomings, they are all our shortcomings as well, and so I ask you to kindly overlook them. I can't help but thank God for the fact that even such faulty people like us can still serve God, and I'm sure that you also feel the same way.

What Is Human Nature in God's Sight?

Let me ask you a question: In God's sight is everyone clean or filthy by nature? You may wonder why I am asking such a question at the beginning of my sermon. I'd like to begin the first day of this revival meeting with a serious issue rather than a light one.

God says that everyone is precious, for God made man in the likeness of His own image. But because Adam fell into

Satan's temptation, he and all his descendants turned into sinners. And because all the descendants of Adam have sin in their hearts, none of them are clean. Even though most people try to forget the fact that their hearts are filthy, it is an undeniable fact that our human hearts are very filthy even in our own eyes.

I have received the remission of my sins by believing in the gospel of the water and the Spirit. But when I look at my fleshly heart, I can see that it still has many carnal desires. It was only after I reached my forties that I could admit this sinful nature of mine to God. Before then, I used to get very angry if anyone called me unclean. Not only did I get offended, but I also protested very loudly, absolutely refusing to accept such an allegation. In time, however, I eventually came to realize just how prone my body was to commit unclean acts in this world, both before God and before man.

So all of us should answer this question God asks of us honestly: "Are you really clean before Me, or just the opposite?" You should admit that you have sin before God and therefore you are unclean. God sees every aspect of us, both of the flesh and of the spirit. Only someone who knows that he is a filthy human being and a vile sinner in God's sight can receive the remission of his sins by believing in the God-given gospel of the water and the Spirit. Put differently, only those who recognize clearly that they are filthy sinners before God can be cleansed by believing in the gospel of the water and the Spirit. Why is this so? It is because God has made it possible only for such honest people to wash their hearts clean with the gospel Truth of the water and the Spirit. Such people who are able to admit their sinfulness to God and recognize that they are doomed to be condemned for their sins—none other than these are the blessed who can receive the remission of their sins by believing in the gospel of the water and the Spirit.

There are countless people living in this world. But it seems that few actually realize that they are bound to be condemned for their sins. Most people carry on with their lives without any concern, forgetting the fact that they themselves will bear the condemnation of sin. Perhaps they live like this because they cannot help it. How about you then? When you consider yourself, do you think that you are a decent and upright person? Why do you think that you are such a wonderful person when you see yourself in a mirror, even though when you look deep side your heart, you know that you are completely worthless? Some of you may be offended to hear me saying that you are worthless inside, but I'm saying this because everyone is a sinner before God until and unless one receives the remission of sins.

Most people refuse to admit their sins because they think too highly of themselves, and they don't like it when they are criticized or called a sinner by someone else. That is why so many people evaluate themselves so generously, all according to their own thoughts. As mentioned, I have received the remission of my sins by believing in the gospel of the water and the Spirit. But before receiving the remission of sins, I did not think that I myself would bear the condemnation of my sins that the Bible spoke about. However, now that I have received the remission of sins, I know that I would have borne this condemnation had I not believed in the gospel of the water and the Spirit.

When God said to me, "You cannot keep the Law. You are a sinner that commits murder and adultery. You steal, you are jealous, you quarrel constantly, you are arrogant, and you act foolishly," I was able to admit that I was such a man and say to God, "Yes, Lord, I am indeed such a man, and that's why I have to believe in the gospel of the water and the Spirit." However, even after receiving the remission of sins by believing in the gospel of the water and the Spirit, it took me a long time before I could really admit that I was committing all of the twelve sins that Jesus spoke of in today's Scripture passage.

Is this not also the case for you? Do you really acknowledge every God-spoken Word in your life? If you heard someone calling you a filthy man, would you be able to keep your face? Only when you accept the Word of God into your heart is it possible for you to truthfully admit your spiritual condition. Everyone is a sinner in God's sight. If you look deep inside yourself, you will realize that you commit sin constantly throughout your life. Yet despite this, too many people do not realize that they themselves are sinners, deluding themselves into thinking that they don't commit any sin at all.

Even among animals, there are some that cleanse and groom themselves. Dogs and cats do this regularly. I recently realized this when I saw my own dog trying to cleanse itself. Even a dog tries to cleanse itself. For instance, when a dog gets mud on its body, it tries to wipe it off by rubbing itself against the floor or the wall.

Even dogs want to be clean like this, but there are many people who refuse to wash away their hearts' sins by believing in the gospel of the water and the Spirit. Even though everyone is destined to be destroyed for the sins that are piled up high in their hearts, too many people have no intention at all to blot them out by believing in the gospel of the water and the Spirit.

The Book of Proverbs in the Old Testament says, *"There is a generation that is pure in its own eyes, yet is not washed from its filthiness" (Proverbs 30:12)*. This means that a lot of people think that they don't have to cleanse away their sins.

Even though they clearly have unclean sins, and they themselves are filthy human beings soiled in grime, they just are not interested in washing. They think on their own that everything is just fine even if they remain unwashed, despite the fact that they can actually cleanse away all their sins by believing in the gospel of the water and the Spirit. Referring to these people Proverbs 30:12 says, *"There is a generation that is pure in its own eyes, yet is not washed from its filthiness."*

If You Recognize That You Are a Filthy Human Being, You Ought to at Least Try to Wash Away Your Sins

Many people living in this world simply have no interest in washing away their sins. This is a vexing conundrum. If there is a way for you to wash away all your sins by believing in the gospel of the water and the Spirit, shouldn't you at least choose this way? What would you do if you were in their shoes? If there is a way for you to wash away your sins by faith, then of course you should choose this way!

However, many people still refuse to expose themselves before God as sinners destined to be condemned for their sins. Some people try to solve the problem of their sins in strange ways, seeking the remission of sins by offering their own prayers of repentance or doing good deeds. These people try to do many good deeds and dedicate their time and effort to what they think is a good and worthy cause, but can all your sins be really washed away once and for all by relying on your own virtuous deeds? No, of course not!

This is because no one can reach salvation through his own work, but our Lord has given us the gospel Truth of the water and the Spirit, the only means by which all our sins can be washed away. However, for you to believe in this gospel of the water and the Spirit, you must first recognize that you are a sinner destined to be destroyed for your sins. It's because of sin that the Bible says that human beings are like the beasts that perish.

From where do the sins of mankind come? Do they arise out of one's circumstances, or do they fundamentally proceed from the human heart? Do people commit sin because of their fundamentally sinful nature, or because of their circumstances? What do you think? This question is answered by our Lord in today's Scripture reading; and so let us turn to His Word and read it once again.

The Lord's Explanation of Our Sins

Let's first turn to Mark 7:14-15: *"Hear Me, everyone, and understand: There is nothing that enters a man from outside which can defile him; but the things which come out of him, those are the things that defile a man."*

What did our Lord say to us here? He said, *"The things which come of him, those are the things that defile a man."* Through His spoken Word, our Lord is saying to us, "Your hearts are filled with filthy sins, and you act out this sinful nature all the time."

Everyone likes to rationalize himself by justifying his actions—that is, people rationalize their actions according to their sinful thoughts. They do this typically by blaming their circumstances for their sins claiming, "It's not my fault that I am committing sin now it is because my circumstances are bad. It's because of I'm living in a bad environment that I've been spoiled." Another common way where people justify themselves is blaming their acquaintances for their own sins, claiming that someone else tempted them and misled them to do such bad things. They protest loudly that they themselves were actually good people in the beginning, but they went astray and fell into sin because of someone else. All their sins and all their misfortunes are therefore traced back to someone else other than themselves, arguing that they are just innocent victims.

Like this, most people think that they are good by nature, and whenever they do anything bad, they blame someone else for leading them astray. However, the Bible clearly says that everyone is born as a depraved sinner. As Adam's descendant, everyone is born into this world as a wicked human being. In other words, all of us were born as a brood of evildoers (Isaiah 1:4).

Let's turn to the Bible and see what our God actually says to us about this issue. It's written in Mark 7:20, *"What comes out of a man, that defiles a man."* What does this passage mean? It means that everyone is born with filthy sins. Put differently, we commit sin in our lives because we were born with filthy sins from the beginning. This is what the Word of God says. And this Word of God is the absolutely undeniable and irrefutable Truth.

Lions sit at the top of the food chain in the animal kingdom and prey upon weaker animals. When a lion hunts down a gazelle, it's just doing what comes natural to it as a carnivorous animal. The same is true for human beings as well. Since we were born with sin, it's only natural for us to commit sin throughout the rest of our lives. That is why all human beings are a brood of evildoers. This is a self-evident and incontrovertible fact.

Yet despite this, countless people still refuse to recognize that they are such sinful beings. But unless they admit their sinful nature, they cannot be saved. It is therefore absolutely imperative for you to grasp your fundamentally sinful nature from the Word of God. You must begin anew by believing in the gospel Truth of the water and the Spirit. If you really want to become a child of God, you must first see and recognize your sinful self. And then you must believe in the gospel of the water and the Spirit with your heart and wash away all your sins by faith. Only then can you become God's own child.

Our Lord came to this earth to save us from all the sins of the world. Why then did He have to be baptized by John the Baptist, and why did He have to be crucified to death? It was to bear all our sins that Jesus was baptized by John the Baptist, and it was because of this baptism that the Lord had to be crucified to death. And Christ had to do all these things because all of us were born with sin.

However, countless people still continue to live in great confusion, dragged around by so many religions that promise salvation but can't deliver. The religious leaders of this world do not admit that they themselves were born as sinners. On the contrary, they teach that everyone is born as a good human being, that people commit sin only because of their bad circumstances, and that only such people need to receive the remission of sins. Yet these religious leaders themselves were born with filthy sins, but they have no inclination whatsoever to admit this. It's actually unimaginable for them to ever admit and call themselves filthy, since they are supposed to be pious as religious leaders. So far from speaking out about the innate sinful nature of humans, they all try to comfort their followers with their mistaken understanding of human nature, saying, "You were born as a decent human being. Your character and integrity are beyond reproach. So don't let anyone make you feel bad about yourself." In other words, these religious leaders only stroke their followers' ego and do not actually speak out about their sins. This is nothing more than whitewashing.

Most people like to listen to someone who says kind words about them. In particular, all churches around the world do this when a new member is introduced to the congregation as someone decent and great. But what would happen if a new church attendee were instead introduced like this: "Today we have a sinner who has come looking for God"? Of course, no pastor would ever say this! Common sense dictates that this just is not feasible. However, in spiritual terms, any and all unsaved people are sinners, even if they attend church.

My Testimony

When I first planted God's Church in a small City, I did not have enough money to open the Church in a nice place. But I still felt compelled to open God's Church, as I yearned to serve the Lord's gospel of the water and the Spirit. So I rented the second floor of a small building by the sea, which was actually little more than a shack. The winds blowing off the sea stirred up so much sand that it even spilled into the church building. If I did not clean the church building even for just one day, sea sand would be all over the floor. So I had to sweep and clean the floor every day, using a large, wet towel to wipe the floor on my knees. The building itself was so old that it was all stained and discolored. But still, I wiped the stairway with a wet towel, thinking that no one would want to come to this church to worship if it was so dirty, and hoping that at least some people would come if the church was clean.

Of course, this was all just my own wishful thinking. After all, no one comes to church just because it's clean. Besides there was only so much I could clean up with such an old shack. Even so I still tried to spruce up the building, painting over stained and dirty areas and doing anything I could just to make it look nice. There was a very important spiritual lesson I learned in those days. While washing the mop which was used to wipe the church floor I thought to myself: "Just as this mop is dirty, everyone's heart is also filthy. When people walk up this stairway into the Church, I will cleanse them all and present them to the Lord as His holy brides. The Lord bore all these people's sins once and for all by being baptized by John the Baptist and saved them all by dying on the Cross, and so I will preach this Truth to them and make them believe that the Lord has washed their hearts from all their sins. The Lord will be happy when their hearts are all cleansed. I will preach the gospel of the water and the Spirit to them and present them all to the Lord as His brides."

I wanted to become a matchmaker of the soul who could say to the Lord, "Lord, here are your brides. They have received the remission of sins once and for all by believing in your gospel of the water and the Spirit. These people are your brides. Please welcome them all into your Kingdom." And in time, I realized that I had indeed become a true matchmaker of the soul before Jesus Christ. Before this moment of awakening, I had considered it only a hypothetical notion that I was a matchmaker of Jesus Christ, but while wiping the church floor and washing the dirty mop, I realized clearly that my purpose on this earth was preaching the gospel of the water and the Spirit to all the sinners of this world, wash their filthy hearts, and present them to the Lord as His brides. It had dawned on me once again that my duty on this earth was preaching the gospel of the water and the Spirit.

"What Comes Out of a Man, That Defiles a Man" *(Mark 7:20)*

Our Lord said in Mark 7:20-23: *"What comes out of a man, that defiles a man. For from within, out of the heart of men, proceed evil thoughts, adulteries, fornications, murders, thefts, covetousness, wickedness, deceit, lewdness, an evil eye, blasphemy, pride, foolishness. All these evil things come from within and defile a man."*

When I stood before this Word of God, I realized that the Lord was speaking about me. And I realized that all human beings were born as a filthy brood of evildoers by nature. Our Lord made this clear to all of us. Indeed, when we acknowledge the Lord's Word and look at ourselves honestly, we cannot help but admit our sinfulness and say to Him, "Lord, You are right. You saw right through me. You are completely right. You have spoken plainly and clearly. Your Word is true. I am indeed who you say I am. I am such a sinner with evil thoughts, adulteries, fornications, murders, thefts, covetousness, wickedness, deceit, lewdness, an evil eye, blasphemy, pride, and even foolishness."

When I accepted the Word of the Lord by faith and examined myself before God, I realized that what the Lord said in today's Scripture passage was spoken to none other than me. This God-spoken Word was a completely accurate description of myself, for I was such a sinner in the Lord's sight whose thoughts were evil, lewd, wicked, blasphemous, proud and foolish. When I looked back at my past, I saw that I was indeed such a depraved sinner who had committed adultery, theft, and murder in my heart.

But you will be surprised to hear that despite my utter sinfulness, people in my hometown actually considered me rather highly. I used to get praised all the time for being such a polite, well mannered young man, and my parents were the envy of the neighborhood for having raised such a good son. But in reality, I had each and every one of the twelve sins listed in today's Scripture passage.

Let me tell you a story from my seminary days to illustrate just how much I struggled with my sins. A professor at my seminary once told the class to never look at any lewd posters when passing by a theatre, instructing us to call on the name of the Lord three times if we felt tempted. I had to pass by a theatre on my way from the seminary to my dormitory. Most times I had no trouble walking pass the theatre. But whenever I saw a poster with a scantily clothed woman, I found myself drawn to the theatre for some reason. It was actually lust rearing its ugly head in my heart. Though suppressed most of the time, all it took was the right circumstances for lust to surface.

It would have been not so bad if I stopped at just stealing a glance at the poster. If the poster was particularly revealing, then I would want to take a closer look at some of the smaller pictures posted by the entrance of the theater below the giant poster. If I had any company, I would say to him, "Why don't you go first; I have some business to take care of." When asked about where I was going, I would say, "It's just I have something to take care of. So you go first and wait for me. I'll catch up with you in ten minutes." And if my friend wanted to go with me, I would say, "Actually, I have to go there alone. So why don't you go first and I will catch up with you later." After sending away my friend like this, I would walk straight to the theater to take a closer look at all the pictures posted beside the entrance and enjoy myself. For one reason or another I could never pass by such an opportunity, even though I always found myself regretting this afterwards. But the reason was actually simple and straightforward: I was caught up in lust.

I never actually entered that theater. But whether I actually watched the movie or just stared at some pictures and entertained lewd thoughts in my mind is not the point, for I was being equally lustful in God's sight. But I still clung onto my pride as I told myself that at least I did not actually watch the movie. So on my way to the seminary residence, I would congratulate myself for not giving into temptation and wasting my money on such a useless movie. I would feel proud of myself for the fact that despite being tempted, I stopped at just seeing some posters and pictures and did not actually walk into the theater to watch the movie. I would then justify my behavior by saying to myself that I did not completely give into temptation. Of course, I never told anyone about lingering around the theatre and glancing at its lewd posters and pictures, but I was satisfied that I didn't actually walk into the theater.

I took it as my pride the fact that as a seminary student purporting to obey the will of God, at least I did not walk into that theatre. When I returned to the residence, my friends would ask me about where I had been. I would then say to them, "Nowhere in particular; I just had some business to take care." However, when our conversation somehow led to movies, I would blurt out without thinking, "Oh, there is a movie playing in the theater, I saw some parts of it today. It looked very good." When asked how I got to see the movie, I would say, "I didn't actually see the movie. I just got a few glances of the poster." But later on, I would eventually discover that I was not alone to have seen the poster, but all my friends had also seen it. But since we were all seminary students, we felt at least a bit guilty about our behavior. So we tried to keep our pride by clinging onto the fact that we had not actually walked into that theater. We were trying to keep our pride as seminary students and Christians.

However, given the fact that everyone is lustful in God's sight, was I not a lewd man just because I did not actually pay to watch any vulgar movies? No, of course not! That's like insisting that the king still has gotten dressed up even as he is stark naked. When I look into my life like this, all my sins are exposed just as the Lord pointed them out here in today's Scripture passage, from wickedness to greed, adulteries, murders, thefts, evil thought and so forth. Indeed, I am a filthy man. I am a completely depraved man. That is why I needed the Lord. I needed the Lord who had blotted out all my sins with the gospel of the water and the Spirit. This is because I was such a filthy man that I believed in the righteousness of the Lord, and that is how I received the remission of all my sins.

I believed in Jesus as my Savior who came by the gospel of the water and the Spirit because I was such a filthy man. Now that I have received the remission of my sins, whenever I look into the Word of God like this, I realize time after time that I am indeed nothing before God. I have absolutely no merit whatsoever in God's sight, other than the fact that I believe that Jesus Christ has blotted out all my sins with the gospel of the water and the Spirit. All that I remember is that the Lord has blotted out all my sins, and this is the only thing that I can speak of boldly. And this alone is my pride and my heart's joy. I have nothing else to present to God. I have nothing on my own to show to Him.

Everyone Is Destined to Do Filthy Things throughout Their Entire Lifetime

Ecclesiastes 9:3 says, *"The hearts of the sons of men are full of evil; madness is in their hearts while they live, and after that they go to the dead."* As the Bible says here, everyone's heart and acts are indeed full of madness throughout their entire lifetime.

I was also a filthy man before God. It's only because the Lord has delivered me from all my sins that I have received the remission of sins and reached my salvation. This evening, all of us must realize and admit clearly here that we are all filthy human beings. Are we clean or filthy before God? Let's set aside Jesus Christ for now and think about our fundamental nature as human beings. Are we filthy or clean in God's sight? Do you feel too uncomfortable to admit that you are a filthy man with so many saints around you? Do you still think that you are not filthy at all? Look back in your past and examine yourself honestly before the Word of God. See for yourself whether or not you are indeed filthy, whether or not your acts are virtuous, whether or not your heart is upright, whether or not your thoughts are godly, whether or not there is anything filthy in your heart, and whether or not you do filthy things in your life.

Look deep inside yourself and say clearly whether you are filthy or clean in God's sight. If you think that you are not filthy, then you ought to be able to say clearly, "I am not filthy. Others may be filthy, but I am truly clean." If you really think that you are not filthy at all, then you ought to be bold enough to say this to God also. If on the other hand, you think that you are a filthy human being, then you must admit this to God and say, "Lord, you are right. I am indeed a filthy man. But even though I am such a filthy man, did you not save me? I thank you for saving such a depraved man like me. I give you all my praise and thanks." Without Christ, all of us are indeed filthy people.

My fellow believers, all of you who have received the remission of sins here should glorify God this evening. On the other hand, if there is anyone here who still has not received the remission of sins—that is, if anyone here has led his life to this very day without realizing clearly that he is indeed a filthy human being by nature—then all such people should draw a clear line this evening. If you still have not drawn this line clearly before God to determine whether you have received the remission of sins or not, and whether you are filthy or clean, then I ask you wholeheartedly to draw the line clearly this evening.

Let me ask you one more time: "Are you clean or filthy?" Why are so many of you still not answering this question? Let me ask you again, for it is absolutely indispensable for us to admit clearly to God whether we are clean or filthy. Are you a filthy or clean human being before God? You are a filthy human being in God's sight. Regardless of whether you have received the remission of sins or not, your existence as a human being in itself is filthy by nature. And it is fundamentally in our human nature to do nothing but filthy things throughout our lives. Don't you agree?

As I see some teenage girls sitting here, I am reminded of just how many filthy thoughts I used to have in my past. I used to have such a filthy mind that when I looked at the girls of my age when I was young, they looked like angels compared to me. But in reality, these innocent-looking girls were actually no better than myself, and some of them might have been even worse.

My fellow believers, all your heart's sins will inevitably come out sooner or later. Whatever you ate this evening may now be in your stomach, but it will soon pass through. If we were born as filthy human beings, then it's destined for us to do filthy things while living on this earth. That is life. If we still try to rationalize ourselves and claim that we have not led a filthy life, then we would not be honest to ourselves. And this should not be the disposition of anyone who is poor in spirit in God's sight. It is not the attitude of anyone asking God for His mercy and grace.

Jesus said in Matthew 5:3, *"Blessed are the poor in spirit, for theirs is the kingdom of heaven."* Whoever is poor in spirit admits to himself readily and says, "I am indeed a filthy man. I was born as a filthy human being from the beginning. And I have led a filthy life to this very day. I cannot help but live a filthy life, for that is my true nature as a human being." Such people who recognize that they have no righteousness of their own at all, that they are filthy, and that they are full of shortcomings—none other than these people are the blessed. And Heaven belongs to none other than such people. Heaven belongs to those who know that they are filthy.

Of course, this does not mean that the Lord would take them to Heaven in their filthy condition. Rather, the Lord cleanses them first and then takes them to His Kingdom of purity and glory. That is why Jesus said that those who truly recognize their filthy selves are blessed.

All of us must reveal and admit ourselves to God, particularly at a revival meeting like this. Even if you have not done that many filthy things so far, in time, you are bound to do them just like everyone else. Everyone is the same; there is nothing that sets anyone apart from anyone else as far as human nature is concerned. No one is better than anyone else.

You are the same as the person sitting next to you.

There are some beautiful lilies in front of the pulpit here. Are any of these lilies different from the rest? No, they are all of the same flower species. Some of them are in full bloom while others are not, but this doesn't mean that they are different flowers. With enough water and time, they will all blossom fully. Just as the lilies in full bloom will eventual wither away, the lilies that still have not blossomed will also wither away in the same way. The same is true for us humans. Since all of us were born as filthy human beings, all of us are equally bound to do filthy things until the day we die. The only difference is the stage and the circumstances in which we find ourselves.

What is our true nature? What is our fundamental portrait as human beings? Ours is a filthy portrait by nature. God Himself has revealed this to us in our journey of life. Do you feel offended by this? I am actually overwhelmed with joy whenever I see my sinful nature laid completely bare. That's because only when I see my fundamental sinful nature can I find the greatness of God's gospel that has solved this problem. That is why I am so happy. It doesn't matter how filthy you are; even the filthiest man can become the cleanest by believing in the gospel of the water and the Spirit.

Let me raise another question to all of you gathered here: "Are you now living a completely perfect and flawless life before God?" I keep raising similar questions repeatedly here because when I asked them before, many of you remained quiet. Don't just stay silent but speak up. Make your decision now and spell it out clearly before God. If you know clearly that you are a filthy human being, you must then admit this when God says to you that you are filthy. You must admit your sinful nature and say to God, "Yes, Lord, you are right. I am filthy even in my own eyes. You are completely right Lord. I am indeed a filthy man just as you say." It's actually a wonderful blessing to discover your true self.

So admit your sinful nature and confess to God that you are indeed filthy. And then say to God, "Lord, please save me. You called me filthy, and so now I ask you to cleanse me. You have pointed out my filthiness. Unlike so many people who have said nothing but good things about me, you alone have exposed my filthy nature. Only you know me completely. You alone are true and right. I am indeed a filthy man just as you say that I am. But I believe that you can cleanse me. Have mercy on me Lord, and cleanse me from all my filthiness." With this confession, hope will spring forth in you to look towards the Kingdom of Heaven.

This age is the age of hypocrisy. So it is impossible for you to see and recognize your fundamental nature as a human being by relying on a worldly religion. Let me illustrate this with a simple example. You can't really tell a woman's face when she has too much make-up. Nowadays the demand for make-up is so strong that there are all kinds of cosmetic products made from all kinds of ingredients. Just a while ago, I saw in a TV commercial where some women were putting mud on their faces. I can't remember what the brand was, but apparently mud is the latest fad in the cosmetics industry. Perhaps it's because human beings were made out of dust, but mud is said to have many ingredients that are very beneficial to the skin.

Whenever I visit Seoul, there is one thing that always confuses my eyes. It's the fact that every woman I see seems to have a similar face. For some reason all these women in Seoul look the same to me, as though they came out of the same cookie oven. They all look the same to me. This is not the case in smaller cities, as the women there at least show some variation, using different colors and shades in their make-up. But here in Seoul, every woman has the same color and shade. It seems every woman in this metropolitan city is a master at disguise. Of course, I am not complaining about make-up per se. Far from it, it's great to see beautiful women. There is nothing wrong with beauty in itself. Rather, my point here is that you should not disguise your heart as you disguise your outside appearance.

It's only a matter of course for us to keep our appearances tidy and neat, but none of us should ever go as far as disguising our hearts before God and man. This world is so full of lies that it's very easy for us to follow the prevailing wind to lay ourselves in. But we must never let the world drag us into lying like this. If you want to live an upright life you should never deceive your heart. There is a different society, a society of the righteous who have put on the grace of God and live an honest and upright life. So even though this world is filthy, not everything is filthy. If you really want to live a clean and upright life, then this is more than possible. You can find grace from God if you expose yourself fully, and none other than God's Church is where you can do this. So I ask you to never deceive your heart before God.

Socrates once said, "Know thy self." He said this because so many people in his days were full of themselves, just as so many people nowadays still think so highly of themselves. But those who come to recognize their sinful nature before dying are the happiest of people. Those who know their true selves, receive the remission of sins, enter Heaven are the truly happy people. No one is happier than they are. In contrast, those who die without reaching this self-realization are the saddest of all. Those who do not know their sinful nature, oblivious to what they really are before God and men alike, and those who are wasting their lives on this earth without realizing what purpose God has for them—these are the most tragic of people. Referring to such people, the Bible says, *"A man who is in honor, yet does not understand, is like the beasts that perish"* *(Psalm 49:20).* Such people who do not know themselves are like the beasts that perish.

All of us must therefore realize our true nature. We must all find grace from God and become our Lord's brides by putting on clean wedding garments and enter His Kingdom after our short lives here on this earth is over. While we are still on this earth, all of us must receive the blessing of becoming God's people—that is, the blessing of becoming heavenly saints and holy people—to enter the Kingdom of Heaven. For what purpose did God put us on this earth? It is to make us His very own people. Therefore, all of us ought to realize our fundamental condition as innate sinners, come to the presence of God, and find His grace.

Have You Received the Remission of Sins by Believing in the Gospel of the Water and the Spirit?

How about you then? Is there really no sin at all in your heart? Is there really no one here who has sin in his heart? I am sure that there are at least a few people here who still remain sinful but are hesitant to admit this. If you are such a person, then you must listen to the Word of God and honestly admit your sinfulness. You will then be able to put on the God-given grace of salvation. Just as many of us here have already received the remission of sins and found God's grace, you will also put on the same grace of salvation. Do you then admit that you and all your family members are filthy human beings? Born as a human being on this earth, you ought to receive the remission of sins from God while you still can, so that you may enter His Kingdom; unless you receive the remission of sins, you cannot attain true happiness no matter how much material prosperity you enjoy on this earth.

The riches of this world, my fellow believers, cannot bring any real happiness to you. True happiness is attained only when you reach your salvation. You must therefore not only receive the remission of sins for yourself, but you must also lead all your family members, relatives, friends, and acquaintances to receive the remission of sins so that they also can enter Heaven together with you. One day, when our Lord decides that it's time for Him to judge the world and take us to His Kingdom, we will entrust ourselves to the Lord and enter this Kingdom according to His will, while everyone else will be left behind to suffer the plagues of the seven bowls that Lord will pour out on this earth.

When our lives on this earth are over, our Lord will surely take us the believers in the gospel of the water and the Spirit to the Kingdom of Heaven. So no matter what tribulations and trials come our way, let us all live out our faith united with God's Church, serve the Lord faithfully and then go to His Kingdom. Where would you go if you fail to receive the remission of sins and instead just live a carnally prosperous life? Where would your destination be?

To find the answer, let's turn to the Word of God. I will end my sermon shortly after looking at the last passage in the Book of Isaiah. It's written in Isaiah 66:24:

"And they shall go forth and look
Upon the corpses of the men

Who have transgressed against me.
For their worm does not die,
And their fire is not quenched.
They shall be an abhorrence to all flesh."

This passage clearly shows that hell does exist. Our lives on this earth are not everything. There is God's Kingdom. Therefore God also has given us the remission of our sins. And it is to make us receive this remission of sins and turn us into His very own people that God allowed us to be born on this earth. This earth is not everything to our lives. I ask you not to place all your hopes on this earth and its vanities. There is another world waiting for you, a new and eternal world that God has prepared for you. So I admonish you all to receive the remission of your sins while you are still on this earth, and then enter this Kingdom of Heaven that God has prepared for you. And to do this, you must first stop deceiving your own heart.

Let me ask you for one last time: Are you a filthy human being, or do you still consider yourself a decent human being? You are indeed a filthy human being. Admit this honestly right here and right now. Everyone gathered here is equally filthy, and so who can condemn whom? The only way to get yourself condemned is to insist that you are not filthy even as all of us here are equally filthy. You will hear people saying, "How can you not be filthy when all of us are filthy like this? That's preposterous! You are no different from us. You are just as unclean as the rest of us. If you think otherwise, you are just making a fool out of yourself! Don't be so ridiculous!" If you deny your true nature, you will only make yourself even filthier.

So let me ask you again: "Do you now admit that you are filthy?" It's not just out of impatience that I keep asking the same question over and over, but it's because admitting your sinful nature is the very first step to receiving the remission of sins. I myself am a filthy man. But I have received the remission of sins thanks to our Lord. That is my only distinction. Do you think that I am somehow cleaner than you? No, that's not true at all. I am just as filthy as everyone else.

My fellow believers! Remember that it is those who are poor in spirits that are blessed by God. It's those who expose their sins to God that receive His blessings. So lay all your sins bare before our Lord, seek His mercy, and believe in the gospel of the water and the Spirit. God will then surely save you from all your sins! ⊠

SERMON

4

Admit Your Fundamentally Sinful Nature and Ask God For His Grace of Salvation

< Mark 7:18-37 >

"So He said to them, 'Are you thus without understanding also? Do you not perceive that whatever enters a man from outside cannot defile him, because it does not enter his heart but his stomach, and is eliminated, thus purifying all foods?' And He said, 'What comes out of a man, that defiles a man. For from within, out of the heart of men, proceed evil thoughts, adulteries, fornications, murders, thefts, covetousness, wickedness, deceit, lewdness, an evil eye, blasphemy, pride, foolishness. All these evil things come from within and defile a man.' From there He arose and went to the region of Tyre and Sidon. And He entered a house and wanted no one to know it, but He could not be hidden. For a woman whose young daughter had an unclean spirit heard about Him, and she came and fell at His feet. The woman was a Greek, a Syro-Phoenician by birth, and she kept asking Him to cast the demon out of her daughter. But Jesus said to her, 'Let the children be filled first, for it is not good to take the children's bread and throw it to the little dogs.' And she answered and said to Him, 'Yes, Lord, yet even the little dogs under the table eat from the children's crumbs.' Then He said to her, 'For this saying go your way; the demon has gone out of your daughter.' And when she had come to her house, she found the demon gone out, and her daughter lying on the bed. Again, departing from the region of Tyre and Sidon, He came through the midst of the region of Decapolis to the Sea of Galilee. Then they brought to Him one who was deaf and had an impediment in his speech, and they begged Him to put His hand on him. And He took him aside from the multitude, and put His fingers in his ears, and He spat and touched his tongue. Then, looking up to heaven, He sighed, and said to him, 'Ephphatha,' that is, 'Be opened.' Immediately his ears were opened, and the impediment of his tongue was loosed, and he spoke plainly. Then He commanded them that they should tell no one; but the more He commanded them, the more widely they proclaimed it. And they were astonished beyond measure, saying, 'He has done all things well. He makes both the deaf to hear and the mute to speak.'"

As we just read in today's Scripture reading, a certain Gentile woman had a daughter possessed by an unclean spirit. So this Gentile woman came looking for Jesus and asked Him to drive out the demon which possessed her daughter. But what Jesus said to her was utterly shocking. He spoke so harshly to her that when we look at it based on our own standard, we may even wonder how Jesus could ever say such things, but if we think about it again more carefully, we can see that what Jesus said was actually more than appropriate. Although it seems impossible to understand what Jesus said to the woman when we think about it from the human point of view, there is an important lesson that Jesus is trying to teach us here in today's Scripture reading.

Let's turn to Mark 7:27 again: *"Let the children be filled first, for it is not good to take the children's bread and throw it to the little dogs."* Now then, what did Jesus say to the woman here? He said, "It is not good to take the children's bread and throw it to the little dogs." This is what Jesus said to the Syro-Phoenician woman. This woman had come to Jesus asking for His help for the sake of her daughter, begging Him earnestly, "Lord, my daughter is demon-possessed. Please cast out this demon. Please deliver my daughter from the evil spirit." But Jesus said to the woman, *"It is not good to take the children's bread and throw it to the little dogs."* These are very harsh words, as they imply that the woman was no better than a dog. We may then wonder here how Jesus could say such a thing to this woman.

But there was a reason why Jesus spoke to the woman like this. The people of Israel used to refer to all Gentiles as dogs. Whenever they came across any Gentiles, they used to think that they were all no better than dogs. Even now, many Jews still think very lowly of any other ethnic groups. Such a prejudiced notion is ingrained deep in the minds of the people of Israel, thinking that they are better than any other nation as God's chosen people.

But this is not what Jesus had in mind when He said to the woman, *"It is not good to take the children's bread and throw it to the little dogs."* Rather, He had a gift that He wanted to give her.

Why Jesus Spoke So Harshly to
the Syro-Phoenician Woman

The reason why Jesus spoke so harshly to the Syro-Phoenician woman as though she were no better than a dog was because He wanted to see the disposition of her heart. In other words, Jesus insulted this woman deliberately so that she would find the grace of God. This woman realized that even if she were treated like a dog, it was fitting so long as she could put on God's grace. Here, our Lord is teaching us that we can receive God's grace only if our hearts are disposed humbly like this woman.

The Lord is saying to us that if we really want to receive God's help and the salvation He is offering to us, then we must have such a humble heart. Put differently, only if we lower our hearts like this woman here can we put on the God-given grace of salvation. This is the lesson that the Lord is trying to teach us through today's Scripture passage, and all of us must grasp it.

What would have happened to the Syro-Phoenician woman if she had come to Jesus with an arrogant heart? What would have happened if she had said to Jesus with such a haughty attitude, "Jesus, my daughter is demon-possessed, and so I would appreciate it if you could just deliver her." If the woman had approached Jesus arrogantly without realizing her true self, and if there had been no sincerity in her heart when she asked for God's help, then the woman would not have found the grace of salvation.

If there are anyone among you sitting here who still has not received the remission of sins, then all such people must have a humble disposition as this woman in today's Scripture passage. They can then all be blessed to receive the remission of sins, so long as their hearts yearn for the grace of God earnestly that they are willing to say to the Lord, "I don't care how you treat me. Please save me." Unless you ask for the grace of God with all your heart, you cannot receive the gospel of the water and the Spirit, the true gospel of salvation. As far as your salvation is concerned, whatever God says to you is right, even if He calls you a dog or far worse things. So what you need is a humble heart to ask God to bestow His wonderful grace upon you. In other words, you must yearn from the depth of your heart to be saved from all your sins.

This Syro-Phoenician woman in today's Scripture passage had such a humble heart that our Lord could not help but answer her request. Our Lord was delighted to see the disposition of her heart. Her attitude was fitting in His sight, for she was asking Him for His grace with all sincerity, accepting His every Word even when He implied that she was no better than a dog.

Let's think in slightly simple terms what the Syro-Phoenician woman said to Jesus. Her response to Jesus was the following: *"Yes, Lord, yet even the little dogs under the table eat from the children's crumbs" (Mark 7:28).* Put differently, she was saying in her answer, "Lord, You are right. I am indeed a dog spiritually. But don't even the dogs eat from their master's crumbs falling under the table?" This Syro-Phoenician woman was approved for her earnest heart, coming to the presence of Jesus and asking Him for His grace with all her heart. Then came Jesus' Word of grace: *"For this saying go your way; the demon has gone out of your daughter" (Mark 7:29).* Hearing this, the woman returned home, and when she arrived, *"She found the demon gone out, and her daughter lying on the bed" (Mark 7:30).* The demon had been cast out just as she had wished.

My fellow believers, the Word of God written in today's Scripture passage teaches us about the proper disposition of a heart that one must have to truly find grace from God. Every heart that yearns to receive God's grace must be just like this woman's heart. Today's Scripture passage, in other words, teaches us that we must admit our true selves to God.

Spiritually speaking, calling a sinner a dog is actually a toned-down expression. When people come to Jesus, they all bring their sins with them. And because everyone is a sinner in Jesus' sight, He says to all, "You are a dog." That's why Jesus said to the woman in today's Scripture passage, *"It is not good to take the children's bread and throw it to the little dogs" (Mark 7:27)*. What did this woman say in her answer then? She said, *"Yes, Lord, yet even the little dogs under the table eat from the children's crumbs" (Mark 7:28)*. When Jesus was saying to the woman, "Why do you ask me for my grace when you are a sinner?" she was ready in her heart to say, "Lord, I am indeed a sinner, and unless you bestow your grace on me, I will go to hell." This is how the woman found grace from God. Today's Scripture passage here contains an extremely important lesson, making it clear that as sinners, unless human beings are humbly disposed as this woman was, they can neither find the grace of God nor reach their salvation.

Our Lord's desire for all of us is revealed here in today's Scripture passage, promising that God will bestow His grace on whoever admits himself as a sinner to the Lord and asks for His grace. However, if one is instead so arrogant and self-conceited that he neither admits himself to our Lord nor asks for His grace, then this person will not put on His grace. This is our Lord's heartfelt desire for all of us revealed here in today's Scripture passage.

If our Lord had called you a dog before you were born again, would you have admitted it readily? Just as it's the ignorant that get easily hurt and offended when their flaws are exposed, so do sinners get very upset when they are called sinners. Most people suffering from an inferiority-complex would be completely incensed if they are called a dog, although a few of them might admit their true colors. My fellow believers, our Lord's heartfelt desire is to bestow His grace on every nation and every tribe. What should one do then? Everyone must humbly admit himself to God and earnestly ask Him for His grace. Today's Scripture passage shows us clearly that only then can one put on the grace of God.

In God's sight, it's our hearts' disposition that is important. Of course, our acts are also important, but they are secondary. How our hearts are disposed is far more important than how we act, for we can change our acts according to our hearts' desire. What really matters is that we should know our true selves and ask God for His grace from the depth of our hearts, and only then can we put on this grace.

Before Receiving the Remission of Sins by Hearing and Believing in the Gospel of the Water and the Spirit, You Must First Distance Yourself from the False Prophets

Let's now turn to the second event recorded in today's Scripture passage. It's written in Mark 7:32, *"Then they brought to Him one who was deaf and had an impediment in his speech, and they begged Him to put His hand on him."* It's written here that some people brought a deaf man with an impediment in his speech, and they begged Jesus to heal him. Here we need to pay particular attention to the fact that when Jesus healed this man; He took him aside from the multitude.

Why did Jesus then take the deaf man aside and healed him far away from the multitude, instead of just healing him in full view of the crowd? This implies that if you really want to receive salvation from our Lord, obtain the remission of your sins, and find His grace, then you must depart from all false prophets first. In other words, no one should be with any false prophets when our Lord is offering His salvation to him. If you side with the false prophets, then even though the Lord is offering His grace of salvation to you, you cannot realize that this is the gospel of salvation nor believe in it, and therefore you cannot receive the grace of salvation either.

There are many records in the Bible showing that while our Lord Jesus was on this earth, He took aside disabled people such as the blind and the deaf to a secluded place and healed them from their ailments. This implies that when it comes to your salvation from sin, if you abide with those who do not believe in the gospel of the water and the Spirit, then you cannot receive the God-given salvation no matter how hard you try. That's because these non-believers would obstruct you from having faith. Everyone who wants to be saved from all his sins must therefore separate himself from any and every false prophet, and only then can he receive grace from the Lord. This is what our Lord is teaching us now.

Let's return to today's Scripture passage. It is written that our Lord spat when He healed the deaf man with an impediment of speech. Where did the Lord spit at? A closer look at the passage shows that Jesus first put His fingers in the deaf man's ear, spat in His hand, and then touched the man's tongue.

There are other accounts elsewhere in the other Gospels where Jesus spat in His hands to heal the sick. For instance, John chapter 9 describes how Jesus opened a blind man's eyes by spitting on the ground, making clay with the saliva, and putting the clay on the blind man's eyes. Spitting usually carries a negative connotation. Across most cultures, to spit at someone is to show one's utter contempt. It is one of the worst forms of insult that shows just how vile and filthy the other person is held. In Korea, some people also spit when they see something or someone disgusting. Perhaps it was out of a similar revulsion at people's sins that Jesus spat, but regardless, the Bible shows clearly that it was not unusual for Him to spit and put His saliva on the tongues, ears, or eyes of the sick.

Looking up to Heaven, our Lord then sighed and said to the deaf man, *"Ephphatha" (Mark 7:34)*. The word "Ephphatha" here means "be opened." Please note here that Jesus *sighed* before saying it. It was out of pity that Jesus sighed; lamenting for the deaf man bound to destruction, for everyone is sinful and must therefore be cast into hell forever. But what happened after Jesus did all these things—that is, after He put His fingers into the deaf man's ears, spat and touched his tongue, looked up to Heaven, sighed, and said to the deaf man, "Ephphatha (be opened)"? The Bible says that *"immediately his ears were opened, and the impediment of his tongue was loosed, and he spoke plainly" (Mark 7:35)*.

Here We Can See Our Lord's Desire for All of Us

What is our Lord's heartfelt desire for all of us? We can see here that He wants to bestow His grace on all who recognize that they are destined to be cursed and cast into hell along with the Devil, who humbly ask for our Lord's grace of salvation no matter what He says and does to them, and who wholeheartedly yearns for the Lord's healing.

Our Lord has remitted away all our sins with the gospel of the water and the Spirit and solved all our problems as well, but before doing so, He made us depart from the false prophets first. The Lord did not work in the lives of those who did not believe in the grace of God. It is God's heartfelt desire to bestow His grace on all who depart from the false prophets. Although we ourselves are not truthful in our sinful state, our Lord wants us to distance ourselves from all the false prophets first. This means that we must recognize not only our own shortcomings but also the fallacy of the faith of those false prophets. Our Lord bestows His salvation on those who recognize their sins and acknowledge that the Lord is offering them the saving grace of the water and the Spirit. All of us must grasp this desire of the Lord. The Lord made it clear that it's on such humble people that He bestows His grace.

In today's Scripture passage, even though the Lord spat at the deaf man and treated the Syro-Phoenician as no better than a dog, they both found the grace of the Lord because they both yearned to put on God's grace with all their hearts. We need to grasp here that God looks at the center of such people's hearts and bestows His grace on such humble people. We should realize that God bestows His grace on those who recognize the Word of the Lord in its entirety no matter what He says to them. And we should also realize here that God bestows His grace on those who distance themselves from any false prophets. This is an absolutely necessary condition for anyone to be born again.

God bestows His grace on those whose hearts humbly accept every Word of God no matter what He says to them, even if He calls them a dog, and who recognize that only God is true and everything He says is right. It's those with such a heart that find grace from God. We must grasp this Truth and believe in it. Everyone in this world who has put on the Lord's grace has such a humble heart. No one can find grace from the Lord unless one humbles his heart like this. After all, how can any heart put on the Lord's grace when it is not even ready to receive it?

Before we heard and believed in the gospel of the water and the Spirit, we did not admit that we ourselves were dogs. But to be saved, one must first admit his sinful state, saying, "I am like a beast. I am no better than a dog, cursed by God to be cast into hell." Unless you admit your sins like this, you cannot be saved. When we look at those who have been saved by the Lord, one common characteristic is that they all admitted their sinfulness and acknowledged every Word of God in obedience, saying, "Yes, Lord, You are right; I am who you say I am." It's on such people that God's grace of salvation was bestowed.

Why do so many people still remain unsaved from their sins? It's because they have not admitted that they themselves are dogs, that they themselves are to be cursed by God and cast into hell, and that they themselves are completely worthless beings who deserve to be spat at. All these people remain unsaved precisely because they do not admit the Word of God to be true.

Therefore, whenever we preach the gospel of the water and the Spirit to people, we must first plow the fields of their hearts deeply. Before we preach this true gospel to them by faith, we need to first awaken them to their sinful state and their need for salvation, letting them know that even though they are no better than a dog, the Lord is still offering them salvation through the gospel of the water and the Spirit. This is an absolutely necessary precondition to preaching the gospel. Before preaching the gospel to anyone, we must first teach this person what a sinner he is in God's sight and completely expose his sinful state. That is what plowing a sinner's heart is all about.

When a farmer sows seed in a field, he first prepares the field by plowing up the ground sufficiently and mixing fertilizers in it, and then he plants the seed on this cultivated field and covers the seed with earth; and he waters that field for the seed to sprout and eventually bear fruit. Likewise, when it comes to leading sinners to salvation, it's absolutely indispensable for us to plow the fields of their hearts sufficiently. We must teach them that they are filthy sinners who are no better than a dog in God's sight, all destined to be cursed and cast into hell in hatred.

My fellow believers, our Lord is perfect in every conceivable way, even when looked at His integrity as a Man. How could He then have spoken so harshly to the Syro-Phoenician woman when she was asking for His grace? Moreover, this woman was asking for the Lord's grace not for herself but for her daughter's sake. How could the Lord then have insulted this woman's character so derisively and said to her, *"It is not good to take the children's bread and throw it to the little dogs" (Mark 7:27)*?

We need to realize what motivated the Lord to say such things. It was not the Lord's intention to insult the woman's character and despise her just for the sake of showing His contempt. Why did the Lord say these things then? He said these things to the woman for no other purpose than to save her, to expose her sinful state and bestow His grace and blessings upon her, and to solve all her problems.

My fellow saints, Jesus did not always say kind things. So it's very important for us to grasp God's intention that's hidden in His Word. The more we grasp God's heartfelt desire, the easier it is for us to live out our faith. We can then follow His every Word by faith.

However, if we do not grasp God's desire, then it's very difficult for us to lead our lives of faith. Therefore, it's imperative for all of us to reach a quick understanding of the will of Jesus Christ from the Bible, and believe in this will. So let us all believe in every Word that Jesus Christ has spoken to us, and let us all follow Him by faith. ✉

SERMON

5

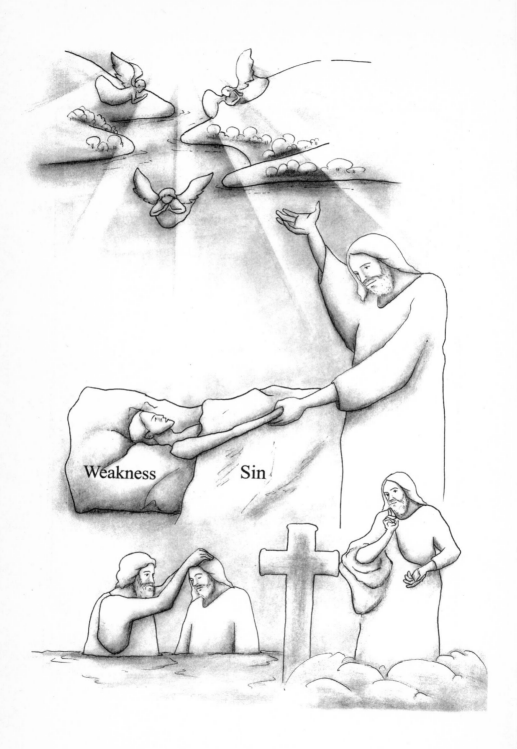

Weakness   Sin

God's Work That
Saves the Hungry Souls

< Mark 8:1-10 >

"In those days, the multitude being very great and having nothing to eat, Jesus called His disciples to Him and said to them, 'I have compassion on the multitude, because they have now continued with Me three days and have nothing to eat. And if I send them away hungry to their own houses, they will faint on the way; for some of them have come from afar.' Then His disciples answered Him, 'How can one satisfy these people with bread here in the wilderness?' He asked them, 'How many loaves do you have?' And they said, 'Seven.' So He commanded the multitude to sit down on the ground. And He took the seven loaves and gave thanks, broke them and gave them to His disciples to set before them; and they set them before the multitude. They also had a few small fish; and having blessed them, He said to set them also before them. So they ate and were filled, and they took up seven large baskets of leftover fragments. Now those who had eaten were about four thousand. And He sent them away, immediately got into the boat with His disciples, and came to the region of Dalmanutha."

At this hour I want to share with you about God's work and blessing through the Word of the Gospel of Mark. When Jesus was in this world, many people followed Him because

He healed many and gave them food to eat. At that time there was not much to eat in Israel. They were really poor.

Therefore, many people followed Jesus wherever He went. Let's look at the Word in chapter 8 verses 1-3, *"In those days, the multitude being very great and having nothing to eat, Jesus called His disciples to Him and said to them, 'I have compassion on the multitude, because they have now continued with Me three days and have nothing to eat. And if I send them away hungry to their own houses, they will faint on the way; for some of them have come from afar.'"*

Who Are These Starving People Spiritually?

There might be some people among you who have at some point experienced starvation for any length of time. Such people know well how a person who does not have anything to eat really feels. Many people who were poor at that time followed Jesus because He gave them food and healed the sick. Multitudes of people followed Jesus. Jesus looked at them and saw that they had been following Him for three days. During that time, they were able to get by with the pack of food they brought with or some fruit from the field, but Jesus saw that they were exhausted because they did not have anything more to eat. Jesus looked at these hungry people and had compassion on them and said that He wanted to give them something to eat right now. So He said to His disciples, *"And if I send them away hungry to their own houses, they will faint on the way; for some of them have come from afar."* Jesus knew the hearts of the people those who did not have anything to eat. Because Jesus came to this world with human flesh, although He is God, He knew these hungry people would faint on the way home because of hunger and if He sent them away without giving them something to eat.

Actually, when one is very hungry he feels very grateful if he gets even a little to eat. Someone who has never experienced such hunger pains holds his head up arrogantly and says, "Why should I take this food from you?" But a person who has actually experienced severe hunger will not do this.

We Koreans ask even the uninvited guests to join us when we have a meal, at least out of courtesy. We usually set another bowl with its utensils on the table and ask them to join us for the meal, but they usually refuse respectfully two or three times to uphold their dignity. They refuse three or four times respectfully, saying, "No, thank you. I had a meal already. I am okay. I just stopped by to ask after your health." However, if we responded, "Oh, okay. Then we will just go ahead and have the meal by ourselves" just because that person refused a few times, if this happened we would be very uncompassionate people. Of course, these days when food is so abundant, it would not matter much even if we responded like this. Rather, it might even be offensive to offer so many times like that. But how was it some two or three decades ago? During those times it would be very improper to say "Okay, we will have the meal by ourselves" just because the person refused a few times. During those times when someone refused like this, it was proper to bring him to the table and sit him down and make him have the meal. We had to make him eat forcibly like this. It's because that person would feel ill-treated if we the host did not do this. Why was this so? It is because we all were lacking in food those days.

I think I told you this story. Before I was in elementary school we had no one at home and there was nothing to eat, and I was so very hungry that I picked out the leftover noodles that were in a slop tub on the street. Even though we were in such dire straits, my parents instructed us, "Don't ever eat at someone else's home. Never go to their home during meal time." At that time, my father had believed in Confucianism ardently. Therefore, even though we did not have anything to eat, we put a pot on the furnace and made the smoke go up out of the chimney just so that people would think that we were cooking. Also, no matter how broke we were, my father always put on a sharp white Korean traditional suit and hat whenever he went out. How could we as mere children live in such circumstances? We often starved all day long because we could not even go to a friend's house during meal times. One day, I saw a slop tub with leftover noodles that someone had eaten and thrown out. At this tender age I calculated this and many thoughts crossed my mind. I thought, "I wish I could at least eat that. But what would the people say if they happened to see me eating it?" I also thought, "That will be embarrassing. And what would my parents say if they found out?" However, I just went for it and ate the leftover noodles in the slop tub because I was so hungry. Of course, it was not enough to fill up my stomach, but I was able to ease my hunger pains momentarily.

That incident came to my mind as we read today's Scripture passage. Anyway, hunger is a great pain for starving people. Jesus who knew such circumstances very well could not just send these multitudes away with an empty stomach. He knew that they would faint on the way if He just sent them away like that. Therefore, when Jesus told them that He would give them something to eat, His disciples asked him, "How can one satisfy these people with bread here in this wilderness?"

Actually the disciples were right. At that time, there probably were at least about ten thousand people following Jesus, and how could He feed all these people? Where could they buy all that bread and rice necessary to make that much bread? It was an impossible situation. But Jesus spoke to them in the Gospel of Mark chapter 8 verses 5-6, *"He asked them, 'How many loaves do you have?' And they said, 'Seven.' So He commanded the multitude to sit down on the ground. And He took the seven loaves and gave thanks, broke them and gave them to His disciples to set before them; and they set them before the multitude."* As it is written in this Word of God, Jesus asked the disciples, *"How many loaves do you have?"* They answered, "Seven." These seven loaves of bread were not sufficient. It was small and only big enough to fit into a lunch box. Nevertheless, the Lord laid hands on this bread and blessed it and gave thanks. Then He gave the bread to the disciples to place it before the multitudes so they could eat.

What do the Scriptures tell us after this? It says that all the 4000 people gathered there ate until they were full. The 4000 mentioned here only included the number of men and not of the women and children who were also gathered there, if everyone was counted it would actually be about ten thousand people. Even so, it records that the Lord gave thanks for this bread and the fish and distributed it to the people and everyone ate until they were full, and when they were satisfied they still had seven large baskets of food left over.

Let's Now Look at the Meaning of the Seven Large Baskets

The Book of Genesis tells us that God rested on the 7th day. Likewise, the number seven implies the perfection of God. Therefore, these seven large basketsful means that God has given abundant blessing to us. God gave the gospel of the water and the Spirit to all the people in this world, and it is a blessing that is more than enough to feed everyone in this world. Furthermore, the two fish mentioned here signifies the Church of God. Therefore, if we interpret it to its fullest content, it means that God has given abundant blessing through God's Church to the people throughout this entire world who are starving spiritually or physically and that there isn't anything lacking in that blessing. We could say that the spiritual teaching of today's Scripture passage is this, "With His work of grace, God bestowed many blessings on everyone throughout the world." We are doing literature ministry now. And about this ministry I think, "God is working through His Church for all the people who are starving spiritually. He is manifesting His work and really making them have much food until they are full and satisfied, and still have much left over. God works so bountifully like this. God works in this world through His Church like this, and this is such a great blessing. I absolutely believe like this.

We have preached so much about the Book of Genesis, haven't we? I did this before, and I am still preaching this Word from the Book of Genesis steadily even now when I preach at our Mission School. Of course, our beginning was insignificant and we lacked many things, but how are we now? God has truly done so many things to the spiritually hungry people of this entire world through His Church. God has truly done much work. It is truly amazing to see how much work He has done. The Lord really distributes more than enough food to these hungry people so that they have much left over. Furthermore, we come to believe that this is the blessing of God as we see such a phenomenon. We are translating the sermons on the Book of Genesis even in these days, and there is so much to preach from the Book of Genesis that we could publish three or four more books from just the first chapter. However, we are preparing it so that we can at least publish one book for each chapter.

There really is so much to say about the Word of God and so much that could become our spiritual food. While doing such works, I feel in my heart, "It would really be wonderful if many people would just read these books and received the remission of sins. God will really do this through His Church. People will no longer be hungry. God really is feeding the spiritually starving ones throughout the entire world through His Church in this era. God is doing such amazing works through His Church." I believe like this.

Today's Word tells that there were seven large baskets of food left over even after all those people had eaten until they were full. In this era also, those who want to eat God's food can receive this food as much as they want through our electronic books or printed books. People do not have God's food because they are not interested, but anyone who is interested in this can really receive the remission of their sins until they are full and also continue to eat to their hearts' content. They can eat and drink such spiritual food through God who works through His Church. I give sincere thanks to God who does all this for us.

Our Lord fed so many people with just 2 fish and 7 loaves of bread and still had leftovers. God also feeds everyone throughout the entire world more than sufficiently these days by making us preach the gospel through His Church. Because we are doing mission works through the internet and Christian literature diligently, anyone who desires to eat God's food can continue to eat this food sufficiently. Truly, this has become such an era that anyone can eat God's food if they really want it. All the peoples dispersed throughout this entire world can receive the remission of their sins and salvation by visiting our website and downloading our electronic books or ordering the printed books. Also, they can continue to receive our books even after receiving salvation if they continue to love God and desire Him. The Lord has done such works through His Church. God gives this spiritual food and blessing to everyone throughout the entire world so that they will not be hungry spiritually. I know this is a truly precious blessing from God. God has given so much physical food and spiritual food and manifested so many amazing works in the world these days where 6.5 billion people live. Therefore, no one can say that they have not received the remission of their sins because they could not find the Truth.

Brothers and sisters, the international situation around the Korean peninsula is really going awry these days. On one map of the United States, the Dokdo Island, a Korean island off the east coast of Korea, is designated as Japanese territory as the Dakesima Island. Actually, what did Rumsfeld, the Minister of Defense of the United States, say? He said, "Korea is an economic superpower. Therefore, we will move towards the military sovereignty of Korea so that they can defend their own country. Actually, the United States had control of the united forces of the Korean military, and they refused to give up that control even when Korea requested to proceed with the program facilitating military sovereignty of itself, and it is really baffling that Rumsfeld said such things.

Actually, the Korean War has not ended in this country. Even now, Korea is in a state of an armistice, a temporary suspension of this War. Strictly speaking, if North Korea or any other army invaded this country again and took control of this country, they would become the owners of this country. And the Japanese are taking steps towards such things now, aren't they? There is so much commotion these days about Japanese claims that Dokdo is their island, and we say it is not, but the truth is we cannot even claim that our mainland is our land, let alone the Dokdo Island. Because the war has not ended in Korea, any superior country with absolutely powerful military can invade this country and become the owner of this country.

But they cannot do as they wish for God's Church preaches the gospel in this land. God does not want such a thing to happen in this land because His children are here. You may think that it would be better for us to just give up our sovereignty and become one of the states of the United States quickly, saying, "Accept us as one of the states of the United States. We want to become the citizens of the United States." I also think that would be the best thing. However, the political leaders of our country do not think like this. What is the reason? It's because nationalism that is prevalent throughout the entire world is also prevalent in Korea. We think that North Korea is an axis of evil because of such nationalism. However, what is the truth. North Korea is neither an axis of evil nor our hatred enemy. They are our people the same as us. They are of the same race and origin. Rather, we can say that North Korea is actually a closer country to South Korea than the United States. This is the reason we are now supporting North Korea, aren't we? This is the so-called "Sunshine Policy."

The international political atmosphere is truly mysterious. South Korea can be invaded by North Korea or Japan if we resorted to humanistic methods and ways. And we do all we can so that we would not lose our sovereignty again. Japanese people say that we must think objectively. They say, "Objectively speaking, Korea is our country. We civilized the Korean people and we taught them all the modern technologies during the colonial period, hadn't we?" However, God does not let any nation invade this land where God's Church is located.

This country would really be in a laughable position if it did not have God's Church that distributes the Lord's food abundantly. Military sovereignty? What military sovereignty? Both North and South Korea would not have anything to boast about. Brothers and sisters, think about it. Would you be scared if some homeless person attacked you? Korea is like such a homeless person if it stands against the powerful countries. Our country would be nothing if it were not for God's Church. Japan has three fleets of Aegis warships. It means that Japan has these great fleets that can attack this country. They can invade this country within a few days if they utilized just these three fleets. We don't have the firepower to effectively resist Japan if we battle against them with the weapons of this world right now. Some people who do not know such political realities say all kinds of things based on the present situation, but they probably would have nothing to say when such a tragedy really happened. Actually, the international political climate is such that it can be construed to have started already.

However, the mysterious thing is that we have still maintained control of our country and even sustained economic development as one of the major economic powers. The IMF that took control of the Korean Economy was induced by the United States and bankrupted a number of significant companies in our country. This means that they tried to make Korea a country out from nothing. Simply put, they tried to buy some leading companies in Korea so that we could not sustain our own economic potential. For example, we have to now import all seeds for strawberries from a foreign country because we sold out all our nursery companies while our economy was under the control of the IMF. Therefore, farmers have to pay a royalty to foreign countries whenever they sell one box of strawberries. Our farmers must indeed give them money when we sell to them even though we worked and grew them in our farms.

From such a perspective we know that we are a funny country that has always been invaded by the other countries. But how is it spiritually? God has given us so much spiritual food now that everyone throughout the entire world can come and visit our website and eat this spiritual food to their hearts' content. And therefore there is no one who can say they are hungry. Thanks to the Lord, we have more than enough food to feed everyone. We have bountiful food in God's Church.

These days, we just have to upload our electronic books on the internet and anyone can read it for free. It means that we have set up the basis for anyone to receive the remission of sins if they just want to receive it. Although we cannot send out sufficient books because of our weak financial situation, I still give sincere thanks to God. God has truly blessed us and has upheld our Church and blessed our country as well. God has done amazing work throughout the entire world through you and me, that is, through God's Church. I give thanks to God. ✉

SERMON

6

I Have No Sin Now.

The Faith That Enables
You to Be Born Again

< Mark 8:22-26 >

"Then He came to Bethsaida; and they brought a blind man to Him, and begged Him to touch him. So He took the blind man by the hand and led him out of the town. And when He had spit on his eyes and put His hands on him, He asked him if he saw anything. And he looked up and said, 'I see men like trees, walking.' Then He put His hands on his eyes again and made him look up. And he was restored and saw everyone clearly. Then He sent him away to his house, saying, 'Neither go into the town, nor tell anyone in the town.'"

In many parts in both the New and Old Testaments, God explains to us what it means to be truly born again. The passage from Mark 8:22-26 which I will share with you today can also be described as one of such passages. Jesus said, *"Not everyone who says to me, 'Lord, Lord,' shall enter the kingdom of heaven, but he who does the will of My Father in heaven" (Matthew 7:21).* This means that those who believe only with their lips cannot enter the Kingdom of Heaven, but only those who truly know the will of God and act according to this will of God.

What then is the will of God mentioned here? The will of God is for every sinner to believe in the gospel of the water and the Spirit and to thus be saved from their sin. The Lord said that the only way for all human beings to be born again from sin is to open up their spiritual eyes by believing in the gospel of the water and the Spirit. For us as those who believe in Jesus as our Savior, to be born again by believing in the gospel of the water and the Spirit is an extremely important issue that cannot be glossed over. This may in fact be described as an indispensable task that God has given you and me alike.

As God the Father sent His Son Jesus to this earth, our Lord was baptized shed His blood on the Cross, and rose up from the dead. In doing this God has blessed whoever believes in this Jesus who came by the gospel of the water and the Spirit as his Savior to be born again and attain all the blessings of Heaven. In John chapter 3, Jesus said to Nicodemus who visited him in the night, "No one can enter the Kingdom of Heaven unless he is born again of water and the Spirit." Therefore, if there are any people among you who still have sin in their hearts, all such people must also be born again by believing in Jesus Christ who came by the gospel of the water and the Spirit and then live their lives of faith properly.

I am sure that you are all familiar with summer visitors called cicadas. These cicadas spend a long time underground as nymphs. Although they vary depending on the species, in general, cicadas live underground for 6-7 years as nymphs, and in some cases, up to 17 long years. Regardless of the particular species, all cicadas are no more than small underground nymphs before they turn into adult cicadas. Also called larvae, these nymphs spend a long time in the dark underground without any light, but when they surface and emerge, they are changed into beautiful cicadas. It's a truly marvelous and amazing mystery that these underground nymphs are transformed into beautiful cicadas. God has allowed such a mysterious phenomenon to occur in nature so that all sinners would be able to realize the mystery of how the gospel of the water and the Spirit works to make them righteous.

Just as the underground nymphs are transformed into adult cicadas that look completely different, all of us living on this earth should also be born again as God's children by believing in the gospel Truth of the water and the Spirit, which is on a completely different dimension from all other religious teachings. Until now, we have all lived as nymphs. Just as the cicada nymphs live in the dark underground without any form of light, likewise, everyone in this world is living imprisoned in the darkness of sin. David, a man of faith in the Bible confessed in Psalms 51:5, *"Behold, I was brought forth in iniquity, and in sin my mother conceived me."* All those born in this world were "brought forth in iniquity" and "conceived in sin" just like David. Because Adam and Eve, our common ancestors, sinned against God, and from then on everyone was born with sin. You and I were clearly sinners born in the darkness of sin and could not help but commit sin from our birth to our deaths.

Where then would our final destination have been as sinners? God said that anyone with any sin can never enter His Kingdom. He has made it impossible for anyone with even the smallest sin to enter the Kingdom of God. The only destination for all who have even a little bit of sin is the fiery hell. That's because God has clearly established it as an unmovable law for anyone whose heart has even the slightest sin to be punished for this sin.

Jesus said in the Gospel of Matthew, *"Assuredly, I say to you, you will by no means get out of there till you have paid the last penny" (Matthew 5:26).* This means that whoever has any sin at all cannot avoid going to hell. It is also written in Romans, *"The wages of sin is death" (Romans 6:23).* This passage means that anyone with sin must face the eternal punishment of hell. It is God's just judgment for whoever is sinful to be cast into hell for his sins. Does this then mean that you and I are all inexorably bound to hell, as we were all born as nothing more than piles of sin? No, that is not necessarily the case. As the Lord is full of love, He has completed our salvation with the gospel of the water and the Spirit so that we the sinners would be able to be saved from all our sins. This salvation is reached by believing in the God-given gospel of the water and the Spirit, and that is also how everyone can receive the remission of their sins and be born again.

Everyone whose heart is sinful is just like a cicada nymph before it undergoes metamorphosis. Just as this nymph lives in the perpetual dark underground, everyone who is living in his sins still has not been born again. For those whose hearts still remain sinful even as they profess to believe in Jesus as their Savior, this in itself is the clear evidence of the fact that they still have not been born again. In contrast, those of us who have been saved by believing in the gospel of the water and the Spirit have now been born again as God's perfect children, just as a nymph is transformed into a cicada. Today, through the Word of God, the Lord is teaching us that everyone must be born again by believing in the gospel of the water and the Spirit.

My fellow believers, can anyone who is blind open his eyes on his own? The Bible says that this is absolutely impossible. Just as no blind person can open his eyes on his own, no one who has sin in his heart can ever blot out his sins on his own. For you and me to blot out all our hearts' sins, we must also find Jesus Christ who came by the gospel of the water and the Spirit. This means that we can receive the true remission of sins only if we meet Jesus our Savior and are born again by believing in Him.

I arrived at Moscow yesterday with my fellow pastors. The trip was long but not boring, as I was full of anticipation to meet you. Today, to all my fellow believers living in Russia, I would like to preach the Truth of being born again through the gospel of the water and the Spirit. Have you still not received the true remission of sins even though you have believed in Jesus as your Savior? Are these sins still remaining in your heart? If so, I am sure that God will wash away all these sins of yours at this hour, while you are listening to the Word of God. I believe that just as the blind man in today's Scripture passage opened his eyes on the day he met Jesus, if only you would completely accept into your heart the Word of Jesus who came by the gospel of the water and the Spirit, your sins will also be cleansed away at this very moment. The living Word of God has the power to wash away all your sins and make you be born again. God is the God of the Word. I admonish you all to believe that God speaks the Truth to us, and He fulfills all His promises through this Word of Truth.

When we turn to the beginning of Hebrews chapter 1, we see that it's written, *"God, who at various times and in various ways spoke in time past to the fathers by the prophets, has in these last days spoken to us by His Son whom He has appointed heir of all things, through whom also He made the worlds; who being the brightness of His glory and the express image of His person, and upholding all things by the word of His power, when He had by Himself purged our sins, sat down at the right hand of the Majesty on high" (Hebrews 1:1-3).* In the Gospel of John we read the following, "The Word of God is God Himself, the Word became flesh, and this God Incarnate is Jesus Christ." The very first thing that you must believe as the Lord's faithful believers is that the Word of God is the Truth. The Bible says in Hebrews, "With the power of His Word, God made the heavens and the earth and He reigns over all its hosts." This means that the very fact that we are breathing today is also thanks to the power of the Word of God.

My fellow believers, what else does this living and powerful Word of God say to us? Let's all turn to Hebrews 1:3. It's written clearly, *"He had by Himself purged our sins."* God has indeed saved you and me from all our sins. Believe in this Word. Then on account of this faith, the Lord will be with you, He will also teach you the gospel of the water and the Spirit, and He will thereby bless your soul to be born again.

To Be Born Again, You Must First Break Out of Your Own Little World Built with Your Own Experiences

My fellow believers, for you to be born again by believing in the gospel of the water and the Spirit, you must first break out of the little world that you have built based on with your own experiences. In other words, you must set yourself free from the confines of your own experiences in order to accept the true Word of God without any obstruction. Everyone in this world lives his own little bubble, formed by his own experiences. You are also all living in your own little world. In this world formed by one's own experiences, everyone knows it so well that he can go anywhere easily even with his eyes closed. You know where everything is located. Even a blind person can live in his own little world without too much discomfort.

While living in this world, we have all come to accept various Christian doctrines and religious experiences into our hearts. Formed out of this is our own little world of faith built with our own experiences. Most people are used to this world of fake faith that they have known, and they are living quite comfortably in it, oblivious to the fact that they are sinners who have neither received the remission of sins nor been born again yet.

However, my fellow believers, if you really want your soul to be born again by believing in the gospel of the water and the Spirit, then it is absolutely necessary for you to break out of your own little world. That's because you can never open your eyes to the Truth as long as you remain inside your own comfortable bubble that you are used to for so long. So long as you remain in this little world of your own experiences, you can't help but continue to live according to your own prejudices and interests. This is far removed from the life that follows God completely. Living in the bubble of your own experiences is completely different from living according to the Word of God.

Here let us turn to the Book of Genesis for a short while. As you yourself know very well, Satan misled Adam, the first man into eating from the tree of the knowledge of good and evil, and the Devil thereby made Adam discern good and evil based on his own standard. Satan deceived Adam with his lies and taught him to judge good and evil on his own so that he would be unable to believe in the true Word of God exactly as it is, and ultimately depart from God. Having thus eaten from the tree of the knowledge of good and evil, from then on Adam and Eve came to have their own standard of good and evil, one that was completely different from God's standard. Before their fall, their thoughts had been exactly congruent with the Word of God, but now each and every thought they had turned completely opposite to the Word of God. And this difference between man's thoughts and the Word of God continues to apply to everyone living in this world as a descendant of Adam today.

My fellow believers, if there is sin in your heart, and if you are living in opposition to the Word of God far from realizing the true standard of good and evil, then you must right now renounce your own little world of experiences. The very first thing that our Lord did to open the eyes of the blind man was to lead him out of his own little town of experiences. All the beliefs that you have held while confined in your own little bubble, such as fallacious Christian doctrines that are focused only on the blood of the Cross, are wrong beliefs. If you want to find the real Truth of the Lord and believe in His Word exactly as it is, you must first be freed from these mistaken beliefs.

The Book of Second Kings chapter 5 gives the account of General Naaman. Naaman was the commander of the powerful Syrian army, but he was a leper. He had failed to cure his leprosy despite trying out every means, and in the end, he had to come before Elisha the servant of God. General Naaman expected that Elisha would lay his hands on him and pray for him. However, Elisha just sent his servant to him and relayed the Word of God, saying to him, "Go to the Jordan River and dip yourself in the water seven times. Your flesh will then be cleansed like a baby."

General Naaman could not understand any of this. That's because the message he got from Elisha made no sense in his own little world that he had known. As Naaman had not yet broken out of his own world of experience, he got angry and said, "In my own country of Syria there are far greater and cleaner rivers than this Jordan River. Wouldn't it be better for me to bathe in one of these rivers in my own country than in the muddy waters of the Jordan River?" He got so angry and felt so insulted that he even thought about returning with his army to invade Israel and lay its land to waste.

This General Naaman speaks volumes about all of us living in the present. Just as he preferred big and clean rivers in his own country of Syria over the dirty and muddy waters of the Jordan River, we also think that we would be born again if we attend a church that has a long history and many members. This, however, is a mistaken thought that still confined to our own little town of experiences. No worldly church can make anyone be born again no matter how big and palatial it may be. The blessing of being born again can be obtained only in a place that preaches the gospel of the water and the Spirit according to the Word of God. In other words, only if you are washed from all your sins by believing in the gospel of the water and the Spirit can you then be cured perfectly from your spiritual leprosy and your body healed to be like that of a little child.

Aroused to anger by Elisha's message telling him to bathe in the Jordan River, General Naaman could not hold down his wrath, and as mentioned, he thought about invading Israel in retaliation. However, one of his subordinates approached him and said to him, "General, if Elisha had told you to do something far more difficult, would you not have done it? If this is so, why wouldn't you then just believe in the Word of God, since this is all that you have to do?" Hearing this, General Naaman changed his mind and believed in this Word, and he went to the Jordan River and dipped himself seven times. That Naaman dipped his body in the water seven times does not imply any human effort or act on his own part. It just means that he believed in the Word. Put differently, Naaman had broken out of his own little world of experience and accepted the Word of God exactly as it was.

What happened to his leprosy? If you are curious, look it up in 2 Kings 5:14: *"So he went down and dipped seven times in the Jordan, according to the saying of the man of God; and his flesh was restored like the flesh of a little child, and he was clean."* It was only a predictable outcome that his leprous skin would be completely healed like that of a little child.

Spiritually speaking, the leprosy mentioned in the Bible can be interpreted as the disease of sin that everyone has. Just as General Naaman was healed from his leprosy by believing in the Word of God exactly as it was, it is when we believe in the Word of God exactly as it is that we can also be washed from all our filthy sins. Yet despite this, countless people who have not left the town of their own experiences think that their sins can be blotted out by volunteering their services to some good cause, practicing asceticism, or exercising self-discipline.

This, however, is a mistaken notion. God said in Jeremiah, *"For though you wash yourself with lye, and use much soap, Yet your iniquity is marked before me" (Jeremiah 2:22).*

This means your sins are washed away clean only when you believe in the gospel Word of the remission of sins, the gospel of the water and the Spirit. Like this, our Lord is making it clear here that all the sins in your heart are blotted out only when you break out of your own little town of experiences and completely accept the gospel Word of the water and the Spirit.

By any chance, is there anyone here who thinks that he can enter Heaven just by offering prayers of repentance diligently and being sanctified? Do you think that you can enter Heaven if you just live virtuously and keep the Law of God zealously? Are you still unsure about the authenticity of the gospel of the water and the Spirit which Jesus has given to you? If so, then this is the very indicator showing that you have not yet broken out of the little town of your own experiences. If there is anyone who thinks like this, now is the time to put away such thoughts of one's own experiences. You must break out of this little town of yours. All this time you have believed in the Lord zealously while living in this little town of your experiences, but how is your condition now? Your heart's sins have not disappeared but continue to remain there. Now is the hour for you to escape from the mistaken beliefs you have held, for you can never enter the Kingdom of God by this faith of your own experience.

There is only one way for everyone to escape from his sins, and it is by encountering the gospel of the water and the Spirit given by the Lord and believing in this gospel with the heart. General Naaman was completely healed from his leprosy once and for all because he had met Elisha the servant of the Lord, heard the Word of God from him, and believed in this Word exactly as it was. Likewise, today, if you also believe with your heart in the gospel of the water and the Spirit, the true Word of God, then at this very moment you can receive the complete remission of all your sins and be born again.

That is why you must first put away all the beliefs and thoughts that you have had until now. You must completely break out of the little town of your own experiences, listen to God's Word, and hold onto this Word of God by faith. God made it clear that anyone with sin can never enter His Kingdom. And the only way to blot out all your sins, if I may reiterate it one more time, is by believing in the gospel of the water and the Spirit which the Lord has given you and thus being born again.

Spiritually Speaking the Many Blind People Appearing in the Bible Refer to Sinners

Hence, that the blind man in today's Scripture passage opened his eyes from meeting the Lord means that a sinner was remitted from all his sins by encountering Jesus. In other words, it means that through the Lord, a man who was living in sins and transgressions had become a righteous child of God by believing in the gospel of the water and the Spirit that brought life to his soul. Like this, the Lord teaches us through His Word that the only way for everyone to be washed from his sins is by having faith in the gospel of the water and the Spirit.

Everyone must be washed from his heart's sins by believing in the gospel of the water and the Spirit without fail. Although we were born as filthy sinners when our mothers gave birth to us, if we believe in God's gospel of the water and the Spirit, the gospel of our spiritual Father, we will obtain the washing of sins and be born again as spotlessly clean righteous people.

For the blind man to open his eyes—that is, for a sinner to be born again—two things were necessary. As we read the Bible, we can find a similar account in John 9:1-7. In this case, the Lord spat on the ground and made clay with the saliva; and He anointed the blind man's eyes with this clay. These two things had to be done before the blind man could open his eyes. This is quite strange. After all, Jesus could have opened the blind man's eyes with a better and neater method. Why does the Bible then say that He spat on the ground and made clay with the saliva? Why did the Lord do this?

My fellow believers, there is nothing written in the Bible that is superfluous. God said clearly that not even one jot or one tittle can ever be changed from His Word until the heavens and the earth pass away. Like this, each and every Word of God contains a profound truth, and such truths can clearly be found in today's account as well.

The spit here means judgment and curse. Think about when we swear at someone. We spit at his filthy soul and curse him. In John chapter 9, that the Lord spat on the ground and made clay with the saliva and then anointed the blind man's eyes with the clay means that He is making it known to us that none other than we deserve to be cursed and judged. My fellow believers, all of us must realize without fail the fact that we ourselves cannot help but be condemned for our sins. We must clearly admit before the Word of God that we are destined to hell for our sins. In other words, we must recognize before God that we were sinful from the moment we were born, and therefore we must be destroyed. You and I alike must make this admission in our hearts, for anyone who does not admit that he is destined to hell cannot receive the remission of sins from Jesus.

When Jesus was on this earth, the Pharisees at that time did not believe that they were destined to hell for their sins. Even as they had met Jesus in person, they were still unable to be born again, and this was all because they had failed to realize their true selves. In contrast, those whose souls were born again from meeting Jesus had clearly recognized that they were sinners bound to hell for their iniquities, and they had believed in Jesus as their Savior. The Lord said, *"Those who are well have no need of a physician, but those who are sick. I did not come to call the righteous, but sinners, to repentance" (Mark 2:17).* This means that the Lord looks for and heals only those who admit that they are sinners.

My fellow believers, are you bound to hell for your sins? I admonish you all to admit this to God. Our Lord will then come looking for each and every one of you who admits to himself that he is a depraved sinner. Is there anyone among you who admits frankly that he is bound to hell? Raise your hand if you admit this. Hallelujah! God is truly pleased by all those who raised their hands. Even for those who have not raised their hands, I am sure that many of them have also admitted in their hearts that they are grave sinners. They probably are too self-conscious to raise their hands. However, everyone who has sin in his heart—that is, all sinners—must raise his hand before God and admit that he is a sinner. It is only to such people that God gives the Word of power that blots out all their sins and enables them to be born again. It is complete nonsense to say that one can go to Heaven even if he is sinful, or that one can avoid hell even if he is not born again. Those who hold this notion have not broken out of their old world yet.

God said to His beloved Abraham, *"Get out of your country, from your family and from your father's house" (Genesis 12:1)*. Abraham then left his country, his family and his father's house—that is, he left his own town of experience—and followed God only by His Word, and for this he was ultimately blessed by God in abundance.

I am sure that you and I must also be like this Abraham. God's blessings are bestowed on those who escape from their mistaken beliefs and admit before the Word of God, "Lord, I am indeed sinful. I cannot help but be cast into hell." Jesus said clearly, *"Blessed are the poor in spirit, for theirs is the kingdom of heaven."* Like this passage, those who admit to God that they are sinful and consequently destined to hell are poor in spirit, and their hearts are sincere which can lead them to Heaven.

Do you grasp this? If you do, then honestly admit to God that your heart is sinful. It is to make us realize this that our

Lord spat on the eyes of the blind man. By spitting on the blind man's eyes, Jesus was saying to none other than us, "You are all destined to hell, for you all have sin in your hearts."

What did Jesus do next? He put his hands on the blind man and touched his eyes. Then the blind man's sight was restored and he saw everything clearly. One's eye is said to be the window to his heart. The Lord also spoke of the importance of the eye, saying, *"The lamp of the body is the eye" (Matthew 6:22)*. That the Lord put His hands on the blind man's eyes, the lamp to his heart, means that the Lord took away all the sins that were in his heart.

That Jesus put His hands on the eyes of the blind man holds an extremely important spiritual meaning to us. In the age of the Old Testament, God established the sacrificial system for His people as the means by which they could wash away their sins and obtain the remission of sins. This sacrifice, however, could not be a perfect sacrifice until the arrival of Jesus Christ on this earth. That's because no matter how diligently one offered such sacrifices to God, his sins were not completely blotted out from his heart. Think about it. Your heart's sins do not disappear no matter how fervently you may believe in Jesus and how diligently you may offer prayers of repentance. Although many pastors teach their congregations that this is possible, in reality, no sin whatsoever is ever blotted out through your own prayers of repentance. There is no record anywhere in the Word of God teaching that your sins are washed away through your prayers of repentance.

God only says, *"For the life of the flesh is in the blood, and I have given it to you upon the altar to make atonement for your souls; for it is the blood that makes atonement for the soul" (Leviticus 17:11)*. In other words, the baptism by water that Jesus received from John the Baptist and the blood He shed on the Cross as a consequence of this baptism is the only means by which you can eradicate all your sins and your condemnation.

As such, because God had compassion for us who were doomed to be condemned and cast into hell for our sins, He gave us a fail safe way to eradicate all our sins and be remitted from them. He taught us the method of the laying on of hands, whereby sinners could pass their sins onto an unblemished lamb by putting their hands on its head. When we turn to the Book of Leviticus in the Old Testament, we can see many passages recording how one's sins were passed onto a lamb by laying his hands on it.

You Must Pass Your Sins onto Jesus by Faith

In the Old Testament's ritual of sin offering, which was performed by the Israelites who were to be forgiven from their sins, the first requirement was an unblemished lamb. Of course, other sacrificial animals such as bulls, cows, and goats were also used, but today, I will use the lamb here as the representative sacrificial animal. In those days, to be washed from his sins, a sinner passed them onto the lamb by laying his hands on its head. Spiritually speaking, this laying on of hands means the passing of sins. As God loved the people of Israel, He gave them the law of the remission of sins by which they could pass their hearts' sins onto a sacrificial lamb by laying their hands onto its head. And He had permitted this sacrificial lamb to be condemned for the Israelites' sins in their place.

What I would like to emphasize here at this hour is the fact that in the age of the Old Testament, the Israelites passed their sins onto a sacrificial animal by laying their hands onto its head. To verify this, let's look up just one more passage in the Old Testament. Evangelist Bae Lydia from our Church in Russia will read two verses from Leviticus 16:20-21: *"And when he has made an end of atoning for the Holy Place, the tabernacle of meeting, and the altar, he shall bring the live goat. Aaron shall lay both his hands on the head of the live goat, confess over it all the iniquities of the children of Israel, and all their transgressions, concerning all their sins, putting them on the head of the goat, and shall send it away into the wilderness by the hand of a suitable man."* Amen.

As you can see in this passage, all the sins of the people of Israel were passed onto the scapegoat when the High Priest laid his hands onto its head. Like this, the laying on of hands means the passing of sins. God had washed away all the sins of the people of Israel by making them pass their sins onto a sacrificial animal through the laying on of their hands.

Let's now return to the New Testament and look up the related Word there. In Hebrews 10:10, the Lord said, *"By that will we have been sanctified through the offering of the body of Jesus Christ once for all."* From this passage we can realize that Jesus Christ became our own Lamb of sacrifice, just like the scapegoat that had taken upon the Israelite's sins on the Day of Atonement in the Old Testament. Jesus is the Lamb of God who had come to this earth to bear all the sins of everyone in this world once and for all by being baptized by John the Baptist; and to wash away all the sins of every sinner, He shed His blood and died on the Cross. Jesus is the Son of God who had come to this earth about 2,000 years ago. It was to accept all your sins and mine through His baptism that this glorious Jesus had come to this lowly earth incarnated in the flesh of man.

When Jesus came to this earth, He was baptized by John

the Baptist (Matthew 3:13-15). Because John the Baptist was a descendant of Aaron the High Priest, he was eligible to become the representative of mankind, and as he put his hands on the head of Jesus Christ on behalf of all mankind, all the sins of the human race were passed onto Jesus. In the Old Testament, Aaron the Highest Priest was able to pass the yearly sins of the people of Israel onto the scapegoat on their behalf as their representative. Likewise, John the Baptist, a descendant of this Aaron, was also qualified to pass all the sins of mankind onto Jesus as the High Priest of this earth.

Referring to John the Baptist, the Lord said the he was the greatest of all those born of women (Matthew 11:11). John the Baptist is the representative of all mankind, including you and me. It's because John the Baptist baptized Jesus in the Jordan River that all the sins of mankind were passed onto Jesus. Spiritually speaking, baptism has the same meaning as the laying on of hands. Put differently, Jesus was baptized in the form of the laying on of hands.

If John the Baptist, the representative of every man and woman, laid his hands on the head of Jesus, doesn't this then mean that all the sins of everyone in this world were passed onto Jesus? Of course they were! I know that there are some people who just can't believe in this Truth. Others may also say that all this is simply beyond their understanding. However, their unbelief stems from the fact that they still have not escaped from their own thoughts which is shaped by their own experiences. If you set yourself free from everything you had believed in thus far, and instead believe in the Word of God alone exactly as it is, then all these things will be engraved in your heart as the clear and unambiguous Truth.

God said in Matthew 3:15 that Jesus "thus" accepted all the sins of this world by this method—that is, by being baptized by John the Baptist. Through this baptism, all the sins of this world were passed onto the body of Jesus once and for all, transcending time and space. None other than this is the power of the gospel of the water and the Spirit that constitutes the Truth of life. God the Father has washed away all our sins once and for all with the mystery of the laying on of hands and the baptism of Jesus. Therefore, if we really believe in the Lord, then it is only our natural duty to learn about the gospel Word of the water and the Spirit and live by placing all our faith in this gospel.

The Lord said,

"Though your sins are like scarlet,
They shall be as white as snow;
Though they are red like crimson,
They shall be as wool" (Isaiah 1:18).

As we have now received the remission of sins and become as white as snow by believing in the gospel of the water and the Spirit, we must never return to our own little world of past experience. At each and every passing moment, until the day we take our last breath, we must all trust in the gospel of the water and the Spirit that has washed away our sins and enabled us to be born again. And by this faith we must follow the Lord. ⊠

SERMON

7

A Christian's Life Is
All about Self-Sacrifice

< Mark 8:27-38 >

"Now Jesus and His disciples went out to the towns of
Caesarea Philippi; and on the road He asked His disciples,
saying to them, 'Who do men say that I am?' So they
answered, 'John the Baptist; but some say, Elijah; and
others, one of the prophets.' He said to them, 'But who do
you say that I am?' Peter answered and said to Him, 'You
are the Christ.' Then He strictly warned them that they
should tell no one about Him. And He began to teach them
that the Son of Man must suffer many things, and be
rejected by the elders and chief priests and scribes, and be
killed, and after three days rise again. He spoke this word
openly. Then Peter took Him aside and began to rebuke
Him. But when He had turned around and looked at His
disciples, He rebuked Peter, saying, 'Get behind Me, Satan!
For you are not mindful of the things of God, but the things
of men.' When He had called the people to Himself, with
His disciples also, He said to them, 'Whoever desires to
come after Me, let him deny himself, and take up his cross,
and follow Me. For whoever desires to save his life will lose
it, but whoever loses his life for My sake and the gospel's
will save it. For what will it profit a man if he gains the
whole world, and loses his own soul? Or what will a man
give in exchange for his soul? For whoever is ashamed of
Me and My words in this adulterous and sinful generation,
of him the Son of Man also will be ashamed when He comes

in the glory of His Father with the holy angels.'"

While Jesus was on this earth, it seemed as though He was also conscious of what people thought of Him. Perhaps for this reason Jesus asked His disciples while traveling to various towns to preach, *"Who do men say that I am?"* So the disciples answered, *"Some say Elijah, others says John the Baptist, and still others think you are one of the prophets."* Jesus then asked them again, "Then who do you say that I am?" Peter then responded and said, "You are the Christ." The word Christ here means that Jesus is the King of kings, our Savior and our God, but at the same time, He is also the Son of God Almighty.

After hearing Peter confessing his faith in front of the other disciples, Jesus openly told them that He would soon be rejected by the elders, chief priests, and scribes, and that He would be killed but rise again in three days. He told them, "Soon I will be rejected by the elders, scribes and chief priests of the day. But I will rise again after my death." Peter, being an impatient and hot-tempered man, objected when he heard this and said to Jesus, *"Far be it from You, Lord; this shall not happen to You!" (Matthew 16:22)*

Our Lord told the disciples what He would do, and what sacrifices He would make for the sake of every soul in the world. He told them that He would sacrifice Himself in order to save the entire human race, enduring suffering and giving up His body on the Cross. Although Peter loved Jesus very much, his love was still too fleshly, and so he tried to dissuade Jesus without thinking about the reason why He had come to this earth, saying to Him, "Teacher, You must not die, nor should You suffer. Why must You do this? This shall not happen to You!" Peter could not understand why his beloved Jesus would have to be rejected by the people and crucified to death. This is because Peter didn't have a full understanding of the exact reason why Jesus had come to this earth. And even though Jesus promised that He would not just die but would also rise up from the dead for sure, Peter just could not believe this, and he was gripped only by the fact that Jesus would die. Of course, our Lord rebuked Peter for this.

Our Lord Came to This Earth to Fulfill His Work

The Lord's work was to offer His own body to God the Father as the propitiation of atonement for the sins of mankind, as everyone's sacrificial offering. It was to thus blot out all the sins of mankind that He had come to this earth. This was His work. Our God had come incarnated in the flesh of man in order to carry out His work. It was to sacrifice Himself, and thereby blot out the sins of all the people in this world and enable them to obtain a new life.

To do His work, our Lord came to this earth incarnated in the flesh, and once He came, He completed this work to perfection. By being baptized in the Jordan River, He bore all the sins of everyone in this world, by giving up His body on the Cross, He paid off all the wages of sins that He had accepted; and by sacrificing Himself like this, He completed His work of salvation to give eternal life to everyone. It is by sacrificing Himself like this that Jesus has saved you and me.

It's only natural for anyone not to want his loved ones to die. Why did Jesus rebuke Peter? The answer is found in what Jesus said to Peter: *"For you are not mindful of the things of God, but the things of men" (Mark 8:33).* Peter was mindful of the work of man rather than the work of God.

What is the work of man? It is about avoiding suffering, neither losing its loved ones nor making any sacrifices. Just getting along with the neighbors, enjoying earthly prosperity, and living in comfort—this is all that everyone is concerned about. Rather than thinking of the real reasons why Jesus had come to this earth, Peter probably also wanted Him to just continue to be with the disciples, showing them miracles and healing the sick. Like this, the disciples just wanted Jesus to be with them for a long time to come, rather than being mindful of the salvation of mankind.

However, God's work was different from man's work. God's work was for Jesus to accept the sins of mankind through the baptism of John the Baptist and to save us by sacrificing Himself on the Cross to death. Those who have been born again in the gospel of the water and the Spirit also carry out God's work. This does not mean that the born-again should actually die on their crosses for someone else, but it means that they should work hard to serve the gospel of the water and the Spirit that has saved every human being, and to spread it to the ends of this world. The challenge, however, is that we are constantly struggling between God's work and man's work.

Between seeking one's own comfort and sacrificing oneself, the former is a much easier course to take. That's because no one wants to sacrifice himself. In fact, even those who have received the remission of sins do not like to sacrifice themselves. After all, anyone who is even marginally intelligent has no wish to do anything that's detrimental to his own interest. However, God's work is all about making sacrifices. This is also what God wants from us.

How do we then sacrifice ourselves? We do so by trying our utmost to bring life to others and help them obtain it, even though this may entail suffering and hardship for us. This is how the righteous who have received the remission of sins must lead their lives. Just as our Lord had come to this earth to do His work, so must we who have received the remission of sins first also carry out the Lord's work. The work of God that all of us must do is none other than sacrificing ourselves to preach the gospel of the water and the Spirit to others, and helping them to receive the remission of sins.

Those who have been truly born again by believing in the gospel of the water and the Spirit are in fact not adverse to self-sacrifice. The Bible says, *"The wicked borrows and does not repay, but the righteous shows mercy and gives" (Psalms 37:21).* Because the Lord dwells in righteous people who have been born again through the gospel of the water and the Spirit, it is natural for them to be infinitely giving. That's because the Lord dwelling in them wants them to give. In contrast, the wicked do not have the Lord dwelling in them, and so they like to borrow rather than to give, and they don't repay even after borrowing. Further in Psalms chapter 37 as quoted above, we read in verse 26, *"He is ever merciful, and lends; and his descendants are blessed."* This means that even though the righteous continue to give, they are blessed and lack nothing. Such are the blessings received for making sacrifices for the Lord's work.

Our Lord, who has entered into us and dwells in us, came to this earth to do His work, and He has given the Holy Spirit to those who have been born again through the gospel of the water and the Spirit. The Holy Spirit has come into our hearts to dwell therein, and our Lord still continues to work to give life to everyone until the day He returns. And He does this work through you and me, who have received the remission of sins through the gospel of the water and the Spirit. That is why our sacrifice is necessary to spread the gospel.

The sacrifice that Jesus made on this earth to fulfill our salvation and to blot out all our sins was the first real sacrifice made on this earth. All the previous biblical figures who were martyred for righteousness were actually shadows to Jesus Christ. God had shown through them that Jesus Christ would come to this earth, carry out His righteous work for the sake of mankind, and endure suffering to give us the remission of sins, new life, and Heaven. Put differently, the sacrifices made by the righteous in the Old Testament were the antitypes of God's work that was actually realized by Jesus.

Just as many prophets had sacrificed themselves, and just as Jesus set a personal example for us, likewise those of us who have receive the remission of sins in the gospel of the water and the Spirit must also make sacrifices. We must be giving. Just as Jesus had worked hard for the entire human race, so must every true Christian work hard for others. All of us are capable of doing this. Since self-sacrifice is only natural for all whose hearts are dwelt in by the Holy Spirit, and since this is what our Lord who is inside us desires from us, we cannot help but to sacrifice ourselves.

To this day, we have made many sacrifices in our lives while following the Lord. However, whoever has received the remission of sins in the gospel of the water and the Spirit must sacrifice his everything. In other words, it's not as though you can sacrifice some things and leave the rest out for yourself. Having met our Lord, we sometimes wonder, "Now that I have received the Lord, will I prosper more or will I have to make more sacrifices? What will happen to me?" Such questions come to our minds because we realize that although we had lived just for ourselves before the Lord came into us, now that we have met the Lord, we have to do God's work first rather than our own work.

This is true for both you and me alike. Now that we have received the remission of our sins, we are not doing own our work but we are carrying out God's work. Nothing is done for ourselves, just as the Bible says, *"For none of us lives to himself, and no one dies to himself. For if we live, we live to the Lord; and if we die, we die to the Lord. Therefore, whether we live or die, we are the Lord's" (Romans 14:7-8).* Everything is done for God. For those who have been truly born again of the water and the Spirit and have been remitted of all their sins, anything that's done just for themselves makes their hearts extremely uncomfortable. That's because it would turn them into the Devil's servants once again. So it is impossible for the born-again Christians to live only for themselves. Is this true for you as well? I certainly hope so.

For Whom Are You Laboring?

When you labor just for yourself, it may please your flesh for a while, but does your heart not feel that there is something wrong, something empty? I am sure that you all had experienced this once or twice. In contrast, when you sacrifice yourself and follow the Lord, and labor hard for His sake, you feel that there is much to be gained. That's because the focal point of a Christian's life is sacrifice. None other than self-sacrifice is the defining characteristic of the life of every Christian.

Exodus 29:18 says, *"And you shall burn the whole ram on the altar. It is a burnt offering to the LORD; it is a sweet aroma, an offering made by fire to the LORD."* When the Day of Atonement came, the altar of burnt offering in the

Tabernacle exuded the aroma of burning flesh throughout the whole day, morning and evening, and God accepted this as a sweet aroma. This is what a Christian's life is all about. When Jesus Christ came to this earth, He put His body on the altar of burnt offering to become our own sacrificial offering. Accepting His death, God the Father blotted out all our sins. For us the born-again as well, our lives must also be sacrificed to be a sweet aroma to the Lord. This is the life of every Christian.

Those who have truly been born again in the gospel of the water and the Spirit and met the Lord do not have a life of their own. They lead their lives entirely for Christ and not for themselves. If you think of this in a fleshly way, such a life may seem rather stupid and idiotic. You may also resent it, wondering, "Why must I live like this?" However, if we sacrifice ourselves to spread the gospel, it will be preached to everyone in this world. We must therefore sacrifice ourselves.

Having come to do His work, the Lord said that He would have to be forsaken by the elders, scribes and chief priests. Why did Jesus have to be forsaken? Did He commit sedition? Did He do anything unethical? Did He go into politics? No, He did none of these things. Why did He then have to be rejected by the scribes and politicians? Why did He have to be forsaken by the chief priests, the religious leaders of the time? Why did He have to be forsaken by lowly human beings when He was the Son of God? Jesus had absolutely no reason to be rejected. Although He had neither any fault nor any sin, Jesus still had to be forsaken because He had to pay off the wages of everyone's sins, because He had accepted these sins. It's because everyone committed sin for himself and only thought of his own human affairs that Jesus sacrificed Himself, even though He was rejected by the people of His days and treated as their enemy.

As those born again in the gospel of the water and the Spirit, we are also persecuted by many people as we carry on with our lives on this earth and do the righteous work of God. It's not unusual for us to be called stupid and foolish, and sometime even idiots. Of course, if you live an ordinary life without doing God's work even as you claim to have been born again, you won't face any persecution. That's because you would be approved by others. But is this life that's led just for yourself without any sacrifice really the kind of life that God desires from you?

We believe that everything we do is God's work, from planting churches to carrying out this literature ministry, working for world mission, taking care of God's Church in Korea and beyond, and praying for all these things. And we are convinced that serving the Lord in this way is sacrificing ourselves. Just as we believe, none of these works is done for ourselves. If we had done them just for ourselves, then we would have sought to receive some sort of compensation. We would have expected God to reward us for our labor, and we would always have thought that our rewards are not enough to compensate for our hard work.

Carrying out God's work is all about giving and sacrificing oneself. In particular, world mission cannot be achieved without sacrifice. We have heard from many brothers and sisters abroad requesting us to send our missionaries to them. But it's not so easy for our missionaries to travel to a faraway country where both the culture and the language are completely foreign to them. It requires a great deal of sacrifice. Like this, when it comes to carrying out the Lord's work, sacrifice is indispensable in all aspects.

Yet some saints still think mistakenly, "Our missionaries must be having fun traveling to all these different places. I wish

I were sent out as a missionary." But is any missionary ever sent out to the mission field on a vacation? If you think our missionaries are out in the field on a vacation, you should put yourself in their shoes and see it for yourself. Some places have such poor water quality that it's not drinkable at all. Take the case of Yanbian in China. The tap water is so bad that when you let it stand for a while, you can actually see sediments at the bottom. Would you be able to drink this water? Furthermore, it's not easy to be all by yourself cut off from your loved ones in a place where you cannot communicate with anyone of your own culture. It requires sacrifice.

Our literature ministry also entails a lot of sacrifice. Seeing our books published, some of you may think, "It's no big deal. Pastor Jong's books are not that great anyways, and so why do we keep publishing more and more books? Just one publication should be enough; anything more is simply a waste of time." But this is not the case. Do you have any idea just how difficult and stressful it is to publish even one book? Everyone involved in this work is facing so much pressure and stress. If you say something wrong, you can easily correct it right away, but once a book is published, that's the end of it. It can't be revised right away. Moreover, it's not so easy to transcribe sermons and edit them into a published format because every context of a sermon must flow smoothly. However, our literary ministry is being carried out well because everyone involved is putting in a great deal of sacrifice.

Whether it comes to your job, your family, or serving the Lord being united with the Church, nothing can be done without sacrifice. Is there anything that's done without any sacrifice? Sometimes you have to do things that you don't want to do, and sometimes you have to forsake your social life to attend church gatherings. All these things entail sacrifice. We can become one only if we sacrifice ourselves like this in various ways and serve the Lord being united with the Church. Even your daily social life requires sacrifice. You can't participate in any social groups unless you sacrifice yourself. As simple as getting involved in the Parent-Teacher Association of your child's school requires some self-sacrifice, and so it's only a matter of course that you should sacrifice even more for God's Church.

It is never an easy thing for you to serve the Lord and live your life united with the Church when you have a job to attend to. Without self-sacrifice, it's absolutely impossible. That is why the Lord said, "Whoever wants to follow Me must deny himself, pick up his cross, and then follow Me." So even when it comes to your job, a great deal of sacrifice is required.

I had also worked in a job for a couple of years, and while holding down this job there were several times when I felt like quitting because of my boss. As a man, my boss was not any better than me, but just because he was the employer, he showed little respect and treated me like an object, ordering me around to do this and that. It was only natural for me to get angry. I was expected to show up at the work on time, but I couldn't leave for home on time. It goes without saying that I couldn't even dream of having any private freedom. When I tried to listen to some sermon tapes or even read the Bible when I had some free time, my boss got on my case and berated me. On average I worked eight hours a day at least. I spent all those eight hours working hard for someone else's business.

But how much did I get paid in return? I just got a pittance, barely enough to make a living. When the payday came around, I felt like ripping up my paycheck, thinking to myself, "Did I work so hard for this lousy pay? It's an insult!" I felt that I could make that much money just by working for an hour elsewhere. I also thought that I should devote all my effort to winning a soul rather than working to death only to make a pitiful sum of money; a soul is more precious than anything else under the heavens and winning it is far more rewarding than any gains to be made on this earth. Since it was such hard-earned money, I also struggled with how to spend it, wanting to put it towards something worthwhile.

I am sure all of you had such experiences before. Money also must be spent wisely. It should be invested appropriately, or otherwise you will end up losing all your hard-earned money. I myself experienced this several times while working at a job. It's never easy to serve the gospel while you are working at a job, attending school, or raising a family, but it's even more challenging to get fully involved in the ministry of the Church. In some ways, you may feel that it's more comfortable to be in the ministry on a full-time basis. Depending on who is looking, it may seem as though our full-time ministers are not doing much else other than raising a racket in the Church and enjoying themselves, but once you step into their shoes, you will realize that it's not so easy as you think. Their ministry is something that can never be done without self-sacrifice.

Our lives are all about making sacrifices. We have been able to serve the gospel and follow the Lord until now because all of us have sacrificed ourselves, from our Sunday school teachers to our brothers and sisters in training and all our saints in the Church. Such sacrifices are continuously necessary in the years to come.

We should not think of the work of man. The work of man is all about worldly prosperity. It's to become a pig with a full stomach. The life that's led in vain without any sacrifice, one that is led not for what is right but for one's own fleshly prosperity only to perish meaninglessly—this is what man's work is all about.

In contrast, those of us who have been born again in the gospel of the water and the Spirit desire to do the righteous work rather than the work of man who die in vain. And we do this righteous work. What righteous work do we do? We do God's work. Small though our sacrifices may be, we sacrifice ourselves to follow the Lord in faith. God does not let these sacrifices go unrewarded. He fills them with blessings without fail. The Lord said in Matthew 16:25, *"For whoever desires to save his life will lose it, but whoever loses his life for My sake will find it."* This means that if we try to live for ourselves, we will lose even more, but if we decide to sacrifice even our own lives for the Lord, He will add more blessings upon blessings.

Even when it comes to the work of man, which is all about fleshly prosperity, sacrifice is necessary. But this work only entails sacrifices and no rewards. In contrast, though it may require self-sacrifice for us to carry out God's work, there is a reward for it, and our sacrifices are worthwhile. That is why we are living a life of sacrifice to follow the Lord. The Lord made it clear to us, "If you lose your life for Me and My gospel, you will live, but if you live only for the work of man, you will lose everything." What does it mean when Jesus said that one must deny himself and follow the Lord in his life? It means that one should follow the Lord even if it entails a great deal of costs. He will then gain many things.

However, if one does not sacrifice himself and gives up following the Lord, he will lose many things. It's written, *"Therefore do not worry, saying, 'What shall we eat?' or 'What shall we drink?' or 'What shall we wear?' . . . But seek first the kingdom of God and His righteousness, and all these things shall be added to you"* (Matthew 6:31, 33). If we are mindful of God's work first, He will provide for all our needs.

All of us must carry out God's work. This means we must all sacrifice ourselves. That's because following the Lord inevitably entails self-sacrifice. Through our sacrifice many people are able to receive the remission of sins. Much is gained even with a small sacrifice. Think about it. We have only made small sacrifices, and yet how much more have we gained? On account of our sacrifice, churches are being planted throughout Korea and more and more souls are being born again. Have we not seen with our eyes just how many souls are saved through the God-established Church and His servants and saints? Although it takes a great deal of sacrifice to plant just a single branch church, we have seen with our own eyes how God blesses us so much more as a result of this.

A great deal of sacrifice was made when Wonju Church was planted, not to mention when the New Life Church was planted in Seoul and another church in Incheon. Many brothers and sisters and God's servants labored very hard, and they made a lot of sacrifices and investments with their material possessions, their bodies, and their hearts, all by faith. That is how they established these branch churches. Even when we planted the Chungju Church, our servants of God invested in many areas. When God's servants minister, they offer there everything to the Lord regardless of how much they own. When we were looking for a place for the Chuncheon Church, we were able to find a building thanks to the Evangelists Jung and Choi and their families, as they offered their material possessions to the Lord. At that time, we had to put down a deposit of around $20,000 and make a monthly payment of around $250. Where else would we have found all this money? It was made possible only because our brothers and sisters and God's servants had offered there everything and sacrificed themselves. It wasn't just our brothers and sisters who made sacrifices. God's servants also made sacrifices and they all served the Lord together.

Sacrifice is necessary for us to follow the Lord. The sacrifices that you have made to follow the Lord, was not made with a conscientious effort, but you nevertheless did this without even realizing them. The very fact that you have followed the Lord to this day is in itself a sacrifice. You could have never followed Him without any sacrifice. Unless one denies and sacrifices himself, it is not possible for this person to follow God's Church, nor can he follow the Lord. Following the Church is following the Lord.

What is the will of the Lord? What is God's work? What's the work of the Lord that He did when He came to this earth? Sacrificing Himself by accepted all our sins in the Jordan River, by being condemned on the Cross in our place, and by thus sacrificing His own body, He saved you and me. This was the work of God. We are now of those who are carrying out God's work. God's work is carried out by those who have received the remission of sins through the gospel of the water and the Spirit.

My fellow believers, the remission of sins is not something that we should receive just for ourselves, but it is something that everyone must receive by hearing the gospel of the water and the Spirit, from those around us and to our families, our fellow countrymen, and everyone else throughout the whole wide world. In China, people are so innocent that most of them receive the remission of sins as soon as they hear the gospel. They are so receptive to the Word. If we work hard just one more year and preach the gospel diligently, God will save many souls there. I also know it takes some time before the gospel is planted firmly in China. But I believe that in a couple of years, the faith of the Chinese saints will become much stronger.

When we planted a church here in Daejeon City, our families and the souls around us will also receive the remission of sins. Planting a church in Daejon to serve the gospel is not only for the sake of the Lord, but it is also for the sake of our own relatives and those around us who have not yet been born again. Just as Jesus sacrificed Himself for everyone's sake, so we must also sacrifice ourselves and serve the Lord in our lives for the sake of other peoples salvation.

I know very well that it's very difficult and hard for you to make sacrifices, and as a result, you sometimes feel like giving it up. I know that you sometimes think, "Can't I now just stop sacrificing so much? Can't I just live my remaining life in ease until the Lord either returns to take me away or I go to His presence?" Even though there is a desire in our hearts to be complacent and indulge ourselves, it is still the will of the Lord for us to sacrifice ourselves. This is what pleases the Lord. And that's why we must have faith. Let us then, we who know the will of God, trust in this will and obey it.

The Bible says that He who is to come will come soon. As the world is so evil, unless we serve the Lord, sacrifice ourselves for Him, and labor for His work, we cannot help but be swept away by the deep undercurrents of sin. The more wicked the times are, the more we must devote ourselves to serving the Lord and follow Him. ✉

SERMON

8

Let's Confess
The True Faith to God

< Mark 8:27-38 >

"Now Jesus and His disciples went out to the towns of Caesarea Philippi; and on the road He asked His disciples, saying to them, 'Who do men say that I am?' So they answered, 'John the Baptist; but some say, Elijah; and others, one of the prophets.' He said to them, 'But who do you say that I am?' Peter answered and said to Him, 'You are the Christ.' Then He strictly warned them that they should tell no one about Him. And He began to teach them that the Son of Man must suffer many things, and be rejected by the elders and chief priests and scribes, and be killed, and after three days rise again. He spoke this word openly. Then Peter took Him aside and began to rebuke Him. But when He had turned around and looked at His disciples, He rebuked Peter, saying, 'Get behind Me, Satan! For you are not mindful of the things of God, but the things of men.' When He had called the people to Himself, with His disciples also, He said to them, 'Whoever desires to come after me, let him deny himself, and take up his cross, and follow me. For whoever desires to save his life will lose it, but whoever loses his life for my sake and the gospel's will save it. For what will it profit a man if he gains the whole world, and loses his own soul? Or what will a man give in exchange for his soul? For whoever is ashamed of Me and My words in this adulterous and sinful generation, of him the Son of Man also will be ashamed when He comes

in the glory of His Father with the holy angels.'"

Long time no see! The Lord's Day has passed and it is now Wednesday. It seems like such a long time has passed since I last saw you all, Monday, Tuesday and Wednesday feels like such a long time.

There is a work that we still don't get through with although it seemed like it would get done soon, and it is the work of publishing the third book of our Christian literature series. Our editors inform us that they are preparing the press today. Someone must inspect the temporary binding after this. We would have to proofread the temporary binding from the beginning again in order to finish the publishing work perfectly, but it will take too long if we tried to make it too perfect and it could actually turn out worse in some aspects. And so we are thinking of finishing it even though it is completed to a certain degree.

There are many saints who have various kinds of gifts in our Church, and I can see that many of them really are not arrogant about their gifts but are humble. The brothers seem very courageous and the sisters seem very humble. Thus, they fulfill all the work that we ask them to do so well although they sometimes say they are not able to do it, and I am so thankful for this. Many workers and saints have worked hard to publish the third volume of our mission book series. I think this book is being published with the love of many workers. Some saints and ministry workers who have been involved directly in this work and others have served with material things. We all have volunteered to serve this literature ministry. It was also very hard for me to publish this third volume of our mission book series. Anyway, we have all worked very hard. But I do not want our efforts to stop here. Rather, I want the evangelization of the gospel of God to continue. I think we have to spread the gospel of the water and the Spirit even more quickly because the world is so gloomy these days.

Message from a Reader of Our Books

Today, I have received an e-mail from overseas just before coming to preach in our Church. This is the e-mail sent to us by "Maria Chejib" who is a secretary of the President of Vista University in South Africa. All the letters and emails sent to the President go through the secretary, and she saw the e-mail we sent to this President concerning our free books on the gospel of the water and the Spirit. This secretary said that she has read two of our books and requested to read more of them. This woman called Maria has been married for 32 years and she said that she has been very diligent in mission activities as well. The translated content of her email is as follows:

"I had not known at all how important it was to know why Jesus received the baptism from John the Baptist. However, these books made me understand according to the Bible what being born again by the gospel of the water and the Spirit is all about. I have finally come to truly understand about the gospel of the water and the Spirit that I had not known before although I have attended church for a long time. I want to share these books to other people that have not heard of it yet. And so I have come to realize that I must speak to my many Christian friends about this gospel so that they can also be born again by the water and the Spirit like me. Now I know that I have absolutely received my salvation. I have the key to salvation. I have been born again by the baptism of Jesus and His death on the Cross. My Savior is alive."

She sent me an e-mail with such contents. Dear beloved saints, have you heard what I have just read to you? I do not know much about the countries in Africa, but some regions of Africa are in such a miserable state. They say that some regions are extremely dangerous because of the AIDS pandemic and rampant crime. They say that 30% of the population of the nation of Zimbabwe is infected with AIDS and many people are dying of this disease each day. Since it is such a miserable country, I want the gospel of the water and the Spirit to go into that country as soon as possible and save many souls from their sins."

Who Do You Say That Jesus Christ Is?

In today's Scripture passage, Jesus asked his disciples, *"Who do men say that I am?"* The disciples answered, *"John the Baptist; but some say, Elijah; and others, one of the prophets."* At this, Jesus asked disciples again, *"But who do you say that I am?"* Peter confessed his faith and said to Him, *"You are the Christ."* Then Jesus said that it was God the Father who made Peter know this. This confession, "You are the Christ," is short, but it is a confession that showed concisely and significantly that the Lord is our Savior.

Most Israelites living in the days of Jesus thought of Him just as one of the prophets of the Old Testament, but Jesus was actually their Savior. Even now, many Jews think of Jesus as just one of the prophets of the Old Testament instead of the Son of God. Therefore, it is very difficult to preach to the Israelites that Jesus Christ is in fact the Son of God and the

Savior of all humanity. They also do not acknowledge the New Testament Scriptures since they do not acknowledge Jesus is the Christ. They are still waiting for their Savior even thinking that only the Word of the Old Testament Scriptures is all that there is. They think like that although Jesus Christ has already come to this world and saved all sinners once and for all by the gospel of the water and the Spirit was resurrected from the dead and now sits on the throne in Heaven. But despite all this, they are still waiting for the Savior.

They are waiting for the Messiah although the Messiah Jesus Christ had already come and fulfilled His righteous salvation as the Son of God incarnated. Therefore, in order to preach the gospel to the Israelites we have to let them know first that Jesus is the Messiah, the One they have been waiting for. They will come to have the genuine faith of salvation if they just come to know this just like us. But I am sure that the Israelites will soon accept in their hearts the gospel of the water and the Spirit and also come to believe in it. Even these days the Israelites pass the sins over onto a sacrificial offering by laying hands on it and offer up this sacrifice of atonement by cutting its throat and sprinkling its blood on the Day of Atonement every year. But if they just accepted the fact that Jesus is the Messiah who they have been waiting for, they will receive salvation from their sins by believing in the fact that Jesus became the Lamb of God through the baptism He received from John the Baptist and His death on the Cross.

Jesus asked the disciples, *"Who do men say that I am?"* They answered, *"John the Baptist; but some say, Elijah; and others, one of the prophets."* Those Israelites did not believe that Jesus is the Messiah or that He is the Son of God. Who is this John the Baptist? He is a servant of God. Then, who was Elijah? He was also a servant of God. They were all one of the prophets or the servants of God, not the Messiah like Jesus. Even so, people of that time considered Jesus the same as such people.

Nevertheless, Peter confessed, *"You are the Christ, the Son of the living God" (Matthew 16:16).* Peter said that Jesus is the Son of God and the Christ. Peter knew and believed through the Father that Jesus is the Son of God the Father and the Christ. Jesus thus is our God and also the High Priest of the Kingdom of Heaven. Jesus Christ took all our sins upon His body once and for all by the baptism, died on the Cross, and was resurrected from the dead, and He is the true Savior who saved us completely. The faith of the gospel of the water and the Spirit is contained in this short confession of Peter.

The word "Christ" means "the anointed King" (Daniel 9:26, John 1:41). In the Old Testament, kings, priests and prophets could receive the anointing with oil. In Israel, they poured oil on the head of a person when they anointed him as a king, a prophet, or a High Priest. God the Father named His Son Jesus Christ and it is because God did the work of saving us from sins through His Son. Therefore, our Lord came to this world and became our King, our Prophet, and also fulfilled the responsibility of the heavenly High Priest who took all our sins upon His body by receiving the baptism. He came to this world as the High Priest of the Kingdom of Heaven and took all our sins upon Himself. The Lord saved us who now believe in the gospel of the water and the Spirit once and for all by fulfilling these three duties of the King, the High Priest, and the Prophet. Therefore, Jesus is our High Priest, our Master, and the Savior who saved us from the sins of the world by the gospel of the water and the Spirit. Jesus was the Prophet of truth who shows us why we were born to this world and what is the gospel Truth of the water and the Spirit that saves us from all our sins. Our

Lord came to this world as the High Priest of the Kingdom of Heaven and took all our sins upon Himself. He took the sins of this world upon His own body instead of passing the sins of the world over onto a sacrificial lamb or goat of the Old Testament. The Lord became the propitiation for us by taking the sins of the world upon Himself once and for all by receiving the baptism from John the Baptist.

When Jesus was dying on the Cross, Pilate wrote a title on the Cross, "JESUS OF NAZARETH, THE KING OF THE JEWS." Then the Israelites seeing this requested, "Do not write, 'The King of the Jews,' even though He said, 'I am the King of the Jews.'" But Pilate answered, *"What I have written, I have written" (John 19:21).* But Jesus is truly the King of all kings and the Master of the entire universe.

A person who knows the righteousness of Jesus in this era is someone who believes in the gospel of the water and the Spirit which Jesus gave us. To us who believe in the gospel of the water and the Spirit, Jesus Christ is the genuine High Priest, the Creator who made this universe, and the Judge who is to come. Jesus will return to this world, resurrect us the saints who have been born again by believing in the gospel of the water and the Spirit, and take us to His Kingdom of Heaven. We will come to live eternally with our Savior in the Kingdom of God. Jesus is our God and the High Priest who has such power. Jesus is the King who dwells with us and rules over us eternally and righteously. I do not know how Jesus Christ appears to a person who does not believe, but Jesus Christ is the King of kings, the Savior of humanity, and the eternal Judge.

The Word of the Scriptures is the Word about Jesus Christ. The Old Testament prophesizes that Jesus would come and save us from all our sins and the New Testament speaks of this promise of the Old Testament being fulfilled. The Word of God contains not only that but also all things like politics, economy, culture, science, future, present, past, purpose of life, human life, and so on. Thus, one comes to receive the remission of sins if one comes to know the Word correctly and realize the gospel of the water and the Spirit.

You and I who live in these end times must also have this genuine confession of faith as that of Peter's. Dear fellow believers, do you have such genuine faith in your heart? We must live with such genuine confession of faith. While living this short life, we must know and believe that Jesus is the King of kings, the High Priest, and also the Prophet. On the other hand, if we do not believe in the righteousness of Jesus Christ and reject it we will be destroyed eternally. I do not want you to become like these foolish people who disrespect and ignore the righteousness of God.

You Must Also Have in Your Heart the Confession of Faith That Says, "Jesus Is the Christ!"

When Peter made the confession of genuine faith to Jesus, He said to him, *"And I will give you the keys of the kingdom of heaven, and whatever you bind on earth will be bound in heaven, and whatever you loose on earth will be loosed in heaven" (Matthew 16:19)*. Jesus said that He will give the keys of the Kingdom of Heaven to Peter who confessed the genuine faith.

Dear fellow believers, what is the "keys of the Kingdome of Heaven"? It is the gospel and the faith in it that cleanses everyone's sins. What kind of gospel makes one enter the Kingdom of Heaven? It is none other than the gospel of the water and the Spirit. This gospel of the water and the Spirit is the gospel of the Lord who took all the sins of the world upon Himself by receiving the baptism from John the Baptist, being crucified and shedding blood on the Cross, and being resurrected from the dead. The key of the Kingdom of Heaven is faith of believing in the gospel of the water and the Spirit which our Lord fulfilled. Hence, we need this faith which says, *"You are the Christ, the Son of the living God" (Matthew 16:16).* This true faith is the faith that believes the Lord is the Son of God, our King and the Savior who came to this world as the High Priest of the Kingdom of Heaven. Thus Jesus took all our sins by receiving the baptism from John the Baptist, was crucified to death on the Cross because of the sins He took upon Himself, and was resurrected from the dead in three days after dying on the Cross. Believing that the Lord has saved us from the sins of the world by the gospel of the water and the Spirit is the genuine faith. Jesus is God who took all our sins upon Himself, blotted them out once and for all, and gave us new life. The Lord knew the beginning and the end of all things and also controlled all things. When Peter confessed such faith, Jesus entrusted him with the work of preaching the gospel of the water and the Spirit, which is the key to the Kingdom of Heaven.

Do you have the faith that you must believe and preach the gospel of the water and the Spirit? The Lord became our Savior and the work He fulfilled is the gospel Truth of the water and the Spirit. Thus, our Savior is Jesus Christ. Do you have faith that the Lord is the Christ, the Son of the living God?

Our genuine Savior is Jesus Christ. We must have this faith that professes the gospel of the water and the Spirit in order to make such a confession of faith. We must have such

faith of believing in this gospel of the water and the Spirit in
our hearts. Dear fellow believers, it does not mean that you
have the knowledge and the faith of believing in the gospel of
the water and the Spirit just because you believe in Jesus as
your Savior. There are many church attendees who believe in
God without knowing that Jesus Christ has saved all
humankind by the gospel of the water and the Spirit. Although
some people have heard and known that Christ means "the
anointed One," many among them do not know that Christ
actually saved us by taking our sins upon Himself and shedding
His blood by the gospel of the water and the Spirit." So when I
ask them, "What is the meaning of the anointed One?" they just
cannot but mumble their preposterous answers to my question.
We can say therefore that only those who believe in the gospel
of the water and the Spirit now know the meaning of the
confession, "The Lord is the Christ, the Son of the living God."
Put differently, faith of believing that the Lord took the sins of
this world by receiving the baptism from John, died on the
Cross, and was resurrected from dead is the faith that is able to
profess, "The Lord is the Christ!"

Have You Believed That the Gospel of the Water and the Spirit Is the Genuine Truth of Salvation?

Do you believe that the gospel of the water and the Spirit
really is the gospel of salvation? If so then do you believe that
Jesus is the Son of God who created the universe and the
Savior who blotted out all your sins once and for all by the
gospel of the water and the Spirit? The faith of people who
have the keys of the Kingdom of Heaven is the faith of
believing that the Lord took over all our sins once and for all

and saved us the believers by the baptism He received from John the Baptist, His blood on the Cross, and being resurrected from the dead. We who are like this have received salvation from the sins of the world.

In order to do this Jesus made us realize and know what treacherous sinners we were through the Law of God. And He resolved the problem of our sins away completely that we could not resolve by ourselves and perfected our salvation. And the Lord taught us how He blotted out all those sins and we were able to become the children of God by receiving salvation from all our sins by believing in the gospel of the water and the Spirit. We have received the grace of salvation once and for all by believing in this genuine gospel which Jesus gave to us. We have been qualified to enter the Kingdom of Heaven by believing in the gospel of the water and the Spirit. You have the keys to the Kingdom of Heaven if you have in your heart the faith that professes, "Lord, You are the Christ."

In today's Scripture passage, Jesus who heard Peter's confession of faith told his disciples not to tell this fact to anyone and that He would soon suffer death at the hands of the chief priest, the elders and the scribes of this world. And He said clearly that he would be resurrected from the dead in three days.

However, Peter tried to stop Jesus from doing His work. Peter protested by saying, "You are the Christ. Why are you suddenly saying that you will die? Why would you be killed by those people?" Peter who had a strong chivalrous spirit was trying his best to stop Jesus from dying on the Cross. He might deserve to be commended for his loyalty to Jesus if we just look at him in a human perspective.

However, Jesus rebuked Peter, saying, *"Get behind Me, Satan! For you are not mindful of the things of God, but the things of men."* Why did Jesus refer to Peter as Satan? Do you think He said this because Peter really was Satan? Jesus said this because Peter thought of things of man and not the things of God. Satan was trying to dissuade Jesus Christ from fulfilling the work of shedding His blood for us by provoking these fleshly thoughts of Peter's. We the believers in the gospel of the water and the Spirit are also like this. We should not think the things of man but instead think of the things of God. If we think the things of man we will also become a slave to Satan. Peter was merely a person who was impatient, a person with a sanguine temperament, but Jesus called him Satan because he tried to stop the work He was doing. The Lord made a clear distinction between the work of man and the work of God and said that one must deny himself and carry his own cross in order to follow Him. I know that all of you understand this Word.

We Should Actually Deny Ourselves and Follow the Lord in Leading a Spiritual Life

There are many times when we struggle to deny ourselves because our flesh is so strong. This is because we cannot follow Jesus if we do not deny our flesh. We cannot follow the Lord if we do not deny our fleshly thoughts because our fleshly thoughts and the Lord's thoughts are totally opposite to each other. Therefore, we must deny ourselves in order to follow the Lord.

And the Lord also states that whosoever is ashamed of believing in Jesus and the Word He has spoken in this adulterous and sinful generation, Jesus will be ashamed of that person when He comes to this world again in the glory of the

Father with the holy angels. It is written, *"For whoever is ashamed of Me and My words in this adulterous and sinful generation, of him the Son of Man also will be ashamed when He comes in the glory of His Father with the holy angels"* *(Mark 8:38)*. Jesus said many things to us while He was in this world, and we come to carry our own cross, deny ourselves, and follow Jesus if we really believe in the works Jesus has done and the Words He has spoken. And we come to realize and believe in the gospel and attain many things through our faith. However, if you don't have faith, or have faith and throw away the Words of Jesus intentionally to follow after your own fleshly desires, and ashamed of believing in Jesus before the peoples of this world, Jesus will likewise be ashamed of you also. If you do not have such faith of salvation that says, "The Lord is the Christ, the Son of the living God" or ashamed of all the Words Jesus had spoken, He will also be ashamed of you when He returns to this world with the glory of the Father and judge the world sitting on the Throne of Judgment.

Believing in the gospel of the water and the Spirit and following the Lord is related to our life. The Lord said in the gospel of Mark chapter 8:35, *"For whoever desires to save his life will lose it, but whoever loses his life for my sake and the gospel's will save it."* You can receive eternal life, salvation, and the blessing if you believe in Him. You will receive everything from the Lord if you believe in the Word God had promised. But what happens if you do not believe in His Word, but instead reject it and are ashamed of it and go far away from it? It means that you will lose your life. You will be cursed eternally. It is the same in this life and the next life as well. Jesus is also ashamed of such a person and does not want that kind of person to enter the Kingdom of Jesus. Then, isn't that eternal death? Yes, such a person will be destroyed forever.

The Lord said, *"Whoever desires to come after me, let him deny himself, and take up his cross, and follow me" (Mark 8:34).* We know this Word well. However, it becomes difficult for us to follow the Lord if we actually face a difficult situation. At such a time, we need to deny ourselves even more and follow the Lord shouldering our own crosses. We cannot follow the Lord without being in a difficult situation and without denying ourselves. And it is impossible to receive salvation without even following like this.

In many places in the Scriptures, the Lord spoke much about faith that will match the affairs and hardships of the end times. One of the incidents that will happen in the end time is that there will be a lot of people who will betray the faith. It means that many believers will leave the Church and from the work of uniting with the Church and serving the gospel, and come to follow after their fleshly thoughts that says, "I am so tired. This is too difficult. Do we absolutely have to live like this when the world is so difficult? It is true that this gospel is genuine. But do I absolutely have to follow the gospel like this?" The Lord said such things would happen much more especially in the end times. And such things are really happening in the born-again Church even now.

If there is a person among us who has betrayed the faith of believing in the gospel of the water and the Spirit and rather following after another gospel, God will not forgive such a person. The Church of God can admonish such a person a few times, but we cannot do anything more if that person does not turn around and return back into the gospel of the water and the Spirit. Who could stop such a person if he says that this gospel is not everything and that he just wants to earn money and live prosperously for his flesh's sake? However, all the basic necessities of food and shelter are resolved by serving the gospel of the water and the Spirit, which is the righteousness of God.

The Lord also said in the Gospel of Matthew chapter 18 verse 15 to 17, *"Moreover if your brother sins against you, go and tell him his fault between you and him alone. If he hears you, you have gained your brother. But if he will not hear, take with you one or two more, that 'by the mouth of two or three witnesses every word may be established.' And if he refuses to hear them, tell it to the church. But if he refuses even to hear the church, let him be to you like a heathen and a tax collector."* This passage says that we should treat such a person as a gentile if he does not listen even after we admonish him once or twice and also if he does not even listen to the admonition of the Church. How can we stop such a person from going out from the Church into the world because he does not want to serve the gospel of the water and the Spirit? When we ask, "Do you dislike this? You do not think the gospel of the water and the Spirit is the Truth, right?" and if the person answers, "I do not think that only the gospel of the water and the Spirit is the genuine gospel of salvation," then the Church will not try to stop him anymore. We would admonish him a few more times, but even God cannot stop him if he says, "The gospel of the water and the Spirit is not the Truth of salvation." When we hold onto such a person forcibly, it only brings about a situation where the sheep entrusted to such people are killed instead. The Lord said, *"And I will give you the keys of the kingdom of heaven, and whatever you bind on earth will be bound in heaven, and whatever you loose on earth will be loosed in heaven" (Matthew 18:18).* If a person denies Jesus, denies the gospel, and also throws away the Word of God, then even Jesus will also treat this person like this. I am sharing this Word because it is written in the Word, not because there is someone like this among us now.

It is actually very difficult for me also. I do not know when the end of this Earth will be. However, one thing I can say is that we do not have much time left over to preach this gospel of the water and the Spirit. We will be able to preach the gospel of the water and the Spirit comfortably only for a few years more in the future. It would be difficult to preach this gospel once this peaceful period passes. It is because this world will become even more treacherous. The Lord said, *"And this gospel of the kingdom will be preached in all the world as a witness to all the nations, and then the end will come" (Matthew 24:14).* This means then that the time has come for calamity to fall upon this world and that time of the Lord's coming has drawn near, if we had already preached the gospel throughout the entire world. I do not know specifically what year, what month, what day and what time the Lord will come to this world. How would I know that? Am I God? The Lord said that no one knows this besides God the Father. But we can know that this day is drawing nearer when we look at it in light of the Word of the Lord.

I am counting the days waiting for December to come around. I feel like facing the New Year as soon as possible. Strangely, this year has been difficult. It is so difficult to wait for December. I do not know why this year has been so difficult like this. Do you feel the same way? Only one person sitting in the rear says this is so. It seems like there are not many people who think it is difficult because there are still many things left to do. Anyway, we must work diligently in the days to come. We must work diligently even if it is difficult and also work even more diligently if it is not so.

We must deny ourselves, carry our crosses, and follow the Lord although we are weak. When we live such a life repeatedly, we come to follow the Lord to the righteous path in due time. There is no one who can deny himself perfectly at once. We encounter such moments when we should deny ourselves while living and experiencing various things in this world, and we gradually become more accustomed to deny ourselves while we are going through such hardships. Denying oneself is difficult, but we come to be able to deny ourselves because we have the Holy Spirit in our hearts. You cannot live the life of denying yourselves and following the Cross if you do not have the Holy Spirit in your hearts.

Those who believe in the gospel of the remission of sins and the Word of God receive the Holy Spirit in their hearts. Therefore, denying ourselves can be possible the moment we come to know our wrong thoughts by the power of the Holy Spirit and acknowledge that we are wrong. We can follow the Lord if we deny like this. And we can fulfill this difficult work and come to follow the Lord properly since the Holy Spirit is inside us and the Lord is with us even if we are in a difficult situation while following Him. We come to follow the Lord thanks to the Lord. However, God is also ashamed of us if we stand against the Lord with our stubbornness and our thoughts, become ashamed of Him, and also throw away the Word of the Lord. Hence, I want you to live out your faith by professing, "Lord, You are the Christ."

Dear fellow believers, let's pray for the translation of our book so that this task of publishing will be finished before the end of December. I want you also to pray much for this. If the third book of our Christian literature series is published before January, we will be able to reap ten times, hundred times the number of souls that were reaped this year. Just as it is written, *"Unless a grain of wheat falls into the ground and dies, it remains alone; but if it dies, it produces much grain" (John*

12:24), we should also sacrifice ourselves for the preaching of the gospel.

The gospel is now spreading even more rapidly throughout the entire world. The evangelization of the gospel is really speeding up hundred times as it was before. Therefore, we must live with faith and hope that the Great Commission will be fulfilled speedily. Dear fellow believers, who comes when the gospel is preached to the end of the world? The Lord comes. Do you believe that the Lord will come? Would it be great if the Lord came? Our joy would be beyond description. All the wishes of your heart will be fulfilled if our Lord comes. This day is not too far away.

I will not mention the name, but a certain brother of ours said that he wants to eat all that he wants when the Lord comes. I asked him what he wants to do in the Millennial Kingdom when the Lord comes and reigns with us, he said that he wants to eat all that he wants to eat without caring for his body. Also, a certain brother who had left the Church said that he wanted to have a romantic relationship to his heart's content. But, will we be able to have a romantic relationship in the Millennial Kingdom? What romantic relationship would we have when our status will all be as same as the angels and we will all be of the same gender at that time? Such relationship is possible when our heart feels such desires like now, but I do not think it will be possible to have a romantic relationship at that time because our hearts will be in a consecrated state.

However, one thing clear is that all our wishes will surely be fulfilled then. Regardless of what kind of wish you have, all your wishes will be fulfilled. The things that are far greater than our wishes, the things that are billions of times better than our wishes, will all be fulfilled to us. It sounds like a story from a dream or a fairy tale, but they are all true. Do you believe this? Yes, I also believe it. This is the very "hope." This hope will definitely be fulfilled. This hope will be fulfilled when the Lord comes. Hence, we must preach the gospel with the heart wishing for the Lord to come quickly.

A person who does not want the Lord to return so speedily because he likes this world so much should live in this world even after the gospel of the water and the Spirit is evangelized completely and we have been raptured in the air to meet the Lord. At that time, human bodies will be destroyed because it will be exposed to natural calamities or radioactivity from the wars. Go ahead and live in this world if you like this world that much. I will follow Jesus and go to that Kingdom of Heaven.

In the Book of Hebrews chapter 10 verse 37 the Lord said, *"For yet a little while, And He who is coming will come and will not tarry."* Therefore, we must live with hope. Dear fellow believers, it is hard and difficult to live for the gospel at times, isn't it? I think this is the case for everyone. Even so, the gospel will be spread to the entire world in a short while. Then the Lord will come. Let's endure in the midst of hope and wait until that time. Let's gather our strength once again and live powerfully. And let's confess our true faith and do the work of spreading the gospel. We have done many works until now, but there is still much work that we must do. ✉

SERMON

9

Be Strong in
The Midst of Difficulties!

< Mark 8:33-35 >

"But when He had turned around and looked at His disciples, He rebuked Peter, saying, 'Get behind Me, Satan! For you are not mindful of the things of God, but the things of men.' When He had called the people to Himself, with His disciples also, He said to them, 'Whoever desires to come after me, let him deny himself, and take up his cross, and follow me. For whoever desires to save his life will lose it, but whoever loses his life for my sake and the gospel's will save it.'"

Today we have read the Word from the Gospel of Mark chapter 8 verses 33 to 35. As we know well when Jesus spoke about suffering death on the Cross after being cast away and suffering hardship at the hands of the elders, the chief priests, and the scribes of Israelites and being resurrected from the dead in three days; Peter, a disciple of Jesus, then tried to stop Jesus from proceeding and told Him that He must not do this. But Jesus rebuked Peter and said, *"Get behind Me, Satan! For you are not mindful of the things of God, but the things of men"* *(Mark 8:33)*. Jesus rebuked Peter and called him Satan. And He gathered His disciples and the crowd around Him and said, *"Whoever desires to come after me, let him deny himself, and take up his cross, and follow me. For whoever desires to save his life will lose it, but whoever loses his life for my sake and the gospel's will save it."*

The Lord Said, *"Whoever Desires to Come after Me, Let Him Deny Himself, and Take Up His Cross, and Follow Me"*

Jesus told us to carry our own crosses, but that does not mean that we should literally carry a wooden cross on our back. The cross Jesus Christ, the Son of God, told us to carry was that we must carry the difficulties that come our way and follow the Lord. The Lord is telling us here to deny ourselves and follow Him, this means that we must throw away our own thoughts and follow Him because we cannot follow the Lord if we have our own thoughts. The Lord thus said, *"Whoever desires to come after me, let him deny himself, and take up his cross, and follow me."*

Actually, we must by now be used to denying ourselves. If we have anything we think is great, then we must deny this, and if we have anything that is shameful then we must deny that also and follow the Lord. We must also deny the things that seem okay to us. There are so many things we must deny. The Lord said that we could follow the Lord only when we deny ourselves like this.

When I just think on fleshly terms, I wish that I did not have any difficulties. The foremost thing I would like is to be healthy so that I can do the Lord's work well. It is difficult because my body is not healthy although my thoughts are running well. It would be wonderful if I at least could think always uprightly, but the difficulties always abound since it is not like this. It is more difficult because I must deny myself even in the midst of my feeble health.

However, in following the Lord, I think there is no other way but to just deny ourselves and follow the righteousness of the Lord, since it is difficult to follow the Lord when we think we are too talented and it is also difficult to follow the Lord when we are totally opposite to this and we become miserable. Sometimes, it seems difficult for us to follow the Lord because we think it will cause damage to us. And on other occasions we find it difficult to follow the Lord because we think we are too lacking to follow Him.

However, our Lord says that we must deny both of these two self-images. We must first deny ourselves in order to follow the Lord. In other words, whenever you and I think that we are great, we must then also deny that greatness, and when we think that we are lacking so much, we must then deny that also in order to be able to follow the Lord. Our Lord said this to His disciples and the multitude of people. Thus, I know that the Lord has spoken this Word to you and me also. How can we follow the Lord without denying ourselves? As I have already said, we could not follow the Lord even if we were so great and we also could not follow the Lord even if we were too miserable. Therefore, a person who is great must bring himself down and a person who is lowly must bring himself up by faith in God's righteousness. It means that we cannot but deny ourselves always by faith of believing in the righteousness of God. This is how we follow the Lord.

It is impossible to follow the Lord by our fleshly thoughts. It would be easy to follow the Lord if we harbor just spiritual thoughts, but it is difficult to follow the Lord without denying ourselves because we often have fleshly thoughts. Therefore, it is difficult to follow the Lord if we cannot cut off these fleshly thoughts when they rise up in our hearts. But I know that it is all possible by faith. We can follow the Lord by the faith of believing in the righteousness of God and we can follow the Lord even in the midst of difficulties by the faith of believing in the gospel of the water and the Spirit. We can follow the Lord sufficiently if we are resolved to follow the Lord even in the midst of difficulties because the Lord holds onto us and leads us.

We have experienced the Word of the Lord in our life. Our spiritual life can actually become better when we face difficulties. It is because our faith does not grow when everything is comfortable and we don't experience any hardship. We are holding onto the righteousness of the Lord during these difficult times, while instead forgetting the Lord when everything is comfortable. That is why the Lord said in the Gospel of Mark chapter 8 verse 35, *"For whoever desires to save his life will lose it, but whoever loses his life for my sake and the gospels will save it."* This Word means, "You will lose your life if you try to save it. However, you will save your life if you lose your life for the gospel of the water and the Spirit. You will receive if you lose your things for the gospel of the water and the Spirit, while on the other hand, you will lose all your things if you try to keep it."

An ex-CEO from Japan wrote a book titled "Throw Away Many Things to Win." That is the fundamental ideology of the Japanese. Japanese people are good at learning. They learn anything with a humble heart. After learning something, they change it according to their own style and recreate it. The author is saying that one must throw away himself in order to win. It means that one must first lower himself to the other person in order to receive something. And then he consequently learns. Japan was able to become successful economically because of such an ideology. Did their leader not lower his heart and attached himself to the President of the

United States in order to win over the entire world? But the President of our country, Korea disputes against the President of the United States concerning many issues, but the Prime Minister of Japan implements a friendly policy with the United States with humanistic wisdom. Anyway, just as the Japanese people were able to become successful because they had that ideology "We must throw away many things in order to win," our Lord also said that we must first lose our things in order to truly save our souls and many other people from sins. The Lord said, *"Whoever loses his life for my sake and the gospels will save it,"* and this Word is the truth.

We really come to receive many things on behalf of our Lord if we lose many things for the gospel of the water and the Spirit. However, the Lord does not give anything to us if we try not to lose the things we have. We instead become people who are cast away by the Lord. We know all too well what this Word means in our spiritual life, but we often forget this in our actual life. We might think that we would be able to do God's work more if we were stronger, healthier, and more prosperous in our life, but our Lord makes us receive even more things when we do His work in the midst of difficulties. The Lord helps us receive life and also makes us save even more souls from sins.

Everyone wants to live a spiritual life in a healthy condition. However, we come to receive many blessings when we follow the Lord while losing many things in the midst of difficulties and also live for the Lord and for the gospel although it is not easy. We do this work, that is, preaching the gospel of the water and the Spirit throughout the entire world, which is not so easy, like this because we have experienced and also believed that the Lord gives even more things when we follow the Lord in the midst of such difficult situations.

Actually the truth be told, we have not followed the Lord until now by our own fleshly strength. We were only able to follow the Lord by the passion our Lord gave to us.

We had followed with passion when we were young and healthy, but how is it now? To follow Jesus is not easy no matter how passionate we are because our body is tired and sick. Now, we live with the resolve, "I just have to go to the Lord after doing all the work the Lord has entrusted to us like this." What more is there to us? The Apostle Paul showed his strong faith by saying, *"Even though our outward man is perishing, yet the inward man is being renewed day by day" (2 Corinthians 4:16).*

But how about someone like me? Even my inner person becomes frustrated and becomes upset when my flesh becomes weak. You might not be like this, but I cannot do anything when I am sick because all my attention is focused on that painful point. However, as time passes and I think about myself before the presence of the Lord, I think it is proper for me to follow the Lord even under such circumstances. Therefore I have set up my mind to do my best in just doing the works the Lord has entrusted to me to do before I go to Him. I can lose all the things that I have if others can just receive salvation by my losing all this. It would be fine to go to the Lord before His return, and it would also be fine to go to Him after serving the gospel of the water and the Spirit until He returns. What a great work the preaching of the gospel is!

How could it not be wonderful to preach the gospel of the water and the Spirit by faith although our life in this world is difficult? When we try to preach the gospel of the water and the Spirit to people these days, most people say, "You try doing better. You believe in it! That is none of my business." because people these days are prone to address their own clear thinking unhesitatingly. Therefore, we are preaching the gospel of the water and the Spirit throughout the entire world by the literature ministry now. We also hope and pray that the Lord would bless us with material things because we cannot even send out our Christian literature if we do not have material things.

The people of this world eagerly join some movement as the supporters when something seems to go well, but they all go away instantly when it does not seem to go that well. Countless number of people followed Jesus when He was performing wondrous deeds like the miracle of the five loaves and two fish and cured the demon-possessed and the sick, but they all ran away from Him when He said, "Eat my flesh and drink my blood." It is the same in doing God's work. Many people follow the Church when the work of serving this gospel goes well and seems like they would receive glory, but they all become disappointed and leave the Church when this work does not go well and things do not seem so great. Not everyone is the same, but unfortunately most people are like this. Anyway, I believe that God blesses us in all our laboring for the preaching of the gospel.

The Lord said, *"For whoever desires to save his life will lose it, but whoever loses his life for my sake and the gospels will save it,"* and we actually only have one life. We will put forth all our resources and methods like this to spread the gospel of the water and the Spirit throughout the entire world. We do not have any other goal besides this. It is because there is no other work in this world besides the preaching the gospel of the water and the Spirit that is worthwhile to live for. The process of a human life is clear. Everyone eventually becomes sick and dies after eating and drinking throughout his entire lifetime. The people of this world really become miserable when they become old. They might live proudly and boastfully while they were young, but they eventually die hopelessly when they get old.

However, those who believe in the gospel of the water and the Spirit and live for the evangelization of this gospel are not miserable at all. Because we have received the Great Commission of preaching the gospel of the water and the Spirit, we live each day with the hope for the Kingdom of Heaven doing this honorable and worthwhile work. Thus, I want you and me to also become people who enjoy the blessings that come from the Lord even though we will lose many of our things for the Lord and the preaching of the gospel of the water and the Spirit. And I want you to have faith that the Lord will absolutely fill up all your necessities.

There is nothing we can gain on this earth if we just calculate it in a fleshly way. However, we can offer ourselves up to the Lord by faith gladly because we will not live in this world for eternity. Moreover, time in this world passes quickly by because our Lord who is to come will come sooner or later. Hasn't my hair become gray already although I first met the Lord at the similar age as these younger brothers and sisters here? Thus, I ask this from you. I admonish you to lose many of your things for the preaching of the Lord's gospel and live for Him. Then, you absolutely will not regret it.

I want you and me to meet the Lord after living by the faith of believing in the gospel of the water and the Spirit. ✉

SERMON

10

Moses, Symbol of the Law; Jesus, Incarnation of Grace and Truth; John the Baptist, the Mediator

< Mark 9:1-13 >

"And He said to them, 'Assuredly, I say to you that there are some standing here who will not taste death till they see the kingdom of God present with power.' Now after six days Jesus took Peter, James, and John, and led them up on a high mountain apart by themselves; and He was transfigured before them. His clothes became shining, exceedingly white, like snow, such as no launderer on earth can whiten them. And Elijah appeared to them with Moses, and they were talking with Jesus. Then Peter answered and said to Jesus, 'Rabbi, it is good for us to be here; and let us make three tabernacles: one for You, one for Moses, and one for Elijah'—because he did not know what to say, for they were greatly afraid. And a cloud came and overshadowed them; and a voice came out of the cloud, saying, 'This is My beloved Son. Hear Him!' Suddenly, when they had looked around, they saw no one anymore, but only Jesus with themselves. Now as they came down from the mountain, He commanded them that they should tell no one the things they had seen, till the Son of Man had risen from the dead. So they kept this word to themselves,

questioning what the rising from the dead meant. And they asked Him, saying, 'Why do the scribes say that Elijah must come first?' Then He answered and told them, 'Indeed, Elijah is coming first and restores all things. And how is it written concerning the Son of Man, that He must suffer many things and be treated with contempt? But I say to you that Elijah has also come, and they did to him whatever they wished, as it is written of him.'"

Do You Know about Elijah?

Prior to today's Scripture passage, in Mark chapter 8, the Lord told His disciples that He would return to God after completing His ministry here on this earth, and that He would die and rise up in three days. Peter then tried to dissuade Him, upon which the Lord rebuked him. After this account we see chapter 8 ending with the Lord saying, *"For whoever is ashamed of Me and My words in this adulterous and sinful generation, of him the Son of Man also will be ashamed when He comes in the glory of His Father with the holy angels."*

Mark chapter 9 then gives the account of the appearance of Elijah and Moses conversing with Jesus. This account is recorded elsewhere in the other Gospels—specifically in Matthew chapter 17 and Luke chapter 9. Let's now return to Mark 9:2-4. *"Now after six days Jesus took Peter, James, and John, and led them up on a high mountain apart by themselves; and He was transfigured before them. His clothes became shining, exceedingly white, like snow, such as no launderer on earth can whiten them. And Elijah appeared to them with Moses, and they were talking with Jesus."*

When Jesus took Peter, James and John to a high

mountain, He was transfigured before them, and His garments shined so white that no launderer on earth could have whitened them. This transfiguration of the Lord foreshadows our own transfiguration which will take place when the Lord returns and take us away. As the Lord was transfigured in today's Scripture passage, we the born-again of water and the Spirit will also be suddenly transformed. This is what the Lord is showing us in today's Scripture passage.

Mark 9:4 says, *"And Elijah appeared to them with Moses, and they were talking with Jesus."* When Elijah and Moses appeared before Jesus who was transfigured into a holy figure and they talked with Him; the disciples were amazed to see this. Upon witnessing this, Peter said, *"It is good for us to be here; and let us make three tabernacles: one for You, one for Moses, and one for Elijah."* But he said this because he was afraid of Jesus' transfiguration. The disciples were so afraid that they did not know what to say, and they were trembling in fear. Then a cloud descended and overshadowed them, and a voice came out of the cloud, saying, *"This is My beloved Son. Hear Him!"* So they looked around, and they no longer could see Elijah and Moses but only Jesus standing there.

As the disciples were coming down from the mountain after seeing this amazing scene, the Lord warned them to "tell no one the things that they had seen, till the Son of Man had risen from the dead." Not understanding what this meant, the disciples just stared at each other trying to figure out what the others were thinking. They were wondering, "What does this all mean? What does He mean by rising from the dead?"

Moreover, the scribes at the time were teaching that Elijah had to come first, and so the disciples became even more puzzled. So they asked Jesus, *"Why do the scribes say that Elijah must come first?"* Jesus then said to them, *"Indeed,*

Elijah is coming first and restores all things. And how is it written concerning the Son of Man, that He must suffer many things and be treated with contempt? But I say to you that Elijah has also come, and they did to him whatever they wished, as it is written of him." This means that Elijah had already come to restore all things, but as the people at that time did not recognize him, they had ignored him and treated him badly. The people of Israel instead revered Moses the most, therefore the disciples understood the appearance of Moses, but they did not quite understand the appearance of Elijah. That's why they asked Jesus about the prophecy of Elijah's return.

Elijah Here Means John the Baptist Who Played the Mediating Role of Linking the Old Testament with the New Testament

This is what God is teaching us through Mark chapter 9. The representative of the Old Testament is Moses. John 1:17 says, *"For the law was given through Moses, but grace and truth came through Jesus Christ."* With the passing of the Mosaic age came the age of Jesus Christ, and the bridge that links these two ages is none other than John the Baptist who came by the heart of Elijah. In Matthew 11:14, the Lord says, *"And if you are willing to receive it, he is Elijah who is to come."* Who is this Elijah "to come"? We can find out by turning to Matthew 11:12: *"And from the days of John the Baptist until now the kingdom of heaven suffers violence, and the violent take it by force."* In other words, Jesus was saying that this Elijah "to come" was none other than John the Baptist. So, as the bridge that links the Old Testament with the New Testament, Elijah's role is extremely important.

As you know yourself, Elijah was God's servant who had delivered the people of Israel from their sin of idolatry. He is the prophet who led the Israelites back to God to believe in Him, and made it possible for them to be saved from their sins. No other prophet in the Old Testament worked as Elijah did. Although Moses received the Law and handed it over to the people of Israel, they broke this Law. In contrast, Elijah was God's servant who, upon being commanded by God, stood before the idolatrous people of Israel, showed them God's power that He was alive, and through this led the Israelites back to God and turned their hearts around from idols.

So God said in Malachi 4:5, *"Behold, I will send you Elijah the prophet before the coming of the great and dreadful day of the LORD,"* promising that He would send Elijah before the last day of wrath. This means that God would send Elijah as His servant who would lead many people living in sin back to God. The Lord said that He would send Elijah, and He also said that this Elijah would come prior to His coming. And according to this Word, John the Baptist had already come in the spirit of Elijah, and yet the people treated this spiritual Elijah very badly.

It is this spiritual Elijah, John the Baptist, who links the Law of the Old Testament with Jesus Christ. John the Baptist is the mediator of mankind. Therefore, the bridge that links the Old Testament and the New Testament is none other than John the Baptist. Without the role that John the Baptist fulfilled in the New Testament as God's servant, it would have been simply impossible for Jesus Christ to save mankind from sin despite coming to this earth. That's because in order to save mankind from sin, God had raised John the Baptist to be the representative of mankind and made him pass everyone's sins onto the body of Jesus, thereby fulfilling His righteousness.

God has ensured that man would be saved from sin with understanding. The mystery of being born again does not mean that God worked on the salvation plan of mankind in a way that no one could understand, but He worked in a way that anyone who really fears God and whose heart is ready to receive Him could understand it.

So, just as Elijah had led the people of Israel back to God, God promised that He would send His servant Elijah to us before the coming of the last day of great wrath. John the Baptist came to us according to this promise. Conceived in the body of Elizabeth, the wife of Zacharias from the house of Aaron the High Priest, John the Baptist came six months prior to Jesus Christ, who was born on this earth through the body of the Virgin Mary. This was God's special providence dispensed to fulfill His righteousness.

Having thus come to this earth, John the Baptist baptized Jesus Christ to pass all the sins of mankind onto Him when He came to the Jordan River at the age of 30. By receiving this baptism from John the Baptist, Jesus Christ bore all the sins of the world. He then carried them all to the Cross, died on it, rose up from the dead in three days, and thereby has saved us all. As John the Baptist baptized Jesus and Jesus received this baptism, all the righteous work of God was fulfilled to save mankind from all sins. That's how John the Baptist became the mediator of the Old and New Testaments.

The Law says that the wages of sin is death. So everyone had no choice but to die for their sins. That's because no one can actually keep the Law of God. However, by being baptized and sacrificing His body, Jesus at once paid off all the wages of our sins in our place. As a real estate agent mediates between a seller and a buyer, Jesus fulfilled the mediation of salvation between God and us. It is to make this mediation of salvation possible that John the Baptist passed all the sins of mankind onto Jesus once and for all. That is why the day after baptizing Jesus, when John the Baptist saw Him carrying the sins of the world, he said, *"Behold! The Lamb of God who takes away the sin of the world!"* John the Baptist bore witness of Jesus Christ as the Savior of mankind who bore on His back the sins of mankind—that is, the sins of the world—and thus he became the mediator between the Old Testament and the New Testament.

We Must Really Understand the Ministry of Elijah

In John 1:6-8, the Bible says the following about John the Baptist: *"There was a man sent from God, whose name was John. This man came for a witness, to bear witness of the Light, that all through him might believe. He was not that Light, but was sent to bear witness of that Light."*

This means that John the Baptist came to bear witness of Jesus, and it is through John the Baptist that everyone can realize properly that Jesus is the Savior. Of course, all of you must also grasp this. That's because no matter how much you want to believe in Jesus as your Savior, unless you know this Truth, you are a practitioner of worldly religion regardless of whether you are a pastor or a layman. If you don't know the gospel of the water and the Spirit, then being deceived by Satan, you will only try to establish your own righteousness in your life of faith, and ultimately turn around to stand against the righteousness of God. No matter how anyone thinks that he has received the remission of sins by believing in Jesus, if he stands against the righteousness of God, then he will indeed turn into His enemy, and therefore this person's soul will be destroyed.

On the mountain of transfiguration, Jesus was suddenly transformed as white as snow, and Elijah and Moses appeared before Him and talked with Him. This shows us that Elijah fulfilled the role of a mediator between Moses and Jesus Christ. John the Baptist passed all the sins of mankind onto Jesus Christ once and for all, and Jesus Christ, in turn, at once accepted all the sins of mankind through this baptism. He then shed His blood and died on the Cross to pay off the wages of all these sins. And having risen from the dead, He has thus completed our salvation; and thanks to this, we have received the remission of sins to be also as shining white as Jesus, and we are now able to enter the Kingdom of God. In other words, God has made us to lack nothing to enter His Kingdom.

Even if you know this gospel message well, when you actually try to explain it to others, you will probably find it very difficult. I have seen many famous pastors appearing in Christian TV making various comments on the baptism of Jesus, but I have never seen any one of them ever providing the right explanation. What is written in Matthew 11:13-14? It says, *"For all the prophets and the law prophesied until John. And if you are willing to receive it, he is Elijah who is to come"*—in other words, John the Baptist is this very Elijah to come.

John the Baptist, the spiritual Elijah, bore witness of Jesus as our Savior, and he testified that Jesus has saved us from all the sins of the world by accepting them once and for all through His baptism. However, many Christian leaders do not know the gospel of the water and the Spirit even as their eyes are wide open, and as a result, they cannot bear its witness to anyone, including their own souls. As these Christian leaders are ignorant of the gospel of the water and the Spirit, when they hear someone else bearing witness of this gospel, they regard this person as a heretic. As we are waging a spiritual battle against Satan, when we tell them about this gospel, their first reaction is to reject it. This is indeed what actually happens. So it's not easy for you to preach the gospel to those who have not been born again yet. Not only do you have to be resolutely determined when preaching this gospel, but your faith must also be unwavering; without this unwavering faith, it is impossible to preach this gospel.

We the believers in the gospel of the water and the Spirit have the Holy Spirit in our hearts, and so we accept this gospel Truth as a matter of course. You need to realize here that accepting Jesus as your Savior without understanding the role of John the Baptist will only turn you into a practitioner of a worldly religion. No matter how ardently you may believe in Jesus as your Savior, you cannot be washed from your sins unless you acknowledge that the sins of the world were passed onto Jesus Christ when John the Baptist baptized Him, and that Jesus shouldered them all at once through His baptism. As those who have received the remission of sins, we believe that John the Baptist played a mediating role between God and us and that Jesus bore all our sins by being baptized by John, died on the Cross, rose up from the dead, and has thereby saved us forever. And it is because of this Truth that we are able to live out our faith despite our weaknesses, and stand even more firmly on our faith in the gospel of the water and the Spirit. Otherwise it is absolutely impossible. I have mentioned this fact clearly in all my writings.

Jesus came to fulfill a meditating role between God the Father and us the sinful mankind. Knowing that we could never approach God because of our sins, Jesus took upon all the sins of mankind once and for all by being baptized by John the Baptist, died on the Cross, and rose up from the dead. Through this, He has completed our salvation, fulfilling His mediating role for us so that anyone who believes in the righteousness of Jesus may approach God boldly. It was possible for Jesus to fulfill His meditating role between God the Father and mankind because of the role of John the Baptist. Of course, this was achieved according to God the Father's plan. Without the role of John the Baptist and the ministry of Jesus, no one could be delivered from sin, nor could anyone recognize Jesus as the Savior.

The Bible says in John 1:6-8, *"There was a man sent from God, whose name was John. This man came for a witness, to bear witness of the Light, that all through him might believe. He was not that Light, but was sent to bear witness of that Light."* This means that John the Baptism came to bear witness of Jesus. John the Baptist passed the sins of mankind onto Jesus through His baptism, and because John the Baptist bore witness of this, we know that Jesus Christ is our Savior, that He bore all our sins by being baptized, that He died on the Cross, that He rose up from the dead, and that He has thereby become our Savior. The next day after baptizing Jesus, John the Baptist therefore said, *"Behold! The Lamb of God who takes away the sin of the world!" (John 1:29)*

It was not so easy in those days for anyone to say that Jesus was the Lamb of God. That's because in those days, if someone proclaimed that Jesus was the Son of God, people would have stoned that person to death right away without hesitation. Yet despite this, John the Baptist boldly preached this truth to everyone. Only those who like John the Baptist doing God's work could say such things. Not just anyone could say them. But John the Baptist bore witness of Jesus, saying, "He is the Son of God; He came to take upon all the sins of mankind; He actually bore them all by being baptized by me;

He will die on the Cross; He will rise from the dead; and He will thereby save us all. He is the sacrificial Lamb of God. He is the Lamb of atonement. He is the Lamb of the redemption of mankind." And according to this testimony, Jesus the Son of God, who had come to this earth as the sacrificial Lamb of God, bore all our sins through His baptism, and just as the sacrificial animals of the Old Testament were killed before the altar of burnt offering, He was crucified to death.

Elijah and Moses appeared on the mountain of transfiguration and talked with Jesus, and here you also need to understand why Elijah appeared with Moses. Although the representative of the Old Testament is Moses, its last prophet and last High Priest is John the Baptist, the spiritual Elijah. If John the Baptist had not born witness of all the facts of salvation, including the fact that Jesus bore all our sins through His baptism, we would not have been able to be transformed as Jesus was transformed. Whether it comes to receiving the remission of sins or being washed from sin as white as snow, it would all have been impossible without the testimony of John the Baptist. As such, the event that occurred on the mountain of transfiguration does not just tell us about Jesus' transformation, but it implies that if you and I believe in Jesus Christ, who came by the gospel of the water and the Spirit, we will be washed from sin as white as snow and become God's children. So, just as Jesus Christ was transformed, so we will also be transformed. But how is this transformation attained? We are transformed by knowing and believing in what was done by Elijah, Moses, and Jesus. This is what today's Scripture passage is teaching us.

Human beings were made in the image of God, but when they fell into sin because of the temptation of Satan and the weakness of the flesh, they lost God's image and became sinners and the Devil's servants. By whom then are human beings once again transformed back into the image of God? It is, of course by God. God gave us the Law through Moses; through the Law we realized our sins; and John the Baptist passed the sins of mankind onto Jesus Christ. Having accepted our sins, Jesus Christ was then crucified and resurrected from the dead, and He has thereby saved us. That is how He has transformed us completely, saved us perfectly, and made us God's children.

However, most Christians do not realize that John the Baptist is the mediator between Jesus Christ and us as mankind, nor do they realize that the Mediator between God the Father and mankind is Jesus Christ. Although they say they believe in Jesus, they don't really understand what John the Baptist did to Jesus, and they just claim to know Jesus blindly. This in reality is just superstition.

Why did Elijah and Moses appear before Jesus in the mountain of transfiguration? They did so because Moses was the representative of the Law, while Elijah was the bridge between Jesus and Moses—that is, the link connecting the Old Testament to the New Testament. And this Elijah implies John the Baptist in the New Testament. As it is written in Matthew 11:11-14, Jesus Himself described John the Baptist as the representative of mankind and the Elijah to come, saying, *"For this is he of whom it is written: 'Behold, I send My messenger before Your face, Who will prepare Your way before You.' Assuredly, I say to you, among those born of women there has not risen one greater than John the Baptist. And from the days of John the Baptist until now the kingdom of heaven suffers violence, and the violent take it by force. For all the prophets and the law prophesied until John. And if you are willing to receive it, he is Elijah who is to come."*

Is there anyone who was not born of a woman? There is no one among you who was born without a mother, right? So when Jesus said, *"Assuredly, I say to you, among those born of women there has not risen one greater than John the Baptist,"* He meant that John the Baptist is the representative of mankind.

Jesus accepted all the sins of mankind through the baptism He received from John the Baptist. Jesus had come to accept the sins of mankind, and John the Baptist was to pass them onto Jesus by baptizing Him. This is sound in principle also. It's because John the Baptist baptized Jesus that Jesus said, *"Permit it to be so now, for thus it is fitting for us to fulfill all righteousness."* That Jesus was baptized by John the Baptist means that John passed the sins of the world onto Jesus, and that Jesus accepted them all. That is why Jesus had to be crucified to death and having risen up from the dead, He has become our Savior. John the Baptist indeed fulfilled the mediating role between the Old Testament and the New Testament.

As John 1:17 says, *"For the law was given through Moses, but grace and truth came through Jesus Christ,"* God gave the Law to mankind through Moses. And through Jesus, He has given us grace and the Truth to set us free from the Law. Why does the Bible mention grace here? That's because it is not by our acts that we sinners and are qualified to enter Heaven. This was not achieved by our own effort, but it was made possible through the sacrifice of Jesus. That's why Jesus has become the Mediator between God and us. We must understand this Mediator properly.

Who is your mediator? Your predecessors of faith are your mediators. Jesus is the Mediator between God and us the born-again, and we who have received the remission of sins mediate between Jesus and those who have not been redeemed yet. Without the mediating role fulfilled by the redeemed, how else could you have known about who Jesus is, and how He accepted your sins through John the Baptist? Could you have known this by yourself? Many Christians believe in Jesus blindly without wondering why He was baptized. They believe in Jesus thoughtlessly. It's because those who have received the remission of sins first played the mediating role that you were also able to know the gospel of the water and the Spirit, and realize and believed that Jesus accepted the sins of the world through John the Baptist, was crucified to death, rose up from the dead, and has thereby become your Savior.

For the wages of sin is death; we in fact had to die for our sins, but because Jesus accepted them all through John the Baptist and paid off these wages on the Cross in our place, we have become righteous by believing in this fact. How can anyone believe in Jesus without knowing this? Worshiping some unknown god is what superstition is all about, and so if you believe in Jesus without really understanding Him, then it's no different believing in some superstition. It is therefore absolutely indispensable for you have the right knowledge of Jesus.

Who is the true Mediator between God and you? It is Jesus. Who then mediates between Jesus and us? It is none other than John the Baptist. Jesus is actually the true God (1 John 5:20). God Himself has linked us back to Him. Jesus was baptized by John the Baptist, and through this baptism, He accepted all the sins of mankind once and for all. He was then crucified to death while shouldering all these sins of the world, and rising from the dead, He has saved us once and for all.

The Old Testament ends with the Book of Malachi, and this Book of Malachi prophesied that Elijah would come again. This Elijah was none other than John the Baptist. And according to this prophecy, John the Baptist was born on this earth six months earlier than Jesus Christ, he bore witness of Jesus, and he passed the sins of the world onto Him by baptizing Him. Because of these sins that Jesus accepted at that time, He died on the Cross, and rising up from the dead, He completed the salvation of mankind. John the Baptist was the mediator in all these things. In this way, he became the mediator between the Old Testament and the New Testament.

John the Baptist also bore witness of Jesus. He bore witness of Jesus as "the Lamb of God who takes away the sin of the world," and he bore witness of what Jesus would do. It's for this work that John the Baptist had come to this earth. Can you now understand the role of John the Baptist? His work was passing all our sins onto Jesus so that it would be possible for Christ to save us. It's because Jesus was baptized by John the Baptist that He could bear all our sins; and to pay off the wages of these sins, Jesus was crucified to death. And rising up from the dead, He completed His work of saving us. John the Baptist bore witness of all these things, testifying that Jesus was actually God and the Son of God the Father.

The Old Testament is represented by Moses. Moses led the people of Israel only to the Jordan River, from where the land of Canaan was visible, and then he passed away to be with God. This implies that the Law's function is teaching us about our sins, and once we realize them, we must go to Jesus Christ. That is the extent of the teachings of the Law and it cannot do anything more for us. The Law itself cannot bring the remission of sins to us. Though Moses saw the land of Canaan in the distance, he died without stepping into it. Likewise, the Law only teaches us about our sins. It is through the Law that we realize that we are sinners before God.

And it is John the Baptist that we realize how Jesus Christ

took upon all our sins. We have become God's people by realizing and believing that Jesus accepted all our sins through the baptism He received from John the Baptist, and that He fulfilled our salvation by dying on the Cross and rising up from the dead. And on the day Jesus returns to this earth, we will also be transformed just as Jesus was suddenly transformed on the mountain of transfiguration. The Bible says that our bodies will be transformed when the Lord returns to this earth, as it is written, *"For this corruptible must put on incorruption, and this mortal must put on immortality" (1 Corinthians 15:53).* This is what God is showing us through the transfiguration of Jesus in today's Scripture passage.

Jesus accepted all our sins once for all through His baptism. Your sins and mine were all passed onto Jesus. While shouldering our sins, He was crucified to death; and rising up from the dead, He has saved us all. The resurrected Jesus Christ is now sitting at the right hand of God the Father. It is by believing in this Jesus Christ as our Savior that we can receive the remission of sins and, even though we are still in our insufficient flesh, we stand unwaveringly before God and live by faith.

How else could we receive the remission of our sins, when the sins we commit in our lives on this earth are so scarlet red? How else could we become God's children, and how else could we become sinless people? Therefore, we must realize this fact clearly, believe in it, and continue to listen to the Word and meditate on this Truth. You must grasp here that your salvation is reached by faith, never by doing something on your own with your flesh.

God has saved you and me, given us wisdom and intellect, and empowered us to do everything. But we are nothing if we don't carry out His work. God has commanded us to do this work, and He has promised us that we will be transformed like Jesus. On our own, we cannot achieve anything to serve God. We must recognize and accept humbly that it is by the strength of the Lord that we are serving Him, and our hearts must be the first to work rather than our bodies. It's our hearts that must stand by faith before God first, and it is by faith that we must work. John the Baptist was humble enough to lower himself before the Lord, saying, *"He must increase, but I must decrease" (John 3:30).* We also need such a disposition of the heart before the Lord. We are just doing what has been entrusted to us.

Whoever does not prepare for the future is bound to turn destitute and live a wretched life as a beggar. If preparing for the future is important like this even when it comes to our fleshly lives, how much more imperative is it when it comes to spiritual affairs? Believing in the fact that John the Baptist became our mediator is preparing for the future of our souls.

Whenever you preach the gospel of the water and the Spirit to others, you need to explain the importance of Jesus' baptism clearly regardless of whether they accept it or not. If you cannot remember the Bible verses that demonstrate this, write them down beforehand and read them to people.

Let us then spread the gospel of the water and the Spirit far and wide, placing our faith in this Truth. United together, let us preach the gospel with all our strength until the end of this world. ✉

SERMON

11

What Will Happen to Those Who Are Rich In Their Hearts?

< Mark 10:17-27 >

"Now as He was going out on the road, one came running, knelt before Him, and asked Him, 'Good Teacher, what shall I do that I may inherit eternal life?' So Jesus said to him, 'Why do you call Me good? No one is good but One, that is, God. You know the commandments: 'Do not commit adultery,' 'Do not murder,' 'Do not steal,' 'Do not bear false witness,' 'Do not defraud,' 'Honor your father and your mother.'' And he answered and said to Him, 'Teacher, all these things I have kept from my youth.' Then Jesus, looking at him, loved him, and said to him, 'One thing you lack: Go your way, sell whatever you have and give to the poor, and you will have treasure in heaven; and come, take up the cross, and follow Me.' But he was sad at this word, and went away sorrowful, for he had great possessions. Then Jesus looked around and said to His disciples, 'How hard it is for those who have riches to enter the kingdom of God!' And the disciples were astonished at His words. But Jesus answered again and said to them, 'Children, how hard it is for those who trust in riches to enter the kingdom of God! It is easier for a camel to go through the eye of a needle than for a rich man to enter the kingdom of God.' And they were greatly astonished, saying

among themselves, 'Who then can be saved?' But Jesus looked at them and said, 'With men it is impossible, but not with God; for with God all things are possible.'"

What Will Happen to Those Who Are Rich in Their Hearts?

Warm greetings to you all! Today, through the passage in Mark chapter 10, I would like to examine those whom God has a close relationship with.

As Jesus was walking on the road, a certain young man came to Him and knelt down before Him, asking, *"Good Teacher, what shall I do that I may inherit eternal life?"* Jesus then said to him, *"Why do you call Me good? No one is good but One, that is, God. You know the commandments: 'Do not commit adultery,' 'Do not murder,' 'Do not steal,' 'Do not bear false witness,' 'Do not defraud,' 'Honor your father and your mother.'"* The young man then said confidently that He had kept all the Law, saying, *"Teacher, all these things I have kept from my youth."* Then Jesus told him of one thing that he was lacking: *"One thing you lack: Go your way, sell whatever you have and give to the poor, and you will have treasure in heaven."* The young man was sad at this Word and went away deeply troubled, for he was a very wealthy man. Seeing him leave, Jesus then turned to His disciples and said that it is extremely difficult for the rich to enter the Kingdom of God, so much so that it is easier for a camel to go through the eye of a needle than for a rich man to enter the Kingdom of God. Then the disciples asked Him, *"Who can then enter the Kingdom of God?"* To this Jesus replied, "With men it is impossible, but with God all things are possible."

Be careful not to misinterpret this passage to mean that you cannot enter Heaven if you are materially rich, for the riches here do not refer to the wealth of the flesh, but the richness of the heart. And through today's Scripture passage you need to grasp why God dislikes those who are rich in their hearts like this. You need to realize why Jesus said that it is more difficult for the rich to enter the Kingdom of God than for a camel to go through the eye of a needle, and with this understanding you need to become a person who is poor in spirit to enter the Kingdom of Heaven.

Jesus says that those who are rich in their hearts cannot enter the Kingdom of God. If one has a rich heart, it means that he is filled with his own things. Such people are too filled with their own thoughts and merits that they have no room for the Word of God to enter. Since God's Word cannot enter them, they naturally reject the gospel and are unable to go to Heaven.

If one's heart is filled with the richness of the flesh, it is impossible for them to enter the Kingdom of God. Those who are rich in their hearts have much of their own merits, and therefore it's impossible for them to enter the Kingdom of God. You all know what a camel is, right? It has a relatively small head, a large body, and one or two humps on its back, quite ideal for transporting both goods and people. Camels are particularly indispensable for a means of transportation in a desert.

The eye of a needle, on the other hand, is a tiny hole. Can any camel ever go through this eye? No, of course not! No camel can go through the eye of a needle, no matter how small and thin it may be. You can try to cram it all you want, but it simply is not possible for a camel to go through the eye of a needle. It's hard enough to put a thread through the eye of a needle even with a perfect vision, let alone a large animal ever going through it? Like this, those who are too arrogant and rich in their hearts cannot accept the righteousness of God with thanksgiving, and therefore they cannot enter His Kingdom.

Why Did Jesus Say from the Beginning That It Is Difficult for the Rich to Enter the Kingdom of God?

Jesus told the young man to keep the Law if he wanted to inherit eternal life. He said this because one must first realize that he is indeed a sinner if he wants to believe in the Lord as his Savior, and it is the Law of God that teaches him this. Put differently, Jesus wanted to see if this young man who desired eternal life knew himself as a sinner. However, this young man considered himself righteous, thinking, "I have never killed anyone, never stolen anything, and never committed any adultery. My deeds are upright." His heart was filled with his own righteousness.

Like this young man, when people today are told to hear the gospel Word of the water and the Spirit and wash away their sins, many claim that they are decent folks who have kept their ethics and morality. And on account of this they refuse to listen to the gospel Word of the water and the Spirit. Such people are all rich in their hearts. It's hard for them enter Heaven because, spiritually speaking, they are too self-righteous to be washed clean from their sins.

To the rich young man who considered himself righteous, our Lord said, *"Sell everything you have and give it to the poor. You will then have treasure in Heaven."* However, this passage does not mean that you can attain eternal life if you sell all your possessions and give them to the poor. Rather, it means that your greed for material possessions prevents your heart from being set on God. In other words, it means that you must throw away all the riches of your heart and the hubris of your flesh for God's Word to enter. However, when this young man who had said that he wanted to obtain everlasting life, heard this Word of the Lord, he turned around in sorrow because his heart was still attached to his possessions. He was so close to emptying his heart and obtaining eternal life, but he had turned away from this opportunity.

Even today, there are so many people in this world who are rich in their hearts just like this young man. Their hearts are filled with their own fleshly arrogance and greed. Some people even boast of how much they can drink. "I drank two cases of beer yesterday. I couldn't carry all that beer on my shoulders, but I could carry them in my stomach." People brag about even such spurious things.

And others boast of their knowledge saying, "I received my musical training at the Julliard School," or, "I graduated from a prestigious university and obtained an advanced degree." There are so many people who brag about their secular knowledge. Every one of them has a rich heart of the flesh. Can they ever enter the Kingdom of Heaven without knowing and believing in the gospel of the water and the Spirit? No, not only is this impossible, but they don't want to place the Kingdom of God in the first place. This is because they are self-satisfied and self-complacent, such people do not have any expectations about the Kingdom of God, nor are they interested in the washing away of their sins. After all, they are so rich in their hearts that they lack nothing from God, and so what more would they need? One looks towards the Kingdom of God and dreams about it when one is lacking, but these people have no need for the Kingdom of God. Would the Kingdom of God ever come across their minds when they are so rich and so satisfied on this earth? No, they never think about God's Kingdom.

What our Lord is telling us in today's Scripture passage is not just addressing this young man, but it is addressed to everyone, including you and me sitting here. Would anyone who is rich on this earth and whose heart is wealthy really think about the Kingdom of God? Those who are meritorious in the flesh do not think about God's Kingdom. On the contrary, they are preoccupied in accumulating even more worldly possessions. Those who have set their minds on studying want to go onto graduate school after college, and then onto a doctoral program. For some of them, having just one doctoral degree isn't enough; they want more degrees, and go abroad to pursue their studies without really giving much thought to it.

The same thing happens when it comes to money as well. Many of you probably remember the scandal surrounding the 1997 bankruptcy of Hanbo, a conglomerate in Korea. The owner of Hanbo, Taesoo Chung had already been convicted of bribery in 1991 and received a suspended sentence of 5 years in another case involving real estate development. In 1997, he was sentenced to 15 years for his role in Hanbogate case. In his greed he had embezzled nearly $10 million dollars and brought down the company with his reckless management. However, far from repenting from this, early this year he was found to have embezzled funds at a private school where he was chairman of the board of directors, and he was once again sentenced to 3 years for this crime. He turned 83 this year. Yet even in such an old age, he could not resist his greed for money, and in his attempt to accumulate even more wealth, he found himself sitting in jail once again.

However, we can't really condemn this man alone, for we also have such greed. What about you? Is your heart also rich, thinking to yourself, "I am good? I am gifted. I am rich. I am better than everyone else"? If you have this kind of mindset, you can never go to the Kingdom of God. What use is it then to be so wealthy in your heart when you can't even enter God's Kingdom? The riches of the heart are not worthy of boasting.

The Young Man Who Claimed Boldly to Have Kept the Law Was Extremely Rich in His Heart

The young man was asked, "Did you keep all the commandments requiring you not to murder, not to commit adultery, not to steal, not to bear false witness, and honor your parents?" Full of self confidence he answered by saying, "Yes, I have kept all such commandments from my youth." What an arrogant heart he had!

Are we really capable of obeying the Word of God faithfully? Do we really obey every written Word of God? James 2:10 says, *"For whoever shall keep the whole law, and yet stumble in one point, he is guilty of all."* This means that if you break even just one statute of the Law, then it's the same as breaking the entire Law. So even if you've never committed murder, if you have lied, then the sin of murder is added onto the sins of lying. This is how God sees it. That's how hard it is to keep the Law to perfection.

Can anyone then say with confidence that he has kept the Law perfectly? If we really understand the Word of God, then we can never be so confident to claim to have kept all the Law from our youth. The Law is such that the more we try to keep it, the more difficult it is to obey it. That's because we are still in the flesh. And that's why we are all insufficient, poor, and ultimately sinners.

What merit do we have? If we examine ourselves carefully, whatever merit we may have is of our own making, and when we compare ourselves to others, there actually isn't much to be proud of. How can anyone claim to be meritorious before God? Everyone is the same. We don't find any particularly gifted or ungifted people; they are all more or less the same. If there is one difference, it is just that some people are rich in their hearts while others are poor. There is no one thoroughly gifted or thoroughly ungifted. We all make the same mistakes that others make, and we all have the same weaknesses that they have. So no one can claim to be meritorious. What's more, before God, all human beings are full of blemishes.

There is a saying in Korea that goes like this, "He is so full of himself even though he doesn't have a dog's horn." What use is it for a dog to have a horn? Of course, no dog has a horn, but even if it did, it would be completely useless, unlike deer antlers that are used for traditional medicine in some parts of the world. Yet despite not having even such useless things— that is, despite having nothing—many people still do not want to relinquish their pride. Stiff necked fools insist they are meritorious.

Siddhartha, the founder of Buddhism, considered himself as the only virtuous man in heaven and on earth, and so he called himself a god. He also was a rich man whose heart was full of ego. If Siddhartha had come to Jesus and said, "What should I do to obtain everlasting life? Since I've shown mercy and done many good deeds, won't I receive eternal life?" Jesus would have said to him, "First throw away your ego that's filling up your heart." Could anyone then attain everlasting life from God through His own acts? Are you sure you can do this? Do you have any merit at all?

It is when you realize that you have no merit at all to even have a hope for the Kingdom of God. It's only then that your spiritual eyes are opened. When these eyes are opened, you will look towards the Kingdom of God rather than this earth. We have nothing to boast of before God. Nor do we have any virtue before man. We have no merit at all in any shape or form. Yet despite this, many people are still conceited. It's such people whom God dislikes the most. He abhors those who are rich in their hearts. The Lord said that it is the poor in spirit who are blessed. Even if one is materially rich, if he is poor in his heart, then this is not a problem. But if one is rich in his heart, then he is destined to hell even if he is poor materially.

The Bible Says That Heaven Belongs to Those Who Are Poor in Spirit

As such, everyone's heart must be poor before God. Those who are poor in their hearts are able to see their souls and their true selves more accurately. They know better to examine themselves and realize their insufficiencies and sinfulness, and they also know how precious the Kingdom of God is. Knowing these things means that the heart is ready to hear the gospel Word of the water and the Spirit. That's why Jesus said that Heaven belongs to those who are poor in their hearts.

To such worthless people like us, the Lord said, "With men it is impossible to enter the Kingdom of God, but with God all things are possible!" It is to save the worthless—that is, depraved sinners—that our Lord came to this earth. It's because we cannot save ourselves that God came to a small town in Israel called Bethlehem over 2,000 years ago. Having grown up in a town called Nazareth and when He reached 30, He was baptized in the Jordan River. Through John the Baptist, the representative of mankind, He was baptized in the exact manner of the Old Testament's ritual, that is, the laying on of hands.

When Jesus was about to be baptized by John the Baptist, He said to him, "You shall baptize me. It is thus fitting for us to fulfill all righteousness. This is necessary to save the poor, those who have no righteousness of their own, those who are insufficient, and those who are destined to hell. It is my duty to receive baptism from you, to thus bear all the sins of all the sinners once and for all, make them sinless, and take them to Heaven. That is what I must do. So baptize me now without raising any objection!"

The baptism that Jesus received entails such a meaning. By being baptized in the Jordan River by God's servant named John the Baptist, the last High Priest of the Old Testament and the representative of mankind, Jesus took upon all the sins of mankind. For all those who have neither any satisfaction nor any riches in their hearts, those who are inevitably doomed to hell, people like you and I, Jesus bore all their sins, died on the Cross in our place, and rose up from the dead. This was impossible with men, but Jesus, who is God, could achieve all these things. By thus laying down His own life, Jesus saved all those who were poor and insufficient in their hearts, and He has made it possible for them to enter Heaven. He has enabled them to enter the Kingdom of God, to receive everlasting life, and to become God's own children. It is because of Him that we were able to become righteous. And we were also saved from ourselves, from our own arrogant hearts. Even though this is impossible with man, God has achieved it all, and He has done it to perfection.

When did we ever think about the Kingdom of God? Did everlasting life ever cross our minds? All that we ever thought of was about our immediate needs and gratification. Did we really take any interest in who God really is, what kind of kingdom His is, and what we must do to enter that Kingdom? We may have thought about traveling or immigrating to another country, but we did not think about entering the Kingdom of God to live there forever. However, when we recognized that we were in fact destitute, we found grace from God and came to have the hope of His Kingdom.

Our Lord Himself took upon all our sins by being baptized. How did He bear our sins? He bore them all at once through the baptism given by John the Baptist. He shouldered them all by the most fitting method, the most appropriate way, and the most Biblically sound way, just as the people of Israel in the Old Testament had passed all their sins over by laying their hands on their sacrificial lambs. He had to come to this earth to save us like this, and He has indeed saved us all perfectly. It's because of His grace that we are now able to enter the Kingdom of God and receive everlasting life. Moreover, we have also become righteous, and we have been saved from destruction. We are no longer children of the earth and darkness, but we have now become God's own children. Just as the Bible says, *"And you He made alive, who were dead in trespasses and sins" (Ephesians 2:1),* Jesus has indeed delivered us from the oppression of the power of darkness.

Because we are poor and we know our insufficiencies, we can see what He has done for us. We were all completely worthless, destined to destruction. Yet the Lord first came looking for such people just like us. And He solved our problem of sin to perfection. Though this is impossible with man, but with God, everything is possible. God has saved us perfectly like this. He has done everything for us. Do you believe in this, my fellow believers? You must indeed believe it all.

If Jesus had not been baptized and crucified to death when He came to this earth, would we be able to enter the Kingdom of God? Our Lord has saved us by coming to this earth, being baptized, and then shedding His blood on the Cross. It's because we believe in this that we have received everlasting life. It is by believing in what Jesus has done for our salvation, and that we have received eternal life and have become God's children, just as the Bible says, *"He who believes in the Son has everlasting life" (John 3:36),* and, *"As many as received Him, to them He gave the right to become children of God, to those who believe in His name" (John 1:12).* It is absolutely not by our own righteousness or merits that our salvation was achieved.

Why Must We Believe in the Gospel of the Water and the Spirit Which Was Given by the Lord?

If we were rich, would we need to believe in the Lord? No. Quite the contrary, it's because we are not rich that we believe in the Lord. Even though we are lacking, we look towards and trust in Jesus Christ who has made us perfect. Because we are poor, we believe in Jesus to attain the righteousness of God. If we had enough merits to solve the problem of our sin on our own, then there would have been no need for Jesus to come to this earth and suffer so much to save us. The Lord came to this earth precisely because none of us had any merit at all, and because we could not solve the problem of sin on our own. And by believing in this fact that God saved us, we are now able to enter the Kingdom of God. If you are too full of yourself, you cannot believe in Jesus. We have come to believe in Jesus because we are worthless and poor. Herein lies the very reason why everyone must believe in Jesus. Because we have no merit, we know just how precious the Kingdom of God is, and we believe in Jesus because we want to go to this Kingdom rather than hell, because we want to enter it, receive eternal life, and inherit this Kingdom.

However, those who are meritorious on their own do not believe in Jesus' gospel of the water and the Spirit. Given how self-satisfied and self-complacent they are, would they even see the sacrifice that Jesus made for them? In contrast, those who lack their own wisdom and whose hearts are poor thank the Lord at the first instance. It's like a starving beggar being grateful for even cold, leftover food and eating it in gratitude. If the beggar gratefully accepted the leftovers that you offered to him, you would like to give him even more and perhaps even set aside some hot meals.

But imagine this beggar throwing the food right back at you and told you to give it to a dog instead. Would you feel like giving him any more food? No, you would want to take back what you offered him and drive him away never to see him again.

Before God, our hearts must be as humble as that of a beggar. As filthy and stinking beggars, we should recognize that we don't deserve hot meals, and we should be begging God to give us anything to eat, even if it were cold leftover food. And if He shows us His mercy, then we should accept it in gratitude. Where would we go if the Law of God were applied to us? All of us would inevitably be doomed to hell. Yet despite this, Jesus saved us by coming to this earth, being baptized and dying on the Cross. Are we then in any position to be so picky about what's offered to us, complaining about the food being too cold or not to our liking? Given the fact that Jesus took away all our sins, can we dare to say that He took away only our original sin or only our past sins? If despite claiming to have received the remission of sins, you say that Jesus did not take away your future sins, and therefore you have to be remitted from them by offering your prayers of repentance, then this too will lead you to hell. You will go to hell because even though Jesus said clearly that He fulfilled all your salvation and took away all your sins, you don't believe in this Word and try to add your own righteousness to it.

If Jesus took away just your original sin and not your personal sins or future sins, then He would have had to come back to this earth again and again, accept your sins through His baptism again, and endure the suffering of the Cross time after time, just as Hebrews 9:26 says, *"He then would have had to suffer often since the foundation of the world."* The Lord created the heavens and the earth and all their hosts in six days. And He rested on the seventh day. Like this, Heaven is a resting place. It's the most wonderful place filled with poetry, music, angels, and everything that is good; a place where we can all rest in peace. Our Lord made this universe and all things in it in six days, and He rested on the seventh day. But would Jesus be able to rest if we were to offer our prayers of repentance every time we commit sin?

When Jesus came to this earth incarnated in the flesh of man, He took upon all the sins of mankind by being baptized in the Jordan River. And to pay off the wages of these sins, He died on the Cross; and rising from the dead in three days He became our true Savior. After His resurrection, while He was still on this earth, He bore witness of the Kingdom of God, gave peace to His remaining disciples, and then ascended to the right hand of the throne of God the Father. He is now resting in Heaven like this because He has achieved everything.

Those who are poor in their hearts believe in what Jesus Christ has done for them and in His every Word. In contrast, those who are rich in their hearts do not believe. That is why the Bible says that it is more difficult for those with a rich heart to enter Heaven than for a camel to go through the eye of a needle. The rich can never go there. Which kingdom is beyond the reach of the wealthy? It's the Kingdom of God. Which kingdom is reserved for the poor? It is God's Kingdom.

One of the hymns that our kids at the Sunday school sing goes something like this, "You can't enter God's Kingdom with money; you can't enter God's Kingdom by power. You can enter it only if you are born again. The Kingdom of God is entered by faith." Our saints in Korea would be quite familiar with this children's praise. Was this praise composed just for the kids at Sunday school to sing and dance? No, it's a confession made by all the people of faith. It's a confession given by God. As the lyrics in this praise say, Heaven can be entered neither with money nor by power. It's a kingdom that can be entered only by those who have been born again of the water, blood and the Spirit.

As We Became Poor in Our Hearts, We Were Saved from All Our Sins

There are so many people in this world professing to believe in Jesus, but how many of them really believe that Jesus is their Savior? How many of them have really received the perfect remission of sins? Countless Christians believe that they have just been remitted from their original sin, and that their personal sins are remitted away by offering many daily prayers of repentance. Arguing that Jesus could not have taken away their sins that they have not even committed yet, and say, "Jesus took away all my past sins, but as far as my present and future sins are concerned, I have to offer prayers of repentance every time I sin. So my salvation is an on-going process. I have been saved, I am being saved, and I will be saved." Does this make any sense? Only someone mentally ill would say such things. Such things are said by those who are confused. It's like saying, "I've come to church, I'm coming to church, and I'll come to church." They might as well say, "I've eaten breakfast, I'm eating breakfast, and I'll eat breakfast." So does this make any sense at all? Such people are suffering from anorexia; less than 3 seconds after having lunch and clearing out the table, they say, "Honey, where is my meal?"

All Christians profess to believe in Jesus. You and I also believe in Jesus, but the difference here is many Christians are rich in their hearts. They keep trying to attain everlasting life through their own acts. But it's all useless. Does God give us eternal life and send us to Heaven only if we do something on our own?

No, our own righteousness is in fact completely useless to God, for Job 35:7-8 says, *"If you are righteous, what do you give Him?*

Or what does He receive from your hand?
Your wickedness affects a man such as you,
And your righteousness a son of man."

This means that even if you do good deeds, it only benefits other people, while it brings no benefit to God. Are you then still trying to obtain everlasting life by keeping all the Law? Will you still say arrogantly, "I have never murdered anyone, nor have I ever committed adultery"? Have you then never harbored any hatred in your heart, nor lusted after anyone of the opposite sex you saw in the streets? God said that He looks at your heart, not your acts. Yet despite this, if you still proudly claim to have kept the Law, then this means that your heart is still rich. Our Lord abhors those who are rich in their hearts. There is no one in Heaven whose heart is rich. Far from it, there only are those who are poor in their hearts, and who therefore believe completely in the water and blood of Jesus Christ.

God has made it possible for us to enter Heaven. We could never have done this on our own, but our Lord has achieved it for us. Even though we were filthy sinners, He came looking for us, saved us, and gave the Word of salvation so that we would receive the remission of our sins by faith.

We are not better than anyone else. If there is one difference, it is just that we have recognized God as our God, and we have admitted ourselves as sinners before His Word. We have neither any merit, nor any righteousness, nor any nobleness, nor any wealth at all. All that we have done is that we acknowledged the Word of God, accepted it into our hearts, and believed in everything that the Lord did on this earth for our salvation. We have done nothing else but believe.

Yet despite this, despite our lack of merit and our insufficiencies, the Lord has saved us all. He has saved us 100 percent by His grace, expecting nothing in return. It is like this because our hearts are poor and devoid of any merit that we have been saved. I ask you to ruminate and meditate on this point one more time, and to give all your thanks to God for such a wonderful blessing. ✉

SERMON

12

The Hundredfold Blessing That Is Received with Persecution

< Mark 10:23-31 >

"Then Jesus looked around and said to His disciples, 'How hard it is for those who have riches to enter the kingdom of God!' And the disciples were astonished at His words. But Jesus answered again and said to them, 'Children, how hard it is for those who trust in riches to enter the kingdom of God! It is easier for a camel to go through the eye of a needle than for a rich man to enter the kingdom of God.' And they were greatly astonished, saying among themselves, 'Who then can be saved?' But Jesus looked at them and said, 'With men it is impossible, but not with God; for with God all things are possible.' Then Peter began to say to Him, 'See, we have left all and followed you.' So Jesus answered and said, 'Assuredly, I say to you, there is no one who has left house or brothers or sisters or father or mother or wife or children or lands, for My sake and the gospel's, who shall not receive a hundredfold now in this time—houses and brothers and sisters and mothers and children and lands, with persecutions—and in the age to come, eternal life. But many who are first will be last, and the last first.'"

The weather has been very hot and humid lately, and I

commend you all for braving the heat wave and still come to Church and listen to the Lord's Word. It's so hot in here that it's difficult to even breathe, and so I will keep today's sermon short.

The Scripture passage we just read today speaks about the wealthy. Here Jesus speaking to the disciples said that it is more difficult for a rich man to enter the Kingdom of God than a camel to go through the eye of a needle. Put differently, Jesus was saying that it's impossible for the wealthy to be blessed by God to enter Heaven. Shocked by this, Jesus' disciples asked Him, "Then does this mean that the rich are excluded from Heaven? Isn't this unfair? Who then can be saved?" Jesus then answered them and said, *"With men it is impossible, but not with God" (Mark 10:27).*

As you know very well, Heaven is God's Kingdom. The Lord said here that those who are rich on this earth cannot enter Heaven. What does this passage really mean? Does it just mean that all the rich people in this world are destined to hell just because they are rich? No, that is not what the passage means. Rather, this passage means that if one's heart is set only on this earth—that is, on the riches of this temporal world that is visible to the eye—then this person's soul is full of sins, and therefore he cannot enter the Kingdom of God.

Who Can Receive This Faith That Allows One to Enter Heaven?

Answering this question, Jesus said the following: *"With men it is impossible, but not with God" (Mark 10:27)*. As Jesus Christ said here, our Lord has saved us by bearing all the sins of the human race through His baptism and being condemned for all these sins on the Cross. That is why He said here that salvation is possible only with God. This means that everyone must understand and believe in the Lord's work of salvation. Through today's Scripture passage the Lord is teaching us that we should not set our minds on just the visible and physical world.

It's not just our bodies that were made in the image of God. The souls that are in our hearts were also made in the image of God. When God created man in the beginning, He made his body first, and then breathed into his nostrils the breath of life. This breath of life denotes the living Spirit of God. It's because we have this spirit that the Bible says that man was created in the image of God. Therefore, just as God is forever living, human beings are also forever living as spiritual beings. Therefore, if you really want to enter the Kingdom of Heaven by faith and live there forever, then you must not allow your heart to be oriented solely towards this visible world and get greedy over its riches. It's inevitable if this happens that people will lose sight of the Kingdom of Heaven, and that is why our Lord said here that it's more difficult for a rich man to enter Heaven than for a camel to go through the eye of a needle.

The Lord has given the gospel of the water and the Spirit to everyone so that all may be able to enter the Kingdom of God, rich and poor alike, for He wants to save everyone from sin. He wants to remit away all the sins of those who listen to the Word of God instead of setting their minds on just this world, such as its fleshly and material riches. That is why He has saved us perfectly from all our sins through His work of salvation, by being baptized and crucified to death. God has thus made it possible for us to enter His Kingdom through our faith in this salvation which was fulfilled by Jesus Christ.

In fact, every Word of God including the Lord's work of

salvation is contained in the gospel of the water and the Spirit. But sadly too many Christians in this world are still interested in material prosperity alone, even as they claim to believe in the righteousness of God and carry out His work. Although the Lord's Word has nothing to do with their fleshly concerns, these people cannot cast aside their greed for the world. Even as such people are completely ignorant of the righteousness of God, they are full of greed for carnal and material prosperity. Since these "nominal Christians" are solely interested in their own material prosperity, their faith is not one that is placed in the righteousness of God, but it is nothing more than simple greed. Therefore, you should be particularly wary of someone who preaches the following: "You can go to Heaven only if you serve Jesus faithfully and offer a lot of money to Him. Only then can you be saved by God." Such sermons are not the genuine teachings based on the pure Word of God. These sermons are given just to rob the congregation of money. Our Lord is the Lord of righteousness who has nothing to do with such false preachers. The Lord made not only this present world that is visible to our eyes, but also the invisible dominion of Heaven. Therefore, the Word of Scripture is fundamentally far removed from our fleshly affairs.

Whose Faith Is Carnal and Materialistic?

It is the fleshly people who make a god according to their own thoughts and pray to this god of their own making to bless them, trying to ensure their material prosperity through this. In other words, they create religions for their own material prosperity, out of their desire to enjoy a wealthy life. This is the fundament motivation for all the religious people of this world.

Ultimately, these religious people just seek their own material prosperity. For such people who are interested only in the riches of this earth rather than the righteousness of God, it's absolutely impossible to enter the Kingdom of God.

Therefore, all who think or say that you can receive many rewards from God only if you store treasures in the Kingdom of God by offering a lot of money to their churches are liars. Such preachers emphasize that one must offer a lot of money to enter Heaven, rather than admonishing their congregation to believe in and preach the righteousness of Jesus. In a church led by such a leader, anyone who offers a lot of money is automatically given a great deal of respect, called a deacon or even an elder. Worldly Christians love it when they are given a title and are called elder so-and-so or deacon so-and-so. And once they receive such titles, they turn arrogant and try to meddle in church affairs, saying haughtily, "This church could not run if I stopped my donations. Had I not offered $100,000, how could the church have purchased that bus?" Such nominal Christians' faith is not genuine but only religious, and their ultimate end is money itself. These people cannot discover the righteousness of God even if they opened the Bible and read the Word of God.

Our Lord has no interest in such shallow people. It's not this temporal world that our Lord speaks of, but it is the dominion of the righteousness of God. In today's Scripture passage, the Lord said that those who are interested in their own material prosperity alone, rely on their own money, and try to reach Heaven by offering their material possessions to God can never enter His Kingdom. He said clearly here that one reaches the Kingdom of Heaven only by believing in the righteousness of God, not by offering the riches of this world.

How did God fulfill His righteousness? The Bible says in

John 3:16, *"For God so loved the world that He gave His only begotten Son, that whoever believes in Him should not perish but have everlasting life."* As this passage says, God the Father saved the entire human race from all its sins by sending His Son to this earth and making Him accept all the sins of mankind by being baptized by John the Baptist, die on the Cross, and rose up from the dead in three days. This is the gospel of the water and the Spirit, the very righteous work that God has fulfilled for us. It proclaims that Jesus Christ has blotted out all our sins by coming to this earth, being baptized, dying on the Cross, and rising up from the dead. And God has made it possible for us to enter the Kingdom of Heaven on account of our faith in this gospel.

Have We Lost Our Everything to Follow the Lord?

It's written in Mark 10:28, *"Then Peter began to say to Him, 'See, we have left all and followed You.'"* Peter had actually been a fisherman by profession. In those days, fishing was considered a good occupation as it provided for a stable source of income. Moreover, a properly equipped fishing boat required at least 5 or 6 men to run it, and so it also generated sufficient employment to hire a whole family and sometimes even relatives or neighbors. Simply put, Peter had a secure job that had enabled him to provide for his family's needs and live a comfortable life.

But one day, while walking along the shore of the Sea of Galilee, Jesus saw Peter and said to him, *"Follow Me, and I will make you fishers of men" (Matthew 4:19).* At that time, Jesus was 30 years old and Peter was a middle-aged man with his hair already turning gray. But upon hearing these Words of the young Lord telling him to follow Him, Peter abandoned not only his boat but also his family to follow Him. Peter had left his everything behind to follow Jesus. That's why he could say boldly to the Lord, "All your twelve disciples including me have forsaken everything to follow You." This was in fact true, but Peter said this because he thought that Jesus would assure the disciples that at least they would enter Heaven if not anyone else.

Jesus then said to Peter, *"Assuredly, I say to you, there is no one who has left house or brothers or sisters or father or mother or wife or children or lands, for My sake and the gospel's, who shall not receive a hundredfold now in this time—houses and brothers and sisters and mothers and children and lands, with persecutions—and in the age to come, eternal life" (Mark 10:29-30).* When the Lord heard Peter saying that he had forsaken everything of this world for Him, the Lord answered him by saying that whoever has left his everything for the Lord will receive a hundredfold in this present age along with persecution, and eternal life in the next age to come. In saying this, the Lord revealed His caring heart to comfort Peter, but this passage contains an even more important meaning. The truth that's revealed in this passage is in the same vein as the one manifested in the previous passage where the Lord said that it was more difficult for a rich man to enter the Kingdom of God than for a camel to go through the eye of a needle. What the Lord listed here—your father, mother, brothers, and sisters' that denotes your immediate family, and your house and lands that symbolize your business or job—are the concrete examples of material prosperity that so many people seek after. In other words, the Lord was saying that whoever left all these things of the world to follow His gospel would not only receive a hundredfold in this present age, but also eternal life in the next age to come.

Our Lord has saved us once and for all by being baptized and crucified to death on this earth. No matter what kinds of sins we might have committed, all our sins were passed onto Jesus through His baptism. And thanks to this, by believing in this Truth of salvation, we have been washed from all our sins. Because the Lord has blotted out all the sins that everyone has ever committed and will ever commit, anyone who believes in the baptism of Jesus and His blood on the Cross can now be saved from all his sins by faith. That is why the Lord said in today's Scripture passage, *"With men it is impossible, but not with God" (Mark 10:27)*. However, those who still pursue only material prosperity to satisfy their fleshly desires rather than believing in this gospel of the water and the Spirit which the Lord has given to them, can neither receive the blessing of entering Heaven nor reach their salvation. What the Lord said to Peter here was spoken to remind us of this Truth of salvation.

Our Lord said that those who forsake their own material welfare to follow the Lord—that is, those who cast aside their attachments to their families, jobs, and riches—will receive eternal life, but at the same time, He also said that they will face persecution along the way. This means that it's inevitable for us to face persecution when we believe in and follow the righteousness of the Lord.

In fact, many sacrifices must be made for us to believe in the gospel of the water and the Spirit which the Lord has given us and follow His righteousness. Jesus has saved us from all our sins once and for all by coming to this earth, being baptized, dying on the Cross, and rising from the dead, and if we really want to believe in this Truth of salvation, then we must pay a price of faith. For us to have the faith of righteousness and follow it, sometimes we must forsake all the attachments that we have to our families, and sometimes we must lose all our material possessions. To believe in the God-given Truth of salvation and follow Him completely, in other words, we must be willing to lose all these things.

For example, let's say that there is a family where each member follows a different religion. Some of them are Christians attending different churches of different denominations, and some of them are Buddhists. Let's now say that one of them came to hear the gospel of the water and the Spirit, the true Word of God, and this person understood and believed in this gospel. But when this man looks around, he sees not only his mother, father, wife, and children all bound by some religious faith of the world, but also his friends and business acquaintances imprisoned by false religions. Since the Truth of salvation is the gospel of the water and the Spirit, and yet all those around him believe in something entirely wrong, this man would feel sorry for them and pity them.

However, far from listening to him, these people reject the gospel of the water and the Spirit. His own family members stand up against him, saying to him, "If you insist on believing in this gospel that you are speaking of, don't even bother to come home! Let's just end our family ties right here and now!" As a result, this man is excluded from his own family, whether explicitly or implicitly. Among those who are on their way to Heaven and wholeheartedly believe in the righteousness of Jesus, there are many who have lost their worldly possessions like this man. In particular, many of us have been estranged from our own parents, brothers, sisters, and relatives; and some of us have suffered financial losses as well. Because these people oppose the gospel of the water and the Spirit, if we continue to hang onto them, we cannot follow the Lord completely by faith, and that is why we cannot be with them. If

we side with them, it's impossible for us to defend the God-
given gospel of the water and the Spirit and preach it in our
lives.

The Apostle John said, *"Do not love the world or the
things in the world. If anyone loves the world, the love of the
Father is not in him" (1 John 2:15).* In other words, the world
or the things in this world —that is, our own family or
money—can sometimes be an obstacle that prevents us from
living out our faith and believing in the Lord's Truth. But the
Lord told us to forsake our everything for Him and also endure
all the persecution that comes from the world because of our
devotion to God. He said that only then can we wholly believe
in and follow the Truth of salvation proclaiming that Jesus has
saved us through His baptism and His blood on the Cross. Our
Lord is saying to us that even if we lose everything in this
world, so long as we hang onto the Truth of salvation
unwaveringly and keep our salvation, we will be blessed by
God a hundred times more than what we have lost. Put
differently, the Lord has promised us that if we suffer any loss
to believe in and follow His righteousness, He will reward us a
hundredfold. If anyone is estranged from his own family of the
flesh on this earth because of his faith in Jesus' gospel of the
water and the Spirit, then this person will surely meet a new
family in Christ and be rewarded a hundred times more than
his loss. This is the Truth that the Lord is teaching us here in
today's Scripture passage.

My fellow believers, we have indeed forsaken many
things to follow Jesus wholeheartedly. Because of our faith in
Jesus, we have lost our own families and riches. However, we
have also gained new brothers and sisters in the Church. We
have gained the true family of God in the Lord. This family we
have attained in the Kingdom of God is on a completely

different dimension from any earthly family. None other than you and I are the members of this family of the Kingdom of Heaven; and we are each other's brothers and sisters. If we are otherwise still too attached to our worldly possessions or lingering family ties rather than believing in and hanging onto the Truth of salvation, then it would be more difficult for us to enter the Kingdom of Heaven than for a camel to go through the eye of a needle. As you know very well, the eye of a needle is a tiny hole through which thread is inserted for sewing. How could such a huge animal as a camel ever go through this tiny eye of a needle? It's obviously totally impossible. But some preachers misinterpret this passage in a strange way, saying, "The word 'camel' (*gamla* in ancient Greek) is a misspelling of the word 'rope' (*gamta*). The Bible scribes made a mistake by misspelling the word 'gamta' in the original text. So, this Scripture passage should be corrected like this: 'It is easier for a rope to go through the eye of a needle than for a rich man to enter the kingdom of God.' This then means that it is very hard, but not impossible, for the rich to enter Heaven. So if you are rich, you need not worry. All that you have to do is offer more money to your church, do more charitable work, and offer more prayers of repentance. That's all that it takes for you to enter the Kingdom of Heaven."

This is a ridiculous interpretation that turns even more preposterous the more you hear it. The Word of Jesus is spiritual in essence, but what He said here in today's Scripture passage is glaringly obvious even in physical terms. Don't ever think about editing the Lord's Word according to your human thoughts to reach your own preferred interpretation. Some of you may think that you can't trust any vernacular translation and insist on seeing the original text, but the same is written in the original text as well. What exactly the word camel refers to in today's Scripture passage is not what's really important. The Lord is speaking of just how difficult it is for a rich man to enter Heaven. He is also saying that no one can be blessed to enter Heaven through his own worldly possessions, but only by believing in what God has done for him, and this is the gist of today's Scripture passage,

The Lord said to all who believe in His righteousness that they would be blessed along with persecutions. Accordingly, it is only a matter of time that we should lose the things of this world if we were to believe in the Lord's righteousness wholeheartedly, receive the remission of sins, and follow Him. It's only natural for us to suffer loss for the Lord. Even when it comes to your own family members, if they don't believe in the gospel of the water and the Spirit nor follow the righteousness of God, then they are not only God's enemies but also your enemies as well. Just as those who have received the remission of sins are enemies to those who have not, those who do not follow this Truth are also enemies to us who follow this Truth faithfully. Since these people are our enemies, what will happen to them? They will be lost and forsaken in the end. In other words, those who don't follow the Truth will be cast into hell along with every enemy of God, while those who follow the Truth will live together in unity with all their fellow saints in the Kingdom of God.

It's by losing the things of the world that we the redeemed receive the Lord's blessings along with the persecutions of the world. Do not think so lightly of this Truth of salvation that has brought the remission of sins and everlasting life to you. Even if you believe in the Lord wholeheartedly and you have received the remission of sins, if you surrender to your family that stands against the Truth, then you will soon lose your everlasting life.

But this doesn't mean that you should casually kick away and abandon your own family without hesitation. Rather, it means that if you believe in the Lord's Truth and continue to follow Him, you will naturally come to drift away temporarily from your family members that stand against this Truth even if you don't forsake them on your own volition. What I am saying is that you should not lose your courage to believe in the Truth, hang onto it, and follow it because of those around you who have not received the remission of sins.

The problem, however, is that most people facing such a difficult situation keep trying to rationalize their circumstances. They allow themselves to be pushed around by their circumstances and let their lives be dictated by lies, thinking that it's best not to stir up any trouble in the family. When this goes on long enough, they come to follow what's appealing to their eyes more and more, eventually succumbing to their flesh to seek religious faith. Ultimately, they end up rejecting the Truth to ensure peace in the family. You should realize here that such people obviously cannot follow the Lord wholeheartedly, nor can they receive everlasting life.

Then what should we do when we face such circumstances? Above all else, we must hang onto the Lord's salvation and everlasting life and follow Him, even if we were to lose our family and the treasures of this world that are visible to our eyes. After this, once our faith is established firmly, rather than abandoning our estranged family members, we should preach the gospel to them and guide them into the gospel so that they may also reach salvation and come into the Truth. None other than this is the Lord's blessing that comes along with persecutions

What Is the Persecution for the Righteousness That the Lord Is Speaking of?

Being hated, beaten, threatened, robbed, and despised for the sake of the Lord is what persecution is all about. To hear others saying the following about us is to be persecuted: "That man used to be a decent guy before he met Jesus and began to attend this church, but ever since then he has changed for the worse. All he does nowadays is preach the gospel. He used to be so friendly before, but now he is so distant." This is how we will be persecuted after we have received the remission of sins by believing in the gospel of the water and the Spirit. We face persecution from our own families, friends, and everyone around us. However, there is something wonderful that we receive along with this persecution, and this is none other than the salvation of our souls—that is, eternal life.

There is no need for you to think of everlasting life too complicatedly. Everlasting life literally means living forever, and this is what's written in the original text. It is all about living happily forever without any imperfections, filled with eternal joy. What ultimately awaits all the righteous, who are persecuted in this world, is this everlasting life which we will be receiving from the Lord. They will all live happily forever in the Kingdom of God.

Therefore, as we believe in the righteousness of the Lord, there is no need for us to feel despondent even if we are persecuted. The Bible says that those who try to save their lives will perish and those who give up their lives will live. Sometimes we feel torn between the need to follow the Truth and the need to take care of our families, thinking to ourselves, "I am persecuted because of the Lord and His Truth. I know that I should do everything possible to take care of my family, but I have neglected this to follow the Truth, and my own family members despise me for this. If I follow the Truth, my own family will suffer, but if I only take care of my family, the Lord's Truth will be neglected." Torn between these two choices, we struggle over what to follow. And it is indeed the case that if we follow the Lord's Truth, this would make some of our family members unhappy. They would say to us in sadness, "How can you do this to us? Our family used to so harmonious, but ever since you believed in Jesus, the ties that bind this family together have come all undone."

But even when you are persecuted like this, you must still follow the Lord's Truth unwaveringly. What will happen then? In the end, you will save your family of the flesh. This is not abandoning them. As God is full of love, He would never tell us to abandon our own families. God promised us that if we are saved and follow the Lord by trusting in His Truth above all else, then even if we are persecuted by this world, God will give us a new family and new lands by a hundredfold.

What are the lands here? They refer to the workplace where we can carry out God's work. And this workplace is found inside God's Church, where we can carry out God's work freely. Those who lose all their worldly things to follow the Lord will surely see their faith strengthened to be rock-solid, they will arm themselves with faith in their workplace, and they will ultimately save their families who still have not been saved. They will lead their families of the flesh into the dominion of salvation. Moreover, they will guide not only their own families to receive the remission of sins but also everyone else.

The Lord said that He would give us lands by a hundredfold. This means that the scope of our activities would be broadened by that much. He also said that we would be blessed in both body and spirit. Therefore, we have no need to be afraid of being persecuted in this world. Because we have the promised blessings of the Lord, there is no reason why we should hesitate to receive the remission of sins through the Word of the Lord and follow Him by faith.

Let's now turn to the last verse in today's Scripture passage. The Lord said here in Mark 10:31, *"Many who are first will be last, and the last first."*

What does this passage mean? It means that those who have not freed themselves from the ties of their unsaved family members will ultimately be last in spirituality, even if they have received the remission of sins first and no matter how long they have believed in the Lord. In contrast, those who believe in this Word of Truth just recently but follow it faithfully will be first spirituality. That is what this passage means. Those who wholeheartedly believe in the Word of God, the Truth of salvation; those who live by faith united with the Church before everyone else; those who expand the scope of their activities by faith; and those who begin a new life by faith—it's such people who have become first. These are our predecessors of faith marching forward ahead of us. By any chance, among our saints who have received the remission of sins just recently, is there anyone who, upon seeing many predecessors in the Church, wants to be at the forefront also to guide other saints? The way to do this is not so difficult. It's actually quite simple. You can surpass everyone else in no time if you just believe in the Word of God and follow the Lord by this faith instead of being bound by your worldly attachments.

Those who believe in and follow the God-given salvation rather than being drawn to material prosperity have received eternal life from the Lord along with persecutions. Along with persecution, they have come into the Church and found a place to carry out God's work. We should remember here that it's inevitable for all who are blessed by God to face persecutions first, even after receiving the remission of their sins and coming into the Church, and even while living by faith under the guidance of the Church. And we should not fear these persecutions. Even though it's an immense struggle for us to bear persecutions, we should think that these persecutions are borne for the sake of the gospel of God, to be united with the Lord. In other words, we ought to embrace persecutions willingly, knowing that God is allowing us to be persecuted like this to bless us by a hundredfold.

If you want to be blessed by the Lord by a hundredfold, then you must follow His Truth. Those who have received the remission of sins and follow the way of faith will all be blessed without fail. They will receive not only material blessings while living on this earth, but also the blessing of everlasting life. This blessing is something that should be received not just by you alone but also all your family members.

Who are your brothers and sisters? Your fellow saints who follow the will of the Lord are none other than your own family, your parents, your brothers, and your sisters. All of us who believe in the righteousness of the Lord are one family. Do you believe that we are one family?

God's Church here is your workplace. Here in God's Church is where you can live according to the law of faith and be blessed by a hundredfold for your faithfulness. I pray to God to give such blessings to all of us. I hope and pray with all my heart that we would all be able to endure persecutions by placing our complete faith in the Lord, and be blessed by a hundredfold along with our trials. ✉

SERMON

13

The Spiritual Wish and The Fleshly Wish

< Mark 10:35-52 >

"Then James and John, the sons of Zebedee, came to Him, saying, 'Teacher, we want you to do for us whatever we ask.' And He said to them, 'What do you want me to do for you?' They said to Him, 'Grant us that we may sit, one on your right hand and the other on your left, in your glory.' But Jesus said to them, 'You do not know what you ask. Are you able to drink the cup that I drink, and be baptized with the baptism that I am baptized with?' They said to Him, 'We are able.' So Jesus said to them, 'You will indeed drink the cup that I drink, and with the baptism I am baptized with you will be baptized; but to sit on My right hand and on My left is not Mine to give, but it is for those for whom it is prepared.' And when the ten heard it, they began to be greatly displeased with James and John. But Jesus called them to Himself and said to them, 'You know that those who are considered rulers over the Gentiles lord it over them, and their great ones exercise authority over them. Yet it shall not be so among you; but whoever desires to become great among you shall be your servant. And whoever of you desires to be first shall be slave of all. For even the Son of Man did not come to be served, but to serve, and to give His life a ransom for many.' Now they came to Jericho. As He went out of Jericho with His disciples and a great multitude, blind Bartimaeus, the son of Timaeus, sat by the road begging.

And when he heard that it was Jesus of Nazareth, he began to cry out and say, 'Jesus, Son of David, have mercy on me!' Then many warned him to be quiet; but he cried out all the more, 'Son of David, have mercy on me!' So Jesus stood still and commanded him to be called. Then they called the blind man, saying to him, 'Be of good cheer. Rise, He is calling you.' And throwing aside his garment, he rose and came to Jesus. So Jesus answered and said to him, 'What do you want Me to do for you?' The blind man said to Him, 'Rabboni, that I may receive my sight.' Then Jesus said to him, 'Go your way; your faith has made you well.' And immediately he received his sight and followed Jesus on the road."

A Fleshly Wish of the Disciples?

In today's Scripture passage we can find two kinds of wishes we can harbor before the presence of the Lord. The first is the wish of John and James, the sons of Zebedee. They asked the Lord to have one of them sit on the left hand side of the Lord and the other sit on the right side when the Kingdom of the Lord comes. Each one of them wanted to take one of the high positions and sit at the side of the Lord when He would take over the power in this world and become the King. It is such a puerile notion from a spiritual viewpoint because it is so far removed from the will of Jesus, but in a human perspective, they could think like this as the people of Israel, which was a tributary nation of the Roman Empire during that time.

As you know, the disciples of Jesus had witnessed the power of Jesus and thus thought that the Kingdom of the Lord would very soon manifest in this world. They had seen the

Lord heal so many people who were dying of sicknesses. The desire to have the power of the Kingdom of the Lord might have been a natural thing since the disciples had seen such miracles of the Lord first hand.

But Jesus spoke to his disciples who had such an outrageous and fleshly thought, *"You do not know what you ask."* The conversation between Jesus and His disciples went like this: *"But Jesus said to them, 'You do not know what you ask. Are you able to drink the cup that I drink, and be baptized with the baptism that I am baptized with?' They said to Him, 'We are able.' So Jesus said to them, 'You will indeed drink the cup that I drink, and with the baptism I am baptized with you will be baptized; but to sit on My right hand and on My left is not Mine to give, but it is for those for whom it is prepared'"* (Mark 10:38-40).

Our Lord came to this world to save the entire humanity from sin, but to some degree the disciples had followed the Lord in order to receive the power of this world although they had also believed in the Lord spiritually. But the Lord asked such disciples, "Can you receive the baptism I receive?" In other words, the Lord asked them whether they could give themselves up as a martyr to save all the peoples of this world from sin. Then the disciples answered Him, "Yes, we can do this." To this the Lord replied, "The thing you are asking will be done according to the Father's will, not according your desires." In other words, the Lord was saying that His Father would bless them if they could also die for the preaching of His gospel just like He would die to fulfill God's work. Therefore, what the Lord was saying was that we would receive as a reward the blessing of sitting at the right or left hand of the Lord if we could be used for the work of God.

Furthermore, Jesus spoke conclusively like this to the

request of James and John: *"For even the Son of Man did not come to be served, but to serve, and to give His life a ransom for many" (Mark 10:45).* The Lord spoke of the reason why He came to this world and said, "Shouldn't you who follow me do the same?" To the request of these two disciples He said, "What position you take when you enter the Kingdom of Heaven is decided according to how God the Father has already prepared it. And those of you who want to be served must also become a person who serves the entire humanity spiritually in this world. And if there are some among you who are like this, then you must become a servant of all the people." The rest of the disciples probably still had much discontentment towards James and John who had made such a request to the Lord.

At that time, the people were very interested in our Lord taking over and becoming the royal power in this world. That is understandable since the Lord had performed so many miracles; like the miracle of the five loaves and two fish in this country Israel that was so poor and did not have a true king. Thus, many people wanted to serve Jesus as the King; and the disciples who followed Jesus also had the same thoughts. The disciples of Jesus had also believed that He would become the King in this world some day. The disciples of Jesus thought and came to the conclusion that Jesus could definitely become a king in this world. They thought that it would not even be so difficult for the Lord to become the king of Israel because so many people in Israel followed Him and not just them.

Think about this for a moment. Who would be more popular and more powerful than Jesus when He performed the miracle of feeding five thousand people with just one small lunchbox by just blessing it once? Jesus was the most popular and famous figure in Israel. Therefore, all kinds of people including the sick, the hungry, and those seeking power gathered around the Lord. Therefore, we can find that not only those who believed and wanted to serve the gospel of the water and the Sprit but also those who were seeking their own greed followed the Lord at that time.

In this scenario the disciples of Jesus, especially James and John, wanted to receive such power through the Lord's fame. Therefore they followed the Lord and helped His work. It is a sad thing, but there also are many people like James and John here in the Church today. There are some people who follow the righteousness of the Lord in order to become prosperous in the flesh and also to live well with security. You are no different from James and John if you just want to become prosperous in the flesh after believing in the righteousness of the Lord. Dear fellow believers, we must have this pure faith and loyal heart toward the righteousness of the Lord. It is not the upright faith for you to serve the Lord with the presumption that you will become wealthy in the flesh, if you believe and serve the righteousness of Jesus. If this is so, then you are someone who commits the sin of serving an idol and using the Lord in order to fulfill your own fleshly desires.

Jesus came to this world in order to give Himself up to save us from all our sins. We must also become the people who throw away all the honor of this world like the Lord, and only preach the gospel of the water and the Spirit to everyone with a pure heart. And we must save them from the sins of this world. Just as the Lord did not seek fame and glory in this world, we must also desire to preach this gospel with such pure faith so that many souls may receive the remission of their sins. We must remove our filthy residues of flesh that seek after power and the material things of this world. We also have many residues of filth now just as there were many residues of flesh in the hearts of the disciples who just wanted to make Jesus their king and attain power owing to Him at that time.

Dear fellow believers, let's face it. Do our hearts desire so much to become prosperous fleshly instead of desiring the prosperity of the spiritual work? Other people might not know this, but you know this fact well. Even amongst the ministers in God's Church, there are some who want fleshly things first, and some who want spiritual things first. But we must grow up as the people who believe and follow the righteousness of God in order for our life of faith to go on the upright path. We must become the people who have this spiritual hope the Lord wants. We have both minds: the spiritual mind and the carnal mind. Therefore, we must first be spiritually minded. We are like the two disciples of Jesus mentioned here if our hearts do not first become spiritual.

Someone Who Has a Spiritual Wish

In the Gospel of Mark 10:46, there appears someone who has quite different wish than the wish of those two disciples. It is recorded, *"Now they came to Jericho. As He went out of Jericho with His disciples and a great multitude, blind Bartimaeus, the son of Timaeus, sat by the road begging."* What did the blind man Bartimaeus want from the Lord? He really wanted his sight restored. He wanted to have his eyes opened so that he could see Jesus and also the beautiful world God had created.

It might sound strange but beggars are actually very comfortable at least in their hearts. Beggars do not have to worry about being robbed or losing everything from a disaster for they do not have anything. I want to share this story with you.

A certain father and a son lived under a bridge as beggars and one day a fire broke out in that area. The people who suffered from this fire were crying and weeping in great tumult, but the indigent father told his son, "Son, you are blessed because you have such a great father. We do not have anything to be burned and we do not have to worry about losing wealth because you have such a great father. We have nothing to lose even if a thief comes. They are crying and weeping, but you do not have to cry because you have a great father." I don't know what his son thought while hearing these words of his father, but anyway this story shows us the comfortable hearts of beggars who do not have anything they should keep. Someone who does not possess anything does not have worries or any anxieties. It is because they do not desire anything more than three meals a day.

This Bartimaeus, a beggar whose heart at least was comfortable even though he was blind, wanted to have his eyes opened by the Lord. From a fleshly point of view, this might seem to be the same as the wishes of the disciples. However, the Lord gives us a very important message through this event. And this is that the wish of the people who have been born again by believing in the gospel of the water and the Spirit does not lie in the riches and glory of this world. They want to open up the eyes of those who are spiritually blind. They are truly concerned about, "How can I make the eyes of the blind see?" In other words, those who believe in the righteousness of God must have such faith that says, "How can I preach the gospel of the water and the Spirit to people who have not been washed from their sins yet, so that they can receive the cleansing of their sins and enter the Kingdom of Heaven?" Do you understand? We have both a carnal wish and a spiritual wish, but we must at least think, "How can I make the blind see?"

This should be the basis of our hearts.

We are the spiritually sick if we do not have such a heart. We will degenerate into the useless ones who have lost our positions and goals as the righteous who have believed in the gospel of the water and the Spirit. Our Lord opened the eyes of the blind and said, *"Your faith has made you well."* Likewise, we must do the work of opening the eyes of people like blind Bartimaeus, if we have been born again through the gospel of the water and the Spirit. We must do this spiritually. The righteous must have this hope of opening the eyes of people who have not been born again yet.

The disciples argued amongst themselves who was the greater and who was the lesser, but this was truly vain. People who just want to boast of their little merits are not the born-again who believe in the gospel of the water and the Spirit. From a spiritual view point they just mumble with their mouths, but their behavior displays something else. They are like a fig tree that is just full of leaves without any fruit. Their life of faith does not have any substance at all. We who believe in the righteousness of the Lord do not have to have such great ability to boast of in a worldly sense. We can preach the gospel of the water and the Spirit to other people if we have faith as small as a mustard seed, that is, if we have this faith that seeks to open up the eyes of the blind. Such people become the precious servants of God who live for the gospel of the water and the Spirit throughout their entire life. Such people can do spiritual work because they have this spiritual heart. If we at least have this spiritual wish like a mustard seed in our hearts, we can do great things with just this heart alone. This small heart can lead many people onto the righteous path and make them receive the remission of their sins. Hence, you and I must become the people who follow after the righteousness of the Lord with a spiritual heart instead of boasting about our fleshly merits.

Dear fellow believers, I want you and me to have this little wish in the heart which is as small as a mustard seed and to open up the eyes of the blind. Do you know how small a mustard seed is? It is so small that one would not even be able to see it if it is placed in the palm of your hand. Also this seed is blown away by our breathing when we try to look at it closely. A mustard seed is so very tiny and light. Therefore the Lord illustrated our genuine but little faith in the Scriptures with a mustard seed amongst so many seeds. Those who believe in the righteousness of the Lord do not need any great power or wealth of this world. They can preach the gospel of the water and the Spirit throughout their entire lives with just this small faith in the grace God. We have this one wish as small as a mustard seed in our heart, and this wish makes us preach the gospel of the water and the Spirit to those around us and save them from the sins of this world, those who are bound for hell. If 50% of a human heart is fleshly and the other 50% is spiritual, we become the true witnesses of the gospel and also become the disciples of the Lord because we have this 50% spiritual heart in us who believe in the gospel of the water and the Spirit. On the other hand, those who do not have the heart of believing in the Lord's perfect gospel of the water and the Spirit do not have a desire in their hearts to live spiritually.

Dear fellow believers, I want you to have such a spiritual heart. God wants us to have this heart of living for the righteousness of God. We must have a spiritual wish in our hearts. We must have a wish which desires to have souls receive the remission of their sins by believing in the gospel of the water and the Spirit. Even if you do not have such great faith and ability, you can still do spiritual works if you just believe in the gospel of the water and the Spirit and follow the

Lord spiritually. You come to serve the gospel of the righteousness of the Lord instead of seeking after fleshly desires although we cannot of course, throw them away completely.

We can follow after spiritual things by just having a little bit of spiritual wishes. And in the end this 50% spirituality in our hearts will come to eat up the other fleshly 50% part there. When a mustard seed is planted, life begins from this little seed. At first, it comes up very weak and small like an annual plant, but it soon grows up to be a very big tree as time passes, and it becomes a blessed space where all kinds of birds of the air can rest in and people rest under its shade. Like this, we can eventually overcome all vain desires and the hearts of flesh and be transformed into spiritual people when we have this faith as small as a mustard seed like this. Hence, we must not disrespect the heart that desires to serve the gospel of the water and the Spirit, which is a spiritual heart like ours. I want you to know that this little wish makes you overcome all fleshly desires. In the hearts of us the born-again who have received the remission of sins, is faith which believes in the gospel of the water and the Spirit, and this faith enables us to grow and be transformed spiritually. However, the problem is that fleshly people among the born-again just bury this spiritual heart under the ground and press it down with a heavy rock preventing it to sprout. You should remember that even such a small wish of faith that is with the Lord will eventually blossom into spiritually beautiful flowers. Therefore, we must at least have such a heart that seeks to preach the gospel of the water and the Spirit to the other people.

What Is the Purpose of a Righteous Person Living in This World?

Does a righteous person live to chase after material wealth and power of this world and enjoy its riches and glory? This should not happen. Such greed only brings calamity to a believer. I will tell you a story from the Scriptures in order to help you understand this lesson well.

Our Lord brought down the city of Jericho through Joshua. Joshua told the people to go around Jericho once a day for six days and seven times on the seventh day according to God's will. The walls of Jericho began to collapse from the inside out when the people screamed and the priests blew their horns after going around the city the last seven times. After the city had collapsed they first saved the family of Rahab the harlot, Joshua said, *"Cursed be the man before the LORD who rises up and builds this city Jericho; he shall lay its foundation with his firstborn, and with his youngest he shall set up its gates" (Joshua 6:26)*. This means that when someone who has received his salvation through the Lord lives for the world that God has personally destroyed, God eventually will destroy him. It does not just end in words, but it actually happens. Actually, when King Ahab ruled over Israel this Word was indeed fulfilled, *"In his days Hiel of Bethel built Jericho. He laid its foundation with Abiram his firstborn, and with his youngest son Segub he set up its gates, according to the word of the LORD, which He had spoken through Joshua the son of Nun" (1 King 16:34)*.

Think about this. Haven't we made so many mistakes while living in this world even though we have thought so many times not to make any mistakes? We do not just act immediately as we feel, but we instead put something into action after thinking about it very carefully and deciding what is right. It is because we, the born-again, cannot receive the Lord's perfect blessing if we build the foundation and the house towards this world and follow the material things and the power of the world. And it's because we become destroyed spiritually. It would not matter even though we lived like that if everything could become prosperous by following the world. However, a person who believes in the gospel of the water and the Spirit will eventually become useless in this world if he does not at least live for the gospel. That is why the Lord says, *"You are the salt of the earth; but if the salt loses its flavor, how shall it be seasoned? It is then good for nothing but to be thrown out and trampled underfoot by men" (Matthew 5:13).* This is the very truth the Lord said to the born again.

Just as all the money one owns would be useless if one should lost one's life, likewise, your entire life will be in vain if you cannot receive the blessing of serving the spiritual gospel no matter how much worldly wealth you have accumulated. Dear fellow believers, we have a great cause to lead a spiritual life. We definitely have reason why we must live like this although it is hard and difficult. Thus, we must have a small wish of the heart, an upright wish of faith, in order to live such a spiritual life. That is, we must have the wish to make other souls receive the remission of sins by preaching the gospel of the water and the Spirit to them, the wish to open the eyes of the blind. This is the true wish that the Lord desires from us.

In some Christian sects, the members are prone to deify their leader so that this leader of that sect who has money and honor would appear more handsome even if he is not. But would someone who looks luxurious and has lots of money become a spiritual person? Regardless of who he is a person who does not believe in the gospel of the water and the Spirit cannot be spiritual. Do you think anyone is able to live spiritually even without believing in this gospel of the water and the Spirit? This is also a wrong notion. You do not even need to look at others. Just look at yourselves. We can at least live serving the Lord according to the desires of the Holy Spirit because we have received the Holy Spirit who has come by the remission of sins we received. Besides this, everything else is of the flesh. People boast of themselves and pretend to be upright as if they have much righteousness, but humans really do not have any genuine righteousness. We must not be deceived by our thoughts. Because we have in our hearts the gospel of the water and the Spirit that opened the eyes of the blind, we must just live our entire life by this faith.

We are prone to boast of our own fleshly righteousness first after receiving the remission of our sins by believing in the gospel of the water and the Spirit. Even while doing this, we think that we actually have much righteousness. However, as time passes, examine and see if your righteousness could be so perfect until you die.

Job who appears in the Old Testament also thought that he was a great person at the beginning. However, when he started facing severe tribulations, he cursed the day he was born and complained against God, saying, "Why did my mother conceive me and gave birth to me? Why did she receive me with her two knees? Why did the sun shine on that day? I would have died in comfort because it would have been too dark if the light had not shone on that day." Then God said to Job, "Job, were you there when I created the universe and all things in it? Were you there when I was putting up the Big Dipper, a constellation up in the sky? Do you know why I made it like this? Do you know the reason why the universe and all the things in it move so wondrously with four seasons? And do you know the reason why this universe that I have created revolves around so orderly like a well toothed cogwheel working with each other? Why do you complain against me and complain about being born to this world? You should acknowledge your shortcomings and your fleshly weaknesses. Why are you instead holding a grievance against me and holding a grievance against your parents?"

Job hears this Word of God and eventually breaks down his own righteousness. He acknowledges, "God, I really did not know. I am truly a treacherous person." Only then did God perfectly accept Job who broke down his righteousness like this. As such, we humans are beings who cannot even reach the feet of God no matter how great we are.

I think about myself and you, the saints and the servants of God. No matter how diligently we do the righteous works until the moment of our death, we do not have anything to boast about besides faith of believing in the gospel of the water and the Spirit. I do not know how you have lived until now, but when we think about it, the days we will live in the future are all in vain on our own. We are insufficient beings before the presence of God. Hence, we live praising the righteousness of the Lord even in the midst of our shortcomings. Therefore, we must spread the gospel of the Lord, which is the salvation of the Lord. We must just boast of the perfection of the Lord rather than boasting of our own greatness, which is vain. We can believe in the perfect gospel of the Lord and preach it because we really are lacking. A person who thinks that he is great in his own thoughts can never preach this gospel of the water and the Spirit. We have the faith that people can receive salvation because they are also weak just as we have received salvation after knowing our own shortcomings. We thus can preach the gospel of the water and the Spirit. Otherwise, we would not even need to receive salvation if we were all perfect on our own.

Dear fellow believers, we are all insufficient always. We have become the workers of the Lord because we are lacking. We dwell in God's Church and serve the gospel because we are weak. Our Lord has also entrusted to us the work of preaching the gospel of the water and the Spirit because we are insufficient beings. The Lord wants to witness the gospel to the blind, the lame, the paralyzed, the poor, the rich, and the powerful, and bestow the grace of God upon them all. The Lord made us receive the grace of salvation by giving us the gospel of the water and the Spirit and made us become the perfect children of the Lord because we are insufficient beings. We cannot serve the righteousness of the Lord if we really are perfect and great in the flesh. We would not even need faith, prayer, and even God, if we were perfect. We pray to the Lord because we are lacking and do His work while believing in the Lord. Do you acknowledge that you are also an insufficient person? I want you to believe that God holds onto us and makes us do his work because we are weak and lacking.

The Kingdom of God awaits us who believe in the righteousness of God. We cannot see it with our naked eyes, but we can see with our spiritual eyes that this Kingdom will definitely come. Jesus Christ who is God has prepared the Kingdom of Heaven for us and is waiting for us to come into that place without fail. And He wants us to open the spiritual eyes of many other people and witness the gospel of the water and the Spirit to them while living in this world. Dear fellow believers, this world and everything in it which is apparent to our fleshly eyes, is not all that it is. There is clearly the Kingdom of God to those who believe in the righteousness of God. Even the Millennial Kingdom that will be unfolded in this land can never be the eternal Kingdom of Heaven. The Kingdom of Heaven is a place where we will enjoy the blessed life for eternity. When people receive the judgment from the Lord He who sits on the white throne, we the righteous who have been born again by believing in the gospel of the water and the Spirit will go to this Kingdom of God; and sinners who have not been born again because of their unbelief will go to the eternal burning fire.

The Lord said that all those who have not received the remission of their sins will be in Hades. The Lord said in the Scriptures that He puts them in the bottomless pit and brings them out in the end times and judges them and then casts them into the eternal fire. I absolutely do not want any of you gathered here to go to that place called Hades. We are the people who shall enter the Kingdom of God.

What must we do in order to enter the Kingdom of God? We must also build God's Kingdom while living in this world just as our Lord came to this world and built the Kingdom of God. We the believers belong to the Kingdom of Heaven, but we must build the Kingdom of God in this world now. We are now gathering people together who shall go and live in the Kingdom of God. This constitutes the preaching of the gospel. We must prepare the Kingdom of God for the people and become the workers who build the Kingdom of God in this world. All the saints must be faithful to the work they have been entrusted with. This is the work God has entrusted to us the believers.

You and I have the Kingdom of God. This world is not all there is to it. I give thanks to God who made us the weak as the workers of the Kingdom of God. I give thanks to the Lord who gave us this spiritual desire to open up spiritual eyes of the blind even though our faith is as small as a mustard seed. I want you to hold onto this wish and fulfill this spiritual wish gracefully and become the saints and the servants of God who faithfully fulfill the will of God in His presence. ✉

SERMON

14

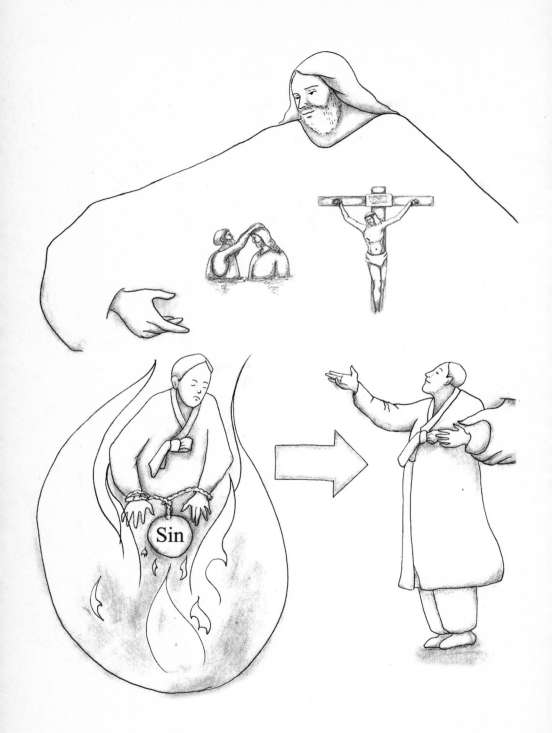

The Faith of Bartimaeus
The Blind Beggar

< Mark 10:46-52 >

"Now they came to Jericho. As He went out of Jericho with His disciples and a great multitude, blind Bartimaeus, the son of Timaeus, sat by the road begging. And when he heard that it was Jesus of Nazareth, he began to cry out and say, 'Jesus, Son of David, have mercy on me!' Then many warned him to be quiet; but he cried out all the more, 'Son of David, have mercy on me!' So Jesus stood still and commanded him to be called. Then they called the blind man, saying to him, 'Be of good cheer. Rise, He is calling you.' And throwing aside his garment, he rose and came to Jesus. So Jesus answered and said to him, 'What do you want Me to do for you?' The blind man said to Him, 'Rabboni, that I may receive my sight.' Then Jesus said to him, 'Go your way; your faith has made you well.' And immediately he received his sight and followed Jesus on the road."

Warm greetings to you all! A revival meeting was held in this City with the Lord's blessings in September 21-24 under the following theme: "The Remission of Sins That's Received Only through the Word." Among those present in that meeting amid God's grace were Sister Hyesook Heo, her mother and sister, and brother Sungrok Hong. Although some of their family members probably have not received the remission of sins yet, God had still given us an opportunity to preach His gospel to these four people. Sister Heo could not be with us today at this hour, but I was pleased to see her rejoicing over the gospel of the Lord, and I shared her joy when she said, "I now know what it really means to believe in Jesus." As she is still young in her faith, she probably does not have the full, detailed spiritual understanding of the salvation that God has fulfilled with the gospel of the water and the Spirit. She did however realize clearly that she no longer had any sins, and so I am sure that her mind will soon reach this understanding thoroughly. Although she said that she will continue to attend her present church for now, if she comes here even just once a month, she will realize what the true Word of God really is. The Holy Spirit who dwells in her heart will teach her clearly that the gospel of the water and the Spirit is the real gospel.

It Is Always Great to Hold Revival Meetings That Preach the True Gospel

As the revival meeting was held over several days, it was physically hard and tiring for us to prepare for it, but the work of God that arose on this occasion made our labor all the worthwhile. Many souls came to these meetings from seeing the pamphlets that we had distributed and the posters we had put up. And these people heard the gospel of the Lord and many of them received the true remission of sins into their hearts. I am sure that God will hold them steadfast to our Church. That's because those who have received the remission of sins know that their own wisdom is completely useless before God no matter how wise they may be, and therefore ultimately, they cannot help but abide in God's Church by faith.

I admonish you to ask God to lead all these new believers to the right path so that they may stand firm on the gospel of the water and the Spirit as soon as possible.

We plan to continue to hold such revival meetings in the future. They will be held under various themes. Other churches that hold only one or two revival meetings a year may wonder why we are holding so many, but we will continue to hold them as many times as we can until the Lord returns to this earth. To every corner of each city and town, we will let everyone know that we are indeed preaching God's Word. To our critics and enemies alike, we will do our utmost to make sure that everyone hears the gospel Word of the Lord.

To this end, we need to make several purchases next week. As it takes financial resources to hold revival meetings, such as paying for winter heating, I would like to ask you to pray diligently about this during this week to see what you could do for the Lord, and consider the possibility of making a financial pledge. It would be good if you could find it in your heart to give willingly to the Lord's ministry. So I ask you to resolve yourself to serve the Lord faithfully and preach His gospel diligently, and to join us in making a pledge next week.

On a different note, the sermons preached during this past revival meeting have been recorded on tapes. As the theme of the meeting has been the gospel, the sermons don't really address the issues that arise in the saints' everyday lives, but anyone who wants the tapes should ask for them from Brother Wongi Choi, a student at our Mission School. He will then give them to you for free. In addition, before this year is over, we are scheduled to establish churches in various regions in Korea, including Wonjoo, and so I also ask you to pray for this as much as possible.

I spent the whole day yesterday resting. I think it's safe to say that all of us at the revival meeting were quite worn out by the end of these meetings. During the revival meeting, I didn't feel tired at all, but once it was over, I felt so exhausted that I could hardly get up, and so I lied down and got some much needed rest. The meeting was over on Thursday, and I took two days off on Friday and Saturday to rest. Perhaps it was too long, as my routine seems to have been broken. This morning, while copying church newsletter, I made some careless mistakes and ended up wasting several papers. But once I am back to my routine, I am sure that everything will return to normal.

In our Church, every sermon is transcribed word by word by Brother Jaedong Park rather than just summarizing it, and in about a month's time, there should be enough sermons compiled to put into another book. There is a huge difference between listening to a sermon just once and reading it carefully in writing. Although it may be boring if you listen or read a sermon that you just heard, if you come across it after some time, when your heart is weary, you will see for yourself how the sermon strengthens your heart and leads your minds to God.

We Are All Fragile Beings before the Lord

This world constantly tries to steal our hearts, but if we wage our spiritual battle for the Lord, we can still abide in the Lord. If, however, we don't fight our spiritual battles, then our flesh will weaken and then we cannot help but fall into the world. That's why we hold revival meetings continuously, so that we may give people spiritual strength. I ask you to pray for this. This last revival meeting was attended by relatively few people, including our newly redeemed brothers and sisters and the students at the Mission School, but I admonish you not to miss any church gatherings in the future. Our Church is such that if you miss just a week, you might as well be a stranger. It makes a huge difference. It doesn't matter whether you are ahead or behind now. It only takes a few weeks of missed gatherings for you to trail behind everyone way in the back. That is how much difference it makes on your heart's desire to run towards the Lord and live for Him.

Let me take this opportunity to introduce to you a new member of our Church. Please welcome her with warm applause. She recently moved to the nearby apartment complex, and as someone who has received the remission of sins, she is your own sister. When this sister moved, she exchanged her TV/VCR combo with the television at my home. I plan to use it when video revival meetings are held in the Church. Until now, there really wasn't any use for a video camera even if we had it, but when I look at how God has given us this television with a video player attached to it, I think He is telling us to use it for our revival meetings. I also believe that the fact that God gave us a copier indicates that He wants us to work even more diligently on our literature ministry. So we will hold our revival meetings in various formats.

As mentioned, next week we will ask you to make pledging offerings for revival meetings. In this week to come, let's all pray hard and serve the Lord diligently. We need various equipment and supplies to hold revival meetings, including heating equipment and ink toners for the copier. Nothing is more tragic than not being able to do what we must do to serve the Lord just because we don't have enough financial resources.

Recently, while reading Romans 11:36, I prayed to God as the following: "Lord, fill our coffer with hundreds of millions of dollars to carry out Your work, so that we may never find ourselves unable to serve You because of any lack of resources." Since everything in the world belongs to the Lord, I have every confidence that if financial resources are needed to spread the gospel, God will provide them to us. I am sure that the Lord will solve everything so that we would never be unable to spread His gospel just because of we don't have enough financial resources. It's already 11:30am. I will end my lengthy preface here and delve into today's Scripture passage.

Bartimaeus the Blind Beggar

It is written in Mark 10:46-47, *"Now they came to Jericho. As He went out of Jericho with His disciples and a great multitude, blind Bartimaeus, the son of Timaeus, sat by the road begging. And when he heard that it was Jesus of Nazareth, he began to cry out and say, 'Jesus, Son of David, have mercy on me!'"*

A blind man named Bartimaeus appears in this passage. In this world there are many blind people like Bartimaeus. How are their lives? First of all, they cannot see the natural beauty of this world. They are not capable of appreciating the intricate beauty of the wonderful natural dominion that God created, from the deep blue autumn sky to the green pines, the splashing seas, and the wild flowers blossoming in the field, nor can they praise God for this beauty. They are also living a very uncomfortable and inconvenient life.

As the blind can't see, they rely on their sense of touch, and their touch is so sensitive that just by relying on a cane, they can tell the difference between a sidewalk and a roadway. Some of them can even ride a bicycle just like us. They know how to get around in a bicycle by the feeling, calculating how many times they have to pedal before turning which way; of course, there is a limit to how far they can go on a bicycle. Despite the heightened sense of touch, not being able to see with one's own eyes is still indescribably inconvenient and unfortunate. The blind could be better prepared for what lies ahead if they could see, but since they have only the sense of touch to rely on, it's unavoidable for them to make mistakes when there are even slightest changes in their surroundings.

For those of us who have a pair of working eyes, it may actually be hard to sympathize with the story of blind Bartimaeus. We may just think that it's a story about some blind man who opened his eyes. However, in this story God is telling us a great deal. First of all, we ought to be grateful that we are able to see, and that we can use our perception to discern, realize, and prepare beforehand. Considering that some people are born blind, the very fact that we have both our eyes working is itself a great blessing. Of course, there also are spiritually blind people, but before anything else we were not born physically blind is itself something for which we should be extremely grateful to the Lord.

Let's imagine that you were really born physically blind. If you were sitting here as a blind person, then you would be listening to this sermon with utmost attention. You'd be all ears, hoping for a small miracle, and thinking that perhaps you could open your eyes if you listened attentively. It may be hard for you to really appreciate this as your eyes are actually open, but whenever this passage is preached to the blind, they show tremendous interest. We too need to pay close attention to it, for this passage is not spoken to just those who are physically blind.

The Blind Man Called Jesus, *"Jesus, Son of David"*

The events described in today's Scripture passage occurred when Jesus and His disciples made a short stop at Jericho while on their way to Jerusalem. Let's quickly go back a little and see what was said in verses 33 and 34: *"Behold, we are going up to Jerusalem, and the Son of Man will be betrayed to the chief priests and to the scribes; and they will condemn Him to death and deliver Him to the Gentiles; and they will mock Him, and scourge Him, and spit on Him, and kill Him. And the third day He will rise again."* The Lord told the disciples something extremely important—namely, that He would go Jerusalem, be crucified to death, and rise from the dead on the third day.

But how did the disciples react at that time? It's written: *"Then James and John, the sons of Zebedee, came to Him, saying, 'Teacher, we want You to do for us whatever we ask.'"* They also said, *"Grant us that we may sit, one on Your right hand and the other on Your left, in Your glory."* Even though the Lord was telling them about the sacrificial death He would suffer to fulfill the work of salvation and to give everlasting life, the disciples were only interested in reaching positions of power, saying to Him, "Allow us to seat in Your glory. In Your sight, who is greater between us two?" Despite the fact they were walking with Jesus their Savior, their hearts were not set on the same thing as the Lord's. So you can imagine just how sad our Lord must have been in His heart.

The two disciples who asked Jesus to allow one of them to sit at His right hand and the other on His left were none other than James and John. These were two of the best disciples of Jesus often considered to be men of good faith. Along with Peter and Andrew, they were particularly cherished by Jesus.

The only consolation is that Peter didn't get into this fray, but he probably was thinking the same also. James and John just beat him to it and spoke to Jesus before he did, thinking, "Let's be the first to ask Jesus to appoint us to some powerful positions when His Kingdom is fulfilled."

After this episode, Jesus and the disciples reached Jericho. Do you remember what happened in Jericho in Old Testament times? Are you familiar with the city of Jericho? Who received the remission of sins here in this city? Jericho is the place where Rehab the harlot received the remission of sins. The word Jericho means aroma, fragrance, or the world, and it's a city located below Jerusalem, which is up in the mountains.

Jesus was passing through this city to go to Jerusalem, and there in this city was a beggar named Bartimaeus. He was sitting and begging by the same road that the Lord was traveling on. Then Bartimaeus the beggar heard that Jesus was passing by. To see what he did when he heard this, let's turn to Mark 10:47 in today's Scripture passage: *"And when he heard that it was Jesus of Nazareth, he began to cry out and say, 'Jesus, Son of David, have mercy on me!'"* As it's written here, Bartimaeus shouted out to the Lord. If he had not cried out and asked Jesus to have mercy on him, Jesus would have just passed him by, and the Bible would have just recorded, "Bartimaeus then spent the rest of his life begging until his death." But Bartimaeus cried out to the Lord and found His audience, and as a result his eyesight was restored.

This account of how Bartimaeus was able to open his eyes has a profound meaning for all of us. Would Bartimaeus the beggar been able to open his eyes if he were to be too reserved? No, of course not! He paid no attention to what others might think, and he shouted out loudly, *"Jesus, Son of David, have mercy on me!"* Was Bartimaeus an educated man?

It's highly unlikely, since there was no special school for the blind, and so it's very likely that he eschewed any formalities and cried out for help out of his desperate heart. Those who considered themselves educated at that time usually called Jesus "Jesus of Nazareth" in reference to His hometown, but Bartimaeus left out Nazareth and just called Him "Jesus, Son of David." He didn't know that Jesus had grown up in a small town called Nazareth, but he had heard over his shoulders that the Savior would be born from the lineage of David.

This was in fact correct. As it is written, *"The scepter shall not depart from Judah" (Genesis 49:10),* God indeed said that of the twelve sons of Jacob, kings would continue to be born from the house of Judah. So the descendants of Judah formed the most important tribe of the people of Israel. It's from this lineage that David was born, and Jesus Himself was born as a Descendant of this David. God had promised through the prophets that the Savior would be born from this royal lineage, and Bartimaeus, having heard about it, had thus believed in it. And having kept this faith all his life, one day he heard that Jesus was actually passing nearby him.

As Bartimaeus believed in his heart that Jesus Christ, who had come as a Descendant of David, was the Messiah, he mustered enough courage to call His name, and through this Jesus he was able to open his eyes. When he called out for Jesus so loudly, the disciples probably told him "Be quiet! Who do you think you are, shouting out so loudly like this? You are just a mere beggar! What do you think you will do if you meet Jesus? Silence! Jesus already has plenty of other people to meet. Don't try anything funny; just get out of here!" But what did Bartimaeus actually do? The Bible says that he cried out all the more. He had remarkable courage. If you really want help, you have to be at least as bold as Bartimaeus. If you fall back intimated by what others say to you, then you have no prospect of finding Jesus. So Bartimaeus shouted out even louder. "Who are you to stop me? I want to see the Son of David! Why are you blocking me? Get away from me!"

As Bartimaeus was blind, he couldn't see anything, but he still tried to make his way through to Jesus unabashedly. Jesus then heard his voice, stood still, and told His disciples to call him. When the disciples came to bring the blind man, he threw aside his garment, jumped up, and dashed to Jesus. Jesus then said to him, "What is your wish? Do you want your eyesight restored? Your faith has saved you." The result of all this is just as it's written in the Bible: Bartimaeus was finally able to see.

For a blind beggar like Bartimaeus, his garment is his most important possession. To a beggar, his money collection can is also a precious possession, though to us it makes no difference whether we have it or not. Without the can the beggar can't obtain any food, and so for him it is a means of survival. A beggar also needs a garment to protect himself from the elements, and yet when Bartimaeus heard that Jesus was calling for him, he threw everything aside including his garment, his can, and whatever little money he had, and he ran to Jesus.

He was a remarkable man. If you really want to find Jesus, you must have as much passion as this man. Without that kind of courage and decisiveness that Bartimaeus had, you cannot really find Jesus. Countless people today also desire to meet Jesus. But if they really want to meet Jesus, then they must first deal with those who are preventing them from meeting Him, just as Bartimaeus cried out to the Lord even more loudly when he was told to be quiet.

Elsewhere in Mark chapter 2, there is a similar account of

four men who tried to bring a paralytic to Jesus but were blocked by the surrounding crowd. There were so many people that there was hardly any place to set a foot down, but if the paralytic and the four men carrying him had given up right there, he would have never been cured and remained paralyzed for the rest of his life until he died. However, the four men carrying the paralytic went over this pressing crowd, climbed up onto the roof, uncovered it, and lowered the paralytic down in his bed to Jesus so that he would be able to meet Him. And as a result of this, he was cured from his disability.

The same persistence is also found in today's Scripture passage. When Bartimaeus called out Jesus' name, not only did the ordinary people but even the disciples of Jesus told Bartimaeus to settle down. They said to him, "Be quiet! You are just a beggar; how dare you be so loud!" But he cried out all the more. Then Jesus saw him, and He became aware that many people were blocking him from coming to Him. When the Lord told the disciples to bring him to Him, Bartimaeus threw aside his garment, his can, his everything, and ran to Jesus.

The Lord then asked him, *"What do you want Me to do for you?"* The blind man answered by saying, "I want my eyesight restored." When Bartimaeus stood before Jesus, he did not ask for money, nor for any expensive garment, far less for a house. His only true wish was to open his eyes in the presence of Jesus, the Son of David.

Compared to the wishes of the disciples who just wanted power and high positions for themselves, Bartimaeus' request was truly honorable. What a blessing is it for a blind man to open his eyes, see this beautiful world of God's creation, and then go to His Kingdom? Bartimaeus wanted nothing else from Jesus but his eyes opened. Even though this man was a beggar and blind, he did everything possible to meet Jesus Christ. If he had given up trying to meet Jesus just because many people were blocking him, or if he had made some other request before Jesus, he would never have opened his eyes. However, he told Jesus that he wanted to open his eyes, and Jesus said to him, *"Go your way; your faith has made you well."* Jesus had opened his eyes for his courage and faith.

Were Those with Two Working Eyes Better Than Bartimaeus the Blind Beggar?

The people at that time had two perfectly working eyes. And with these eyes they had seen Jesus passing by. However, it was the blind man who ran to Jesus and asked Him to open his eyes, and it was his wish that was granted. The blind man Bartimaeus refers to every sinner who is born spiritually blind. Therefore, the real lesson of this story is that every sinner can receive the remission of sins by the Word of power that Jesus has given. You need to grasp here that no one today has any sin, whether he believes in Jesus or not.

Many cannot understand when I say this, but I can proclaim it by faith. People have no sin. Just as they were born with open eyes, they were also born with their sins already remitted away. However, many people live in a spiritually blind state, as though they have sin when in fact they are sinless. Those who don't know the dominion of God think that there are only sinners in this world. If there are such people among us, they must have courage like Bartimaeus and receive the remission of sins from the Lord.

All the sins in this world have disappeared thanks to Jesus. We are living in a bright world in this sinless state. However, countless people are still living in their sinful state unable to open their eyes, in their depressed state. Since they believe that they have sin, just how dark, gloomy, and restless must they be? How frustrated must they be to live thinking that there are sins in this world?

There is a huge difference between those living with their eyes opened and those living with their eyes closed. Those who have opened their eyes think that this world is a bright and beautiful place. They know that this world that God made is beautiful and good. In contrast, those who have not opened their eyes think the very opposite. For them, this world is nothing but a wearisome, frustrating, and depressing place.

Those who have opened their spiritual eyes believe that Jesus Christ has blotted out all their sins with the gospel of the water and the Spirit, and they confirm in their hearts that they are indeed sinless. They are then able to live in this world in joy and happiness, for all their sins have disappeared. In contrast, those who believe that there is still sin in their hearts cannot help but live in frustration, suffering and darkness. However, mankind truly has no sin. There is no sin in this world. As we are living in a sinless world, we ourselves are also sinless.

Whenever anyone asks me, "Pastor, do you have no sin?" I answer confidently, "Yes, of course I have no sin." Because my response comes so naturally, some people react adversely sometimes. That I have no sin does not mean that I don't commit sin anymore. Rather, it means that regardless of whether I commit sin or not, the Lord bore all my sins and was condemned for them, and therefore I have no sin. And because I am sinless, I can laugh and praise the Lord even in my most difficult circumstances. That is how I lead my life.

When Bartimaeus the beggar was blind—that is, when he was sinful—how miserable must his life have been? The routine things that we take for granted must have been a constant struggle for him, even such mundane things as going to the bathroom and trying to eat his meals. However, once he met the Lord, opened his eyes, and received the remission of his sins unto salvation, there was no need for him to put up with such hassles anymore.

The same is true for us as well. Once we receive the remission of sins, all the hassles and sufferings of the past are gone. Of course, there still are times in our lives when we feel depressed, gloomy, dark, and frustrated. But is this what our lives are really about? Must our souls really suffer like this? No, of course not! As those who have received the remission of sins through the Lord, we are not such people. We need to realize here that whenever we feel that this world is depressing and dark, this is not real, but it's just the Devil deceiving us. We are those who have opened the eyes of the soul. We are the righteous. It's so wonderful to live in this world with our eyes open, to walk with the Lord, and to lead our lives for Him. I am sure that Bartimaeus, who was saved by the Lord, also lived the rest of his life in happiness with his eyes open.

That We Have Opened Our Spiritual Eyes Does Not Mean That the Circumstances of Our Remaining Lives Have Changed Suddenly and Entirely

It's just that the angle of our view has changed. Before, we could tell a flower only by touching it, but now, we can find it out with our eyes. My fellow believers, if one receives the remission of sins and completely opens his spiritual eyes through the Lord, then his heart will change profoundly, even though his natural surroundings made by God remain unchanged, as his outside appearance also remains unchanged. Because this person has opened his eyes, if he just gives some effort, he will be more than able to live a wonderful life in this dark world, lead countless people to Jesus Christ, and make the rest of his life worthwhile. I believe that just as such a life was granted to the beggar Bartimaeus, it is also granted to you and me.

While living in this world, if we believe unwaveringly with our hearts that there is no sin in this world, then we can all live happily in bright and shining light. When we realize and believe that there is no sin, this world turns into a truly beautiful and spotlessly clean place. However, if we think that this world is filled with sin, then it is a dark, depressing, filthy, and all around unlivable world. Our hearts' faith makes such a huge difference. This world is often a wearisome and depressing place for not only those who have not received the remission of sins, but also for those who have. However, those who have received the remission of sins through the Lord, those who have opened their spiritual eyes, know that there is no sin in this world, and therefore they see this world as a beautiful place. Think about it. Think about the blue sky, the brilliant stars all the creatures teeming with life, the beautiful flowers that blossom in time without anyone telling them, and the abundant harvest in the fall. Can't you see just how wonderful this world is? Our view of the world ought to change in this way.

Among those who insist that they have received the remission of their sins, there are some who still lead a pathetic life in this world. It's because they still think that there are sins in this world. Even after opening their spiritual eyes through the Lord, they judge the world with the same touch that they had when they were blind, and so they cannot see the true beauty of this world. In other words, they are unable to live in a spiritually bright world. You and I should realize what a beautiful and wonderful world we are living in.

However, if there were still sins, how filthy and dirty would this world be? One would be hopeless in such a world, since he sees everyone, including himself, as nothing more than a pile of sin. We need to have the right view of the world. There is no sin anymore. There is no sin in this world. If you think there is sin, it is not real, but you are just being deceived by the Devil. It means that you have the Devil's eyes and remain spiritually blind, even though there is no sin. There is a huge difference between remaining spiritually blind and opening your spiritual eyes to see that there is no sin in this world. For those who know and believe that there is no sin in this world, the condition of their hearts is completely different from those who believe that this world is filled with sins. My fellow believers, I admonish you all to realize that there is a huge gap between those who live by faith and those who don't, and those who live with their spiritual eyes opened and those who live with their spiritual eyes closed.

How wretched was Bartimaeus' life when he was blind? And how depressed are the lives of today's people who still have not opened their spiritual eyes? They are just interested in how to make money and live a comfortable life. And whatever they do, there is no beauty in their hearts. The only joy of their lives is to fill their own stomach, and to gossip about others. There is no eye in their hearts to see the world clearly. They see no beauty.

But in reality, how wonderful is this world? Just how beautiful has our Lord made it? How happy has He made us and blessed us? God made both this world and the next world beautiful. He made the whole universe beautiful, both the heavens and the earth. Bartimaeus had been living in a depressing and dark world, but when he found the Truth, he opened his eyes and saw the beautiful world of God's creation. Likewise, rather than looking at the world pessimistically, we should also have spiritual eyes and see the true beauty of the world.

Though we were blind, we have now opened our eyes— this is the truth. To believe that we have no sin is to believe in the truth. Despite having the eyes of the flesh, we were all spiritually blind. But now that we have opened our eyes through the Lord, we should not look at this world in the same way we did when we were blind. Once our spiritual eyes are opened, we must see the world as a beautiful and wonderful place. Similarly, when we deal with other people, we should believe that they have no sin, and we should shine the light of this faith on them. Believe from the depth of your heart that you and I are both clean and spotless, and that there is no sin in this world.

You and I have received the remission of sins. However, sometimes we still get depressed. Other times we feel unhappy. Why are we unable to live happily in this beautiful world? Why do we stumble as though we were going through a dark tunnel, instead of building our happiness? Why are we walking on a dark road when there clearly is a bright road ahead of us? As spiritually born-again people, we must open the eyes of our hearts once again. Just as Bartimaeus opened his eyes, so must we also open our spiritual eyes completely, and only then can we realize that this world is indeed beautiful. Otherwise we will live like a blind person who can't see ahead, trapped in a dark and frustrating world of pessimism.

The same goes when we bear witness of the gospel to others. Whenever you approach people, you should never see any of them in a negative or dark light. Don't think pessimistically, "How could this person ever receive the remission of sins?" Cast aside all such cynical thoughts. They are clean, sinless people. No matter what anyone says, you should approach them boldly and lift up the scale covering their eyes. You have to thus open their spiritual eyes and make it possible for them to receive the remission of sins. For those who have opened their spiritual eyes, there is a breathtakingly beautiful and expansive world before them. In their lives there is neither any curse nor any darkness. There is only wonderful happiness waiting them.

If you see this world through your eyes of faith in bright light, you will see that the world is indeed filled with blessings. Of course, even among those who have received the remission of sins, there are some who live in darkness as if their eyes were still tightly closed. But this is wrong. We the redeemed should never live like this. If there are any such people among the saints gathered here, they must escape from this flawed thinking as soon as possible.

Countless people have received the remission of sins since we began our literature ministry. Myriads of people are coming into the light of the Lord, and His Church is becoming evermore beautiful. We must believe with our hearts that all our past sins have disappeared from our lives, and that we have now begun to lead a new, happy, and joyful life in the Lord.

It's precisely for this reason that the Lord has saved us, and so it is completely foolish for any of us to lead a miserable life bound by our past sins even after receiving the remission of sins. No beautiful flower can blossom in our lives if we live like this. That's the same as living in the past mindset as slaves in Egypt and trembling in fear, unable to take the expansive land of Canaan that the Lord has opened up for us, the wonderful world that the Lord has given us. We must escape from this mindset. Just as Bartimaeus the beggar escaped from darkness, so must we also shake it off and set ourselves free.

It's now time for me to bring this sermon to its conclusion. All of us need to realize how God has made our lives so blessed, and abiding by this faith in the Lord, we also need to think about whether there really is any sin in this world or not. I admonish you to believe from the depth of your heart that there is no sin in this world, and to live and work in this sinless world as its light, both at your home and your workplace. I ask you to abide by your faith in the Lord, who has illuminated the world, to give thanks to Him for what He has already given you, and to bear witness of the Light before God. This beautiful world that God has given us is so large that our entire lifetime would still not be long enough for us to enjoy it all. All that remains for us to do is to just enjoy it by faith and take what God has given us.

My fellow believers, we can never become blind again. If we have indeed opened our spiritual eyes through the Lord, then all of us must live a new life. Bartimaeus had lived in misery begging in the dirty and grimy street all his life, but once he opened both his eyes, he saw this beautiful world and truly came to appreciate all its beauty. So we must also live like him. So let us not bind our lives in our past. The Bible says, *"Old things have passed away; behold, all things have become new."* Just like this passage, God has indeed opened our world anew, so that we may live in all its expanses, blessings, and beauty.

Do you believe in this? Then live by this faith. The flowers of happiness will then blossom in your home, the flowers of the Truth in the Church, and the flowers of blessings in our lives.

God has blessed us to enjoy everything in the world. I hope and pray that you will enjoy it all in the Light, bear even more fruits before God, and give all the more glory to Him. ⊠

SERMON

15

The Lord Has Need of You

< Mark 11:1-10 >

"Now when they drew near Jerusalem, to Bethphage
and Bethany, at the Mount of Olives, He sent two of His
disciples; and He said to them, 'Go into the village opposite
you; and as soon as you have entered it you will find a colt
tied, on which no one has sat. Loose it and bring it. And if
anyone says to you, 'Why are you doing this?' say, 'The
Lord has need of it,' and immediately he will send it here.'
So they went their way, and found the colt tied by the door
outside on the street, and they loosed it. But some of those
who stood there said to them, 'What are you doing, loosing
the colt?' And they spoke to them just as Jesus had
commanded. So they let them go. Then they brought the
colt to Jesus and threw their clothes on it, and He sat on it.
And many spread their clothes on the road, and others cut
down leafy branches from the trees and spread them on the
road. Then those who went before and those who followed
cried out, saying:
'Hosanna!
Blessed is He who comes in the name of the LORD!
Blessed is the kingdom of our father David
That comes in the name of the Lord!
Hosanna in the highest!'"

Whom Does the Lord Say He Will Use?

Have you been peaceful, my fellow believers? Before I

commence preaching today's sermon, I want to tell you that our life is extremely busy. Yesterday morning I went to Kimpo Airport on business, and in the afternoon I went down to Injae Discipleship Training Center where I helped set up a large plastic greenhouse of about 300sqm with my co-workers. Since returning from the hard work, I feel exhausted today. I am very busy. And you also are very busy living in this world, aren't you? I'm deeply thankful to Lord that He allows us time to share His Words.

Loose a Colt That Is Tied Up and Bring It Here

Today we read from Mark 11 verses 1-10. Our Lord said, "Loose a colt that is tied up and bring it," and the colt mentioned here refers to everyone living in this world, that is, you and me. The Old Testament also records this: *"But every firstborn of a donkey you shall redeem with a lamb; and if you will not redeem it, then you shall break its neck. And all the firstborn of man among your sons you shall redeem" (Exodus 13:13)*. This means, if the owner of a colt wanted to save the colt because of his compassion for it, he should kill a lamb instead to save this colt. This is the Word of God which was spoken to His people to illustrate the remission of their sins. I believe you know this very well that in the Old Testament times, there was the ritual of the imposition of hands where people laid their hands on the sacrificial animals before they were killed and offered them as the propitiation for their sins before God.

By the way, the characteristic of a colt, the offspring of a donkey, is that it is stubborn and does not heed to the words of its master very well. Also, it always carries something on its back throughout its life until it dies. Humans are also like this. Humans do not heed to the Word of God very well, and they are very stubborn and carry the burden of their sin throughout their entire lifetime. A donkey and a human are really very similar in this respect.

Because of this, even in today's Scripture passage in the New Testament, the Lord speaks of us using this illustration of a colt. The Lord said, *"You will find a colt tied, on which no one has sat. Loose it and bring it. And if anyone says to you, 'Why are you doing this?' say, 'The Lord has need of it.'"* The Lord was telling us here what kind of people God calls when He calls for His workers. The Lord wanted a colt that no one had ever sat on. This means, the Lord wants to use people who have not become slaves to worldly people as His servants or as His workers. No matter who it is, once a person has become a servant to another human, the Lord cannot use him. This is because he already has an owner.

The saints whom the Lord is using currently and all the true workers of the Lord are people who have not become a servant of another. I want to say this Word of the Lord, "You will find a colt tied, on which no one has sat. Loose it and bring it," especially to our young brothers and sisters who have not yet become a servant of another human in this world. Of course, it's the same for the older brothers and sisters as well. Even if you are an older person with not much strength, our Lord can lead you and use you as a perfect servant if you think "I am not a servant of another human. I do not serve another human being as my master."

Anyone Who Has Not Become a Servant of Another Can Become a Worker of God

The Lord calls such people and wants to use them as His workers. However, as a colt is tied to a post by its owner, we humans are also tied to this and that. Jesus said, "If it is tied to something, untie it and bring it to me." What does this Word mean? It means that a person who wants to become a true servant of God must untie himself from many things he is tied to. Although we humans are prone to be tied to all kinds of things in this world because we are fundamentally weak, we have this hope of becoming the servants of God and becoming His workers in our hearts. I want you to carry the Lord on your back and also become His approved workers instead of carrying other people around. I want you to untie all things of this world that bind you, and when the Lord calls you like this through the servants of God, I want you to run towards the Lord and really become precious workers of the Lord.

From a humanistic perspective, the way Jesus works in some aspects can seem really one-sided and difficult to understand. Jesus told the disciples abruptly and unilaterally, *"Go into the village opposite you; and as soon as you have entered it you will find a colt tied, on which no one has sat. Loose it and bring it. And if anyone says to you, 'Why are you doing this?' say, 'The Lord has need of it,' and immediately he will send it here."* Then the disciples did as the Lord had commanded them even though they could not understand it, and there really was a colt tied by the front gate of a house when they went to that village. One of the people standing there asked them, "What are you doing, loosing that colt?" And the disciples replied as Jesus had told them to, and the owner unbelievably gave them permission to take the colt away.

Dear fellow believers, do you think the Lord really needed the colt? Actually, even a colt can carry luggage only after growing up a little bit, but a young colt cannot carry much luggage at all. It only takes much effort to feed it but the truth is it cannot do much work. Then, what does this Word imply? We must understand the deep meaning of this Word well. The Lord is speaking here about the matter of calling and making us as His workers. The Lord said that He calls people who have not yet become the servants of another and uses them as His servants. The Lord said to His disciples, "Loose it and bring it," and it means that although we who have been born again have not matured fully and our faith is still young, the Lord nevertheless calls us through His servants if the Lord wants to use us.

The Lord calls many believers as His servants through the born-again workers of the Church. Although a person who has been called does not have any ability now, the Lord will make him into His precious worker later if he continues to follow the Lord obediently according to the calling of the Lord. And the Lord personally rides into the City of Jerusalem riding on this young colt, and the colt receives much glory along with Jesus at that time. Therefore, although your faith is still young, do not doubt, "What can I do? Would God really use me as His servant?" If you are not bound to this world and want to follow only the Lord, our Lord said here that He will call you through His servants. At that time, we just need to obey His calling and follow Him by faith. Then, like this young colt that appears in today's Scripture passage, we can be used by God preciously.

When the disciples untied that young colt and brought it to Jesus, someone took off his outer garment and put it on the back of the colt as a saddle. When Jesus rode on the colt, the people spread their clothes on the road, and others cut down leafy branches from the trees and spread them on the road and followed Him, crying out, *"Hosanna! Blessed is He who comes in the name of the LORD!"* Our Lord rode into the city of Jerusalem on the back of the colt like this. Plainly speaking, this young colt became a success in a single day. That someone took off his outer garment and put it on the back of the colt means that God will entrust His work to us soon. It means that God will command us who have been called by the Lord to do His work and put God's luggage on our back.

Do Not Refuse When the Lord Wants to Use You

Dear fellow believers do not ever refuse to obey when God calls you, when God wants to use you, and when God needs to use you. You do not need to refuse His calling, thinking, "I am still too young and I do not know anything." If the Lord really wants to use you, He gives all the necessary ability to you first, and then uses you. Therefore, I want you to obey the Lord totally and follow Him without doubting. God really wants to continue to call workers and use them in His Church.

Of course, when one is first called to do His work, the person can feel an enormous burden, thinking, "Can I do this work when I am still so young? I am not confident about this." However, the thing we must remember is that although we receive hardships with the Lord when we follow Him, we also receive glory with Him. That the Lord wants to use you means that you have been chosen by the Lord. The Lord does not call just anyone. He chooses His servants amongst the people who have received the remission of their sins perfectly and have not been tainted by this world yet even though he might seem immature still; He does not call people who serve others or follow after power and honor of this world because they are completely bound to this world.

Actually, I know that there are not many saints who are old enough to enjoy their lazy days. This means that there are that many people that God will call as His workers. If God calls you, I want you to really follow Him by faith. And I want you to do the Lord's work joyfully. I want you to do His work along with Him. Although there probably will be some hardships as well, even more glory awaits His servants. Even the young colt of the Lord wanted to carry Jesus around on its back, not a drunk or a terribly wretched person of this world. Dear fellow believers, don't you really want to carry Jesus on your back and live as His servant? You must serve the Lord perfectly as much as you can since you have received the remission of your sins after being born to this world. I want each one of you to become a colt like this who serves the Lord.

I reiterate this Word of the Lord again, which says, *"You will find a colt tied, on which no one has sat. Loose it and bring it."* This is the Word of God calling His workers in the Church. I want you to follow obediently if God calls you to use you like this. Actually there would be no justification in Him saying that He would use the colt that already had an owner. But the owner gave up the colt willingly when the disciples said, *"The Lord has need of it."* When our Lord calls us like this, there is no need to apply any justified reason for it. If the Lord wants to use someone, the Lord just tells him to come. We just have to bring ourselves to the Lord just as the Lord said, "You will find a colt tied on which no one has sat. Loose it and bring it." When you bring yourself to the Lord, you become the servant of the Lord naturally.

We are bound to this world like the colt that is tied to a

leash. We are tied to our families, jobs, and even to some businesses. However, the Lord said that the servants of the Lord go and untie the leash that binds you when He calls for you. It means that the servants of God explain to you what the really important things are and what are not. Then you just need to hear this and obediently shake off the things that are not important. Even if there are some losses, you just have to accept some loss before the presence of the Lord and not worry about it anymore. The Lord will eventually use you if He decides to use you. When the Lord calls you as His servant, the Lord does not ask for your understanding first. The Lord calls us we who have been living as the servants of this world and then uses us as God's servants according to His will. The Lord rides on our back and entrusts the Lord's work to us and also wants to use us as His servants to enter the City of Jerusalem. Therefore, when the Lord calls you like this, I want you to discuss with the servants of God and untie many things that bind you even if you are tied to the world in many aspects. I want you to become the servants that serve the Lord faithfully like this.

The Lord Truly Wants You to Use You for Many Tasks

Is there anyone among you who happens to think "I cannot be a servant of God" and refuses like this? How will you reply to His invitation when the Lord calls you to use you? Will you say that you cannot follow His calling? Or, will you say, "I am tied to many things, but I am willing to untie those things and follow you if you want to use me. Use me, Lord"? You must be brought to the Lord feigning yourself to be forced and be used by the Lord like this young colt in today's Scripture reading. We must thereby become the servant of God who serves Him while living in this world and receive glory along with God and along with it also receive hardship at times. Do you understand?

There are some saints that God has already called, and there are others that God will call in the future. The important thing to remember is that the Lord does not come and speak to you personally, but that He calls His workers through His servants like the disciples of Jesus who went to fetch the colt as mentioned in today's Scripture reading. And so when the servants of Jesus Christ, His disciples, want to use you, I want you to obey them and really be used preciously by the Lord. This is the main point of today's sermon.

Dear fellow believers, do you think God is calling you? You will have either one of the following thoughts: "God will not call me" or "God will definitely call me." And I know that there probably are some brothers and sisters who stubbornly refuse even though the Lord calls them. But when this happens to you, you must say "yes" and follow the Lord when it definitely is His calling you. It will never be a loss for you. God will call you some day through His servants, just as God called Samuel the prophet. I want you to live out your faith by believing in this Word. ✉

HAVE YOU TRULY BEEN BORN AGAIN OF WATER AND THE SPIRIT?

HAVE YOU TRULY BEEN BORN AGAIN OF WATER AND THE SPIRIT?

PAUL C. JONG

Among many Christian books written about being born again, this is the first book of our time to preach the gospel of the water and the Spirit in strict accordance with the Scriptures. Man can't enter the Kingdom of Heaven without being born again of water and the Spirit. To be born again means that a sinner is saved from all his lifelong sins by believing in the baptism of Jesus and His blood of the Cross. Let's believe in the gospel of the water and the Spirit and enter the Kingdom of Heaven as the righteous who have no sin.

RETURN TO THE GOSPEL OF THE WATER AND THE SPIRIT

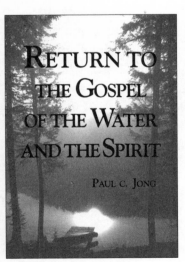

RETURN TO THE GOSPEL OF THE WATER AND THE SPIRIT

PAUL C. JONG

Let's return to the gospel of the water and the Spirit. Theology and doctrines themselves can't save us. However, many Christians still follow them, and consequently have not been born again yet. This book clearly tells us what mistakes theology and doctrines have made and how to believe in Jesus in the most proper way.

The Fail-safe Way for You to Receive the Holy Spirit

In Christianity, the most significantly discussed issue is salvation from sins and the indwelling of the Holy Spirit. However, few people have the exact knowledge of these two topics. Nevertheless, in reality people say that they believe in Jesus Christ while they are ignorant of true redemption and the Holy Spirit.

Do you know the true gospel that makes you receive the Holy Spirit? If you want to ask God for the indwelling of the Holy Spirit, then you must first know the gospel of the water and the Spirit and have faith in it. This book will certainly lead all Christians worldwide to receive the Holy Spirit through the remission of all their sins.

Our LORD Who Becomes the Righteousness of God (I) & (II)

The teachings in these books will satisfy the thirst in your heart. Today's Christians continue to live while not knowing the true solution to the personal sins that they are committing daily. Do you know what God's righteousness is? The author hopes that you will ask yourself this question and believe in God's righteousness, which is dealt in detail in these books.

The Doctrines of Predestination, Justification, and Incremental Sanctification are the major Christian doctrines, which brought only confusion and emptiness into the souls of believers. But, dear Christians, now is the time when you must continue in the Truth which you have learned and been assured of.

These books will provide your soul with a great understanding and lead it to peace. The author wants you to possess the blessing of knowing God's righteousness.

IS THE AGE OF THE ANTICHRIST, MARTYRDOM, RAPTURE AND THE MILLENNIAL KINGDOM COMING? (I)

After the 9/11 terrorist attacks, traffic to "www.raptureready.com," an Internet site providing information on the end times, is reported to have increased to over 8 million hits, and according to a joint survey by CNN and TIME, over 59% of the Americans now believe in apocalyptic eschatology.

Responding to such demands of the time, the author provides a clear exposition of the key themes of the Book of Revelation, including the coming Antichrist, the martyrdom of the saints and their rapture, the Millennial Kingdom, and the New Heaven and Earth-all in the context of the whole Scripture and under the guidance of the Holy Spirit.

This book provides verse-by-verse commentaries on the Book of Revelation supplemented by the author's inspired sermons. Anyone who reads this book will come to grasp all the plans that God has in store for this world.

IS THE AGE OF THE ANTICHRIST, MARTYRDOM, RAPTURE AND THE MILLENNIAL KINGDOM COMING? (II)

Most Christians today believe in the theory of pre-tribulation rapture. Because they believe in this false doctrine teaching them that they would be lifted before the coming of the Great Tribulation of seven years, they are leading idle religious lives steeped in complacency.

But the rapture of the saints will occur only after the plagues of the seven trumpets run their course until the sixth plague is all poured-that is, the rapture will happen after the Antichrist emerges amidst global chaos and the born-again saints are martyred, and when the seventh trumpet is blown. It is at this time that Jesus would descend from Heaven, and the resurrection and rapture of the born-again saints would occur (1 Thessalonians 4:16-17).

The righteous who were born again by believing in "the gospel of the water and the Spirit" will be resurrected and take part in the Rapture, and thus become heirs to the Millennial Kingdom and the eternal Kingdom of Heaven, but the sinners who were unable to participate in this first resurrection will face the great punishment of the seven bowls poured by God and be cast into the eternal fire of hell.

The TABERNACLE: A Detailed Portrait of Jesus Christ (I)

How can we find out the truth hidden in the Tabernacle? Only by knowing the gospel of the water and the Spirit, the real substance of the Tabernacle, can we correctly understand and know the answer to this question.

In fact, the blue, purple, and scarlet thread and the fine woven linen manifested in the gate of the Tabernacle's court show us the works of Jesus Christ in the New Testament's time that have saved the mankind. In this way, the Old Testament's Word of the Tabernacle and the Word of the New Testament are closely and definitely related to each other, like fine woven linen. But, unfortunately, this truth has been hidden for a long time to every truth seeker in Christianity.

Coming to this earth, Jesus Christ was baptized by John and shed His blood on the Cross. Without understanding and believing in the gospel of the water and the Spirit, none of us can ever find out the truth revealed in the Tabernacle. We must now learn this truth of the Tabernacle and believe in it. We all need to realize and believe in the truth manifested in the blue, purple, and scarlet thread and the fine woven linen of the gate of the Tabernacle's court.

The TABERNACLE: A Detailed Portrait of Jesus Christ (II)

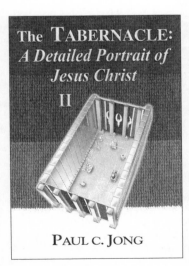

As God had commanded Moses to build the Tabernacle in the Old Testament, in the New Testament, God wants us to also build a Sanctuary in each of our hearts so that He may dwell in us. The material of faith with which we can build this Sanctuary in our hearts is the Word of the gospel of the water and the Spirit. With this gospel of the water and the Spirit, we must wash away all our sins and be cleansed. By telling us to build Him a Sanctuary, God is telling us to empty our hearts and believe in the gospel of the water and the Spirit. We must all cleanse our hearts by believing in the gospel of the water and the Spirit.

When we cleanse away all the sins of our hearts by believing in this gospel Truth, God then comes to dwell in them. It is by believing in this true gospel that you can build the holy Temples in your hearts. It is highly likely that until now, at least some of you have probably been offering your prayers of repentance to cleanse your hearts, trying to build the Temples by yourselves. But now is the time for you to abandon this false faith and be transformed by the renewing of your minds by believing in the gospel of the water and the Spirit.

The Elementary Principles of CHRIST

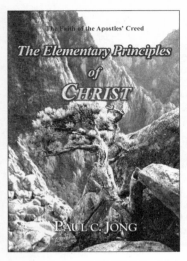

We must have the faith that the Apostles had and believe as they did, for their faith and beliefs came from the Holy Spirit. The Apostles believed in Jesus Christ, His Father, and the Holy Spirit as their God.

The Apostle Paul confessed that he died with Christ and was brought to new life with Him. He became an instrument of God by believing that he was baptized into Jesus Christ (Galatians 3:27). In God's gospel are found the baptism that Jesus received, the blood that He shed on the Cross, and the gift of the Holy Spirit that He has bestowed on everyone who believes in this true gospel of the water and the Spirit.

Do you know and believe in this original gospel? This is the very gospel that the Apostles had also believed. We, too, must therefore all believe in the gospel of the water and the Spirit.

The Gospel of Matthew (I), (II), (III), (IV), (V), (VI)

There are countless new Christians throughout the world, who have just been born again by believing in the gospel of the water and the Spirit that we have been spreading. We are indeed yearning to feed on the bread of life to them. But it is difficult for them to have fellowship with us in the true gospel, for they are all far away from us.

Therefore, to meet the spiritual needs of these people of Jesus Christ, the King of kings, The author proclaims that those who have received the remission of their sins by believing in the Word of Jesus Christ, must feed on His pure Word in order to defend their faith and sustain their spiritual lives. The sermons in these books have been prepared as new bread of life that will nourish the born-again to edify their spiritual growth.

Through His Church and servants, God will continue to provide you with this bread of life. May God's blessings be on all those who have been born again of water and the Spirit, who desires to have true spiritual fellowship with us in Jesus Christ.

The First Epistle of John (I) & (II)

He who believes that Jesus, who is God and the Savior, came by the gospel of the water and the Spirit to deliver all sinners from their sins, is saved from all his sins, and becomes a child of God the Father.

The First Epistle of John states that Jesus, who is God, came to us by the gospel of the water and the Spirit, and that He is the Son of God the Father. The Book, in other words, mostly emphasizes that Jesus is God (1 John 5:20), and concretely testifies the gospel of the water and the Spirit in chapter 5.

We must not hesitate to believe that Jesus Christ is God and to follow Him.

Sermons on Galatians: From Physical Circumcision to the Doctrine of Repentance (I) & (II)

Today's Christianity has turned into merely a world religion. Most Christians nowadays live in a situation of being sinners because they haven't been born again by spiritual faith. It is because they have only relied on Christian doctrines without being aware of the gospel of the water and the Spirit until now.

Therefore, now is the time for you to know the spiritual fallacies of the circumcisionists and keep distance from such faith. You have to know the contradictoriness of the prayers of repentance. Now is the time for you to stand firmer than ever on the gospel of the water and the Spirit.

If you haven't believed in this true gospel so far, you have to believe in our Savior who came to us by the gospel of the water and the Spirit even now. Now, you have to be complete Christians with the faith of believing in the gospel Truth of the water and the Spirit.

The Love of God Revealed through Jesus, The Only Begotten Son (I), (II), (III)

It is written, "No one has seen God at any time. The only begotten Son, who is in the bosom of the Father, He has declared Him" (John 1:18).

How perfectly did Jesus reveal the love of God to us! How perfectly did Jesus deliver us! What perfect Truth of salvation is the gospel of the water and the Spirit! We have never regretted receiving our salvation through our faith in Jesus, who came by water and blood (1 John 5:6).

Now, we have become His sinless people. Whoever believes in the gospel of the water and the Spirit can receive the eternal remission of sins and earn eternal life.

Eat My Flesh And Drink My Blood

Until now, most Christians have not known the Truth, but only inherited religious acts. From the gospel to Holy Communion, today's Christianity maintains its orthodoxy not through the knowledge of the Truth, but by emphasizing only formal procedures and consecrated rites.

As a result, when today's Christians come across the bread and wine that signify the flesh and blood of Jesus during Communion, they are thankful only for the sacrifice of His blood, and they can't help but remain completely ignorant of the fact that Christ took upon Himself all their sins once and for all by being baptized by John the Baptist.

Therefore, I admonish all Christians throughout the whole world to learn, even from now on, what the flesh and blood of Jesus mean within the gospel of the water and the Spirit, to believe in it, and to thereby receive their salvation and also partake in Holy Communion with the right faith.

The Relationship Between the Ministry of JESUS and That of JOHN the BAPTIST Recorded in the Four Gospels

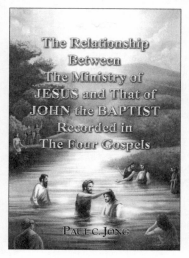

Do you perhaps think that it doesn't matter whether there needs to be the ministry of John the Baptist or not? You must believe according to the written Word of God. We must understand and believe in the ministry of John the Baptist within the frame of the ministry of Jesus Christ. John the Baptist in the New Testament was the prophet Elijah promised to be sent down to this earth according to the Book of Malachi chapter 4, verses 4-5. As the prophet Elijah to come, John the Baptist was born six months before Jesus, and he was the one who had pass on the sins of this world at once by giving Jesus the baptism at the Jordan River at the age of thirty. Thus, we must become the recipients of God's blessing by knowing the ministry of John the Baptist and accepting the ministry of Jesus Christ.

THE WILL OF THE HOLY TRINITY FOR HUMAN BEINGS

Through the Book of Genesis, God wants us to realize His good intentions toward us. Where is God's will for us revealed? It is revealed in the gospel Truth of the water and the Spirit that God accomplished through Jesus Christ. We must come into this good intention of God by faith, manifested in the gospel of the water and the Spirit. To do so, when we consider God's Word, we need to cast aside our existing carnal thoughts we have had, and believe in God's Word exactly as it is. All of us must throw away our mistaken knowledge accumulated until now, and open our spiritual eyes by placing our faith in the righteousness of God.

The Fall of Man and the Perfect Salvation of God

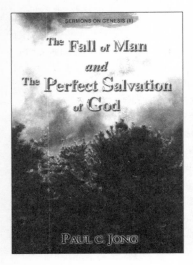

In the Book of Genesis, the purpose for which God created us is contained. When architects design a building or artists draw a painting, they first conceive the work that would be completed in their minds before they actually begin working on their project. Just like this, our God also had our salvation of mankind in His mind even before He created the heavens and the earth, and He made Adam and Eve with this purpose in mind. And God needed to explain to us the domain of Heaven, which is not seen by our eyes of the flesh, by drawing an analogy to the domain of the earth that we can all see and understand.

Even before the foundation of the world, God wanted to save mankind perfectly by giving the gospel of the water and the Spirit to everyone's heart. So although all human beings were made out of dust, they must learn and know the gospel Truth of the water and the Spirit to benefit their own souls. If people continue to live without knowing the dominion of Heaven, they will lose not only the things of the earth, but also everything that belongs to Heaven.

Heretics, Who Followed the Sins of Jeroboam (I) & (II)

Christians today do not know what the gospel Truth of the water and the Spirit that the Lord has made and given us is. Thus, they continue to believe in the doctrines of Christianity and not the gospel of the water and the Spirit. For that reason, the fact of the matter is that despite their claim of having faith in Jesus, they continue to believe in and follow golden calves.

We must discern those that worship golden calves as God within Christianity. And by coming back before God of the Truth, we must offer the sacrifices of righteousness to God. The sacrifice that God receives with rejoice is the sacrifice of righteousness that people offer by faith after having received the remission of sin by having faith in the gospel of the water and the Spirit. Before God, you must seriously think about whether or not you are offering the sacrifice of God-given righteousness by the faith of believing in the gospel of the water and the Spirit.

The Lord's Prayer : Misinterpretations and Truth

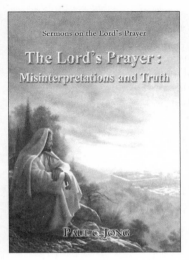

In order to interpret the Lord's Prayer correctly, we must first correctly understand the gospel of the water and the Spirit, which was spoken to us by the Lord. We have Truth in us when we not only know and understand the gospel of the water and the Spirit but also believe it with our hearts. The true gospel, which we believe in, has led us so far, so that we can lead truly faithful lives that the Lord wants from us in the Lord's Prayer.

Exegesis on the Book of ROMANS (I)

The righteousness of God is transparent. God's righteousness cannot be substituted by anything. That is because His righteousness is different from the righteousness of man. We need to know what God's righteousness is, and we need to believe in it.

God's righteousness is fundamentally different from human righteousness. The righteousness of mankind is like a filthy rag, but the righteousness of God is like a brilliant pearl shining forever. God's righteousness is the Truth that is absolutely needed by every sinner, transcending all ages.

HAVE YOU MET JESUS WITH THE GOSPEL OF THE WATER AND THE SPIRIT?

It is written, "No one has seen God at any time. The only begotten Son, who is in the bosom of the Father, He has declared Him" (John 1:18).

How perfectly did Jesus reveal the love of God to us! How perfectly did Jesus deliver us! What perfect Truth of salvation is the gospel of the water and the Spirit! We have never regretted receiving our salvation through our faith in Jesus, who came by water and blood (1 John 5:6).

Now, we have become His sinless people. Whoever believes in the gospel of the water and the Spirit can receive the eternal remission of sins and earn eternal life.

Sermons on the Gospel of Luke (I), (II), (III), (IV), (V), (VI), (VII)

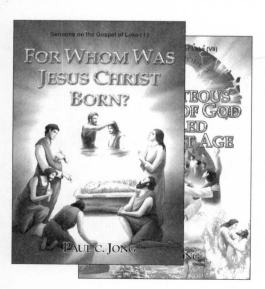

It is Jesus Christ who moves the entire history of this world. Our Lord came to this earth to save all humans from the sins of the world, and He has become the bread of new life for those of us who believe in the gospel of the water and the Spirit. In fact, it was to give this new life to us, who were all destined to hell for our sins that our Lord came looking for you and me.

No More Chaos, Void or Darkness Now (I) & (II)

Although we may be powerless and because the Word of God has power, when the Word falls to the ground it bears fruit without fail. Further, because the Word of God is alive we can see for ourselves that it is the same today and tomorrow, and forever unchanging. Unlike the words of man, God's Word never changes, for it is ever faithful. When God speaks, He fulfills exactly according to His Words.

For the Word of God has power, so when God said, "Let there be light," there was light, and when He said, "Let there be a greater light and a lesser light," it was fulfilled just as He had commanded.

THE DIFFERENCE BETWEEN ABEL'S FAITH AND CAIN'S FAITH

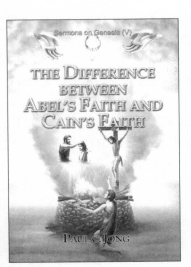

Whenever we stand before the presence of God to glorify Him, we should not approach Him through some religious rituals, but instead we have to approach Him by trusting in what He has done for us and thanking Him for His love. Only then does God accept our worship and pour the Holy Spirit on us abundantly.

FOR THE LOST SHEEP (I) & (II)

What God wants to do is to make us into His children by making us born again through the gospel of the water and the Spirit.

We humans are born as God's creations first, but if we receive the remission of sins by believing in the gospel of the water and the Spirit, we are born again as the children of God. This means that, after the Lord came and remitted all our sins, we who were blind could now obtain our sight.

WISDOM OF THE PRIMITIVE GOSPEL

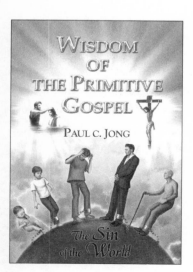

The primitive gospel is the Truth of salvation that's absolutely indispensable to everyone. Transcending all denominations, this primitive gospel will clearly teach every Christian how God's blessings could be bestowed on them. This true gospel will now fill your heart with God's overflowing love. And it will be the most precious gift to all your loved ones.

BE A GOSPEL WITNESS WHO SAVES
THE HUMAN RACE FROM DESTRUCTION

Mankind, who had eaten the fruit of the knowledge of good and evil, came to have the different standard for good and evil from God's. Then, which is correct, God's Word or our judgment? Our standard is always relative and selfish. Therefore we should cast away our own ideas and simply trust and follow God's Word focusing on "What does the Word of God say?" Ignoring God's Word and seeking self-righteousness is Cain's faith and religious belief. Abel put his faith in the Word of God he heard from his father, Adam, and offered the firstborn of his flock and of their fat. But self-conceited Cain brought an offering of the fruit of the ground to the Lord. God accepted Abel's offering but refused Cain's offering. It is God's lesson that faith in man-made religions cannot bring salvation.

THOSE WHO POSSESS ABRAHAM'S FAITH

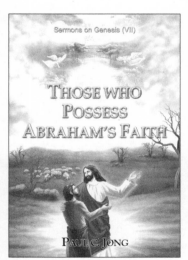

There are two kinds of righteousness in this world which are constantly in conflict and struggle with each another; these are the righteousness of God and the righteousness of man. Although God's righteousness faces many obstacles, it always prevails over the righteousness of man and leads us to the victorious way. That's because the Word of God is almighty. Because God's almighty power is with us, we are able to taste His blessings, for the Word of God has the power to reach our hearts, thoughts and souls, and brings all His blessings to us.

WHAT SHOULD WE STRIVE TO BELIEVE AND PREACH?

The Gospel of Mark testifies that Jesus Christ is the Son of God and God Himself. And it also testifies that He is our Savior. So we can see the writer of the Gospel of Mark bearing witness of Jesus forcefully, testifying that He is the very God and our Savior. This is why I would like to bear witness of this Jesus Christ who is manifested in the Gospel of Mark as much as possible based on the gospel of the water and the Spirit. What is obvious is that the core Truth of Christianity is found in the gospel of the water and the Spirit. Jesus said to Nicodemus, "Most assuredly, I say to you, unless one is born of water and the Spirit, he cannot enter the kingdom of God" (John 3:5).

Paul C. Jong's Christian books have been translated into 65 major languages at this point: Afrikaans, Albanian, Arabic, Bengali, Bulgarian, Burmese, Cebuano, Chichewa, Chin, Chinese, Croatian, Czech, Danish, Dioula, Dutch, English, French, Georgian, German, Greek, Gujarati, Hebrew, Hindi, Hungarian, Indonesian, Iranian, Italian, Japanese, Javanese, Kannada, Khmer, Kirghiz, Kirundi, Latvian, Luganda, Luo, Madi, Malagasy, Malayalam, Marathi, Mindat, Mizo, Mongolian, Nepali, Polish, Portuguese, Romanian, Russian, Serbian, Shona, Slovak, Slovene, Spanish, Swahili, Swedish, Tagalog, Taiwanese, Tamil, Telugu, Thai, Turkish, Ukrainian, Urdu, Vietnamese, and Zou. They are also available now through our free e-book service.

E-book is digital book designed for you to feel a printed book on screen. You can read it easily on your PC monitor in your native language after downloading the viewer software and a text file. Feel free to visit our web site at http://www.nlmission.com or http://www.bjnewlife.org to download our e-books, and you will get the most remarkable Christian e-books absolutely for free.

And, would you like to take part in having our free Christian books known to more people worldwide? We would be very thankful if you link your website to ours so that many people get an opportunity to meet Jesus Christ through our inspired Christian books. Please visit our site at http://www.bjnewlife.org/english/about/take_banners.php to take our banners to your website. In addition, we would be also very thankful if you introduce our website to the webmasters around you for adding our link.

The New Life Mission
Contact: John Shin, General Secretary
E-mail: newlife@bjnewlife.org

*W*orldwide websites of

The New Life Mission

Please find your vernacular websites below.
You can download Christian e-books and request Christian books for free.
Feel free to visit our websites below right now!

A www.nlmafghanistan.com
www.nlmafrikaans.com
www.nlmalbania.com
www.nlmamharic.com
www.nlmangola.com
www.nlmarabemirates.com
www.nlmarabic.com
www.nlmargentina.com
www.nlmarmenia.com
www.nlmaruba.com
www.nlmaustralia.com
www.nlmaustria.com

B www.nlmbahamas.com
www.nlmbahrain.com
www.nlmbangladesh.com
www.nlmbelarus.com
www.nlmbelgium.com
www.nlmbengali.com
www.nlmbenin.com
www.nlmbhutan.com
www.nlmbolivia.com
www.nlmbotswana.com
www.nlmbrasil.com
www.nlmbriton.com
www.nlmbrunei.com
www.nlmbulgalia.com
www.nlmburkinafaso.com
www.nlmburundi.com

C www.nlmcameroon.com
www.nlmcanada.com
www.nlmcebuano.com
www.nlmchichewa.com
www.nlmchile.com
www.nlmchin.com

www.nlmchina.com
www.nlmcolombia.com
www.nlmcongo.com
www.nlmcostarica.com
www.nlmcotedivoire.com
www.nlmcroatia.com
www.nlmczech.com

D www.nlmdenmark.com
www.nlmdioula.com
www.nlmdominica.com
www.nlmdutch.com

E www.nlmecuador.com
www.nlmegypt.com
www.nlmelsalvador.com
www.nlmequatorialguinea.com
www.nlmethiopia.com

F www.nlmfinland.com
www.nlmfrance.com
www.nlmfrench.com

G www.nlmgabon.com
www.nlmgeorgian.com
www.nlmgerman.com
www.nlmgermany.com
www.nlmghana.com
www.nlmgreek.com
www.nlmgrenada.com
www.nlmguatemala.com
www.nlmgujarati.com

H www.nlmhaiti.com
www.nlmhindi.com
www.nlmholland.com
www.nlmhonduras.com
www.nlmhungary.com

Turn over

© Some of these websites may not work because they are still under construction.

Worldwide websites of

 The New Life Mission

I www.nlm-india.com	www.nlmpoland.com
www.nlmindonesia.com	www.nlmportugal.com
www.nlmiran.com	www.nlmportuguese.com
www.nlmiraq.com	www.nlmprcongo.com
www.nlmisrael.com	**Q** www.nlmqatar.com
www.nlmitaly.com	**R** www.nlmromania.com
J www.nlmjamaica.com	www.nlmrussia.com
www.nlmjapan.com	**S** www.nlmsaudiarabia.com
www.nlmjavanese.com	www.nlmserbian.com
K www.nlmkannada.com	www.nlmshona.com
www.nlmkazakhstan.com	www.nlmsingapore.com
www.nlmkenya.com	www.nlmslovakia.com
www.nlmkhmer.com	www.nlmslovene.com
www.nlmkirghiz.com	www.nlmsolomon.com
www.nlmkirundi.com	www.nlmsouthafrica.com
www.nlmkorea.com	www.nlmspain.com
L www.nlmlatvia.com	www.nlmspanish.com
www.nlmluganda.com	www.nlmsrilanka.com
www.nlmluo.com	www.nlmsuriname.com
M www.nlmmadi.com	www.nlmswahili.com
www.nlmmalagasy.com	www.nlmswaziland.com
www.nlmmalayalam.com	www.nlmsweden.com
www.nlmmalaysia.com	www.nlmswiss.com
www.nlmmarathi.com	**T** www.nlmtagalog.com
www.nlmmauritius.com	www.nlmtaiwan.com
www.nlmmexico.com	www.nlmtamil.com
www.nlmmindat.com	www.nlmtelugu.com
www.nlmmizo.com	www.nlmthailand.com
www.nlmmoldova.com	www.nlmtogo.com
www.nlmmongolia.com	www.nlmtonga.com
www.nlmmyanmar.com	www.nlmturkey.com
N www.nlmnepal.com	**U** www.nlmuganda.com
www.nlmnewzealand.com	www.nlmukraine.com
www.nlmnigeria.com	www.nlmurdu.com
www.nlmnorthkorea.com	www.nlmusa.com
www.nlmnorway.com	**V** www.nlmvenezuela.com
P www.nlmpakistan.com	www.nlmvietnam.com
www.nlmpanama.com	**Z** www.nlmzambia.com
www.nlmperu.com	www.nlmzimbabwe.com
www.nlmphilippines.com	www.nlmzou.com